THE PERFECT EDGE

The Ultimate Guide to Sharpening For Woodworkers

RON HOCK

POPULAR WOODWORKING BOOKS
CINCINNATI, OHIO
www.popularwoodworking.com

READ THIS IMPORTANT SAFETY NOTICE

To prevent accidents, keep safety in mind while you work. Use the safety guards installed on power equipment – they are for your protection.

When working on power equipment, keep fingers away from saw blades, wear safety goggles to prevent injuries from flying wood chips and sawdust, wear hearing protection and consider installing a dust vacuum to reduce the amount of airborne sawdust in your woodshop.

Don't wear loose clothing, such as neckties or shirts with loose sleeves, or jewelry, such as rings, necklaces or bracelets, when working on power equipment. Tie back long hair to prevent it from getting caught in your equipment.

People who are sensitive to certain chemicals should check the chemical content of any product before using it.

Due to the variability of local conditions, construction materials, skill levels, etc., neither the author nor Popular Woodworking Books assumes any responsibility for any accidents, injuries, damages or other losses incurred resulting from the material presented in this book.

The authors and editors who compiled this book have tried to make the contents as accurate and correct as possible. Plans, illustrations, photographs and text have been carefully checked. All instructions, plans and projects should be carefully read, studied and understood before beginning construction.

Prices listed for supplies and equipment were current at the time of publication and are subject to change.

METRIC CONVERSION CHART

TO CONVERT	TO	MULTIPLY BY
Inches	Centimeters	2.54
Centimeters	Inches	0.4
Feet	Centimeters	30.5
Centimeters	Feet	0.03
Yards	Meters	0.9
Meters	Yards	1.1

Distributed in Canada by Fraser Direct
100 Armstrong Avenue
Georgetown, Ontario L7G 5S4
Canada

Distributed in the U.K. and Europe by
F&W Media International, LTD
Brunel House, Ford Close
Newton Abbot
TQ12 4PU, UK
Tel: (+44) 1626 323200
Fax: (+44) 1626 323319
E-mail: enquiries@fwmedia.com

Distributed in Australia by Capricorn Link
P.O. Box 704
Windsor, NSW 2756
Australia

Visit our website at www.popularwoodworking.com, or our consumer website at shopwoodworking.com.

Other fine Popular Woodworking Books are available from your local bookstore or direct from the publisher.

20 19 18 17 16   7 6 5 4 3

ACQUISITIONS EDITOR: David Thiel (david.thiel@fwmedia.com)
SENIOR EDITOR: Jim Stack (jim.stack@fwmedia.com)
DESIGNER: Brian Roeth
PRODUCTION COORDINATOR: Mark Griffin
PHOTOGRAPHER: Ron Hock
ILLUSTRATOR: Martha Garstang Hill

ABOUT THE AUTHOR

Ron Hock is the owner of Hock Tools, a twenty-five-year-old cottage industry that makes acknowledged superior blades for planes and other woodworking tools. Hock started the business when, as a struggling knife-maker, students at James Krenov's Fine Woodworking program at The College of the Redwoods in Fort Bragg, California, came to him for plane irons for the wooden planes they were making at the school. He tooled up for plane irons, learned about plane-making and found a niche-market of discerning wood-workers who appreciate a superior tool.

Ron earned a B.A. and M.F.A. in studio art from the University of California at Irvine. In the ensuing quarter-century since making his first plane blades he's learned about tool steel metallurgy, cutting edge geometry, hand woodworking tools and sharpening. His interest and expertise regarding sharp edges comes from a blade-maker's perspective and he has given countless lectures about steel, tools and heat-treatment.

DEDICATION

Through his uncompromising craft, teaching and writings James Krenov has inspired and launched the careers of thousands of woodworkers … but maybe only one metalworker.

Thanks, Jim.

ACKNOWLEDGMENTS

A large number of people helped me with this book either directly, by sharing their knowledge and wisdom, or by providing tools, abrasives and technical assistance. I am grateful for their generosity in sharing their expertise. I hope this list is complete yet I doubt it is – I'm sure I have forgotten to mention someone or two; if so, I apologize and thank them, too:

First and foremost is my wife, Linda Rosengarten, for being selflessly supportive and endlessly helpful as my primary editor. Thank you, Sweetie, there is no way I could have done this without you. And my son, Sam Hock, for letting me be a bit less attentive as the fatherly fig-ure that I hope he's otherwise come to expect.

For hands-on help, advice and lots of tool lend-ing and kibitzing, my immense gratitude to: Kevin Drake of Glen-Drake Toolworks; Paul Reiber, artist and woodcarver; Dan Stalzer, green-wood furniture maker; Joaquin Leyva, woodworker; Earl Latham, tool expert and collector; Joel Moscowitz of Tools for Working Wood; Mike Wenzloff of Wenzloff & Sons Sawmakers, and Christopher Schwarz, editor, *Popular Woodworking* magazine.

True experts in their fields, generous with their tools and expertise: Wally Wilson of Veritas; Jeff Farris of Tormek USA; Don Naples of Wood Artistry; Kyle Crawford of Work Sharp; Valerie Gleason of Chef's Choice; Peter Moore of One Way; Linda Jones of Woodsmith; Cindy Martin, Kris Spofford, Dave Long and Trish Dawson of Saint-Gobain Abrasives (Norton); Brian Burns; Stan Watson of DMT; Harrelson Stanley of HMS Enterprises; Rich Bohr of 3M; Bill Kohr of Craftsman Studio; Dave Bennet of Flexcut; Joyce Laituri of Spyderco, and Kent Harpool and Tim Rinehart of Woodcraft Supply.

The professionals, tops in their fields, who helped me with some difficult technical materials: Dr. Abraham Anapolsky, metallurgist; Caroline Schooley, microscopist; Steve Anderson, Sonoma State University SEM technician; Dr. William R. Hoover, metallurgist, LLC; Brian Ross, metallurgist, Latrobe Steel; Hans Nichols, metallurgist, Precision-Marshall Steel; Katherine Cockey, corrosion engineer; Charles Beresford of Cryogenics International; and Jeff Wherry of the Unified Abrasives Manufacturer's Association.

And, for making this book happen in the first place, and look and read the way it does: Rick Droz, photog-raphy advisor; Martha Garstang Hill, creator of the illustrations; Brian Roeth, designer, and David Baker-Thiel, executive editor, Popular Woodworking Books.

Thank you, one and all.

(TABLE OF CONTENTS)

(INTRODUCTION)

Give me six hours to chop down a tree and
I will spend the first four sharpening the axe.

– ABRAHAM LINCOLN

"RELAX. YOU KNOW MORE THAN YOU think you do." Reassuring words for new parents from Dr. Benjamin Spock's classic *Baby and Child Care* (that's Doctor Spock, not Mister Spock, jeesh …) and, amazingly, these classic, reassuring words are applicable to this book, too. A perfect edge is the intersection between two surfaces, one that performs its assigned task the way you want it to. You need only:

1. Determine the correct angle for that intersection.
2. Rub the tool at the appropriate angle on an abrasive surface until that intersection is created.
3. Repeat #2 with successively finer grits until the desired degree of "polish" is obtained.

That's it. Really. And you can do it. The perfect edge is all about angles and grits, and what follows here is, I hope, information that will help you make good decisions about them. Clear away all the hype and hoopla, all the myth and magic, all the gear and gadgets and what you have is rather simple: a metal edge and an abrasive means of removing some metal from that edge. Every cutting tool in your shop needs an edge – ground to some angle and honed such that it can perform its intended task.

It's impossible to describe how to sharpen every tool for every task but it is my sincere hope that, with study and practice, you will understand more and more about what is involved in cutting wood with steel. The more you understand, the easier, less stressful and more intuitive your woodworking will become. Relax.

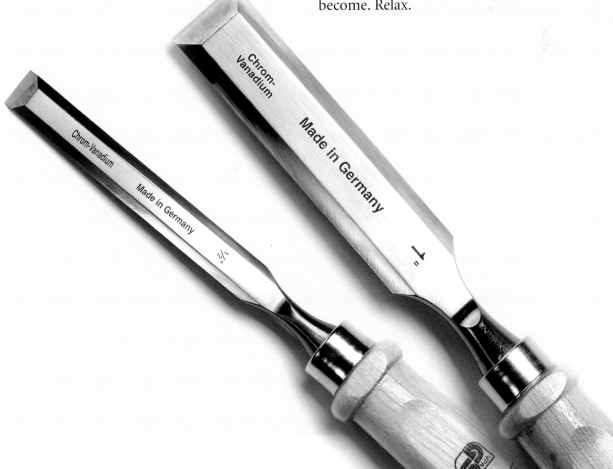

1 Why Sharpen?

FIRST, A DEFINITION OF WHAT "SHARP" MEANS: A sharp edge results from the zero-radius intersection of two planar surfaces. In other words, where the back of a plane blade meets the bevel is the cutting edge. If that edge is honed as close to zero radius as is possible, that edge is as sharp as it can be – a perfect edge. A true zero-radius edge is a purely theoretical thing, but it represents the bull's-eye of all sharpening techniques and practice. The reason a zero-radius goal is only a dream is because the blade you are sharpening has to be made from something – for instance, steel – and that something is made up of crystals, which are made of molecules, which are made of atoms; and all of these microscopic building blocks have size. However small these microscopic building blocks may be, there is still some "there" there and it is that little bit of size which determines how close to the goal of zero radius the laws of physics allow you to get. The smallest radius possible is the diameter of the largest discrete particle in the metal's mixture that can't be abraded away. I discuss a lot more about edge-tool metallurgy in Chapter Two: What is Steel?

Your fresh and painstakingly-honed perfect edge begins to wear the instant you put it to use; its radius increases, becomes rounder, on its way to becoming dull. If you're a glass-half-empty type, you might say that there are no truly sharp edges, just ones that are dull or duller. So, it seems that "sharp" needs a yet more practical definition. A blade is sharp when it cuts what it is supposed to cut according to the specifications of the person doing the cutting. Put simply: sharp is as sharp does.

I tolerate a not-so-perfect edge for certain purposes that for others would be intolerable. How sharp is sharp enough is a function of how much pressure I am willing to apply to the edge and how critical is the surface left behind. Sometimes when I cut a sandwich in half, I cut it with the table knife that I just used to spread the mayo. That knife isn't very sharp compared to the chef's knives in the kitchen, but the table knife is handy, will do the job adequately and I don't have to clean and dry a chef's knife after I'm done (no stainless steel knives in my kitchen – only old-fashioned, high-carbon steel, treated with care). I may need to push harder with that table knife to cut my sandwich than I would have with a sharper knife, but the difference in this instance is inconsequential.

The sharper the edge, the less effort required to cut with it and the cleaner and smoother the just-cut surface will be (still no biggie where the sandwich is concerned). Similarly, for certain woodworking tasks an extreme degree of sharpness would also be a waste of sharpening time. A scrub plane is used for dimensioning rough lumber quickly, where the surface finish is not the goal, just the final dimension. Yes, it needs to be sharp, but a stropped, mirror finish is unnecessary for the rough work that it is to perform. Save the strop, and your valuable time, for a blade intended for more precise work – where the surface left behind is more important than a sandwich.

This last statement assumes, however, that you don't enjoy sharpening and that sharpening blades is a means to an end, a necessary function from which to carry on. As it turns out, many people live to sharpen – finding sharpening a satisfying endeavor in its own right. Me? I actually like to mow my lawn because of the way it looks (and smells) when I'm done. And

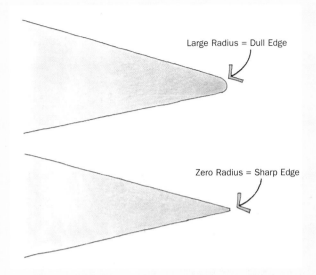

A dull edge has a large radius. A sharp edge approaches zero radius.

I appreciate the time I spend doing it as a sort of outdoors meditation, away from the phone and all. Others so dislike mowing that they'll pay a neighbor kid to do a so-so job and are happy with that. By the same token, some woodworkers will hone and polish their scrub plane blades all the way to a mirror-like finish and all of their edged tools are carefully sharpened and maintained to the same degree. Others want tools that are sharp enough to do the work at hand and want the sharpening process to be as fast and easy as possible: "Get it done and get back to the woodworking."

I've included tips to help the spectrum of sharpeners achieve their goals with both "get it done" minimal techniques to keep you productive, as well as the "gnat's eyelash" types that seek the optical-mirror-flat-back edge-radii that can be measured only using wavelengths of light.

Sharpening is a fundamental woodworking skill – as vital to your woodworking success as any skill you apply to the wood. In his book *Woodcarving*, Chris Pye says, "A master woodcarver once told me that when costing a piece of work, he would allow up to one third of the allotted time for sharpening and maintaining his tools." You weren't born with this skill – it must be learned. To learn any skill takes practice. Give in to the learning process. The time you spend learning to sharpen will pay off later as it will become second nature to know which grit to use and when, how sharp any given tool needs to be for the task at hand, and when it is time to re-sharpen an edge.

I mentioned that some people like sharpening simply because the activity of sharpening can be so satisfying, like the activity of waxing the car or, in my case, mowing the lawn. We resonate with the results on a fundamental, aesthetic level. But in addition to being aesthetically satisfying, a sharp, polished edge will last longer in use. At some microscopic level, every edge appears as a row of "teeth." The size of a tooth is in direct proportion to the size of the abrasive particle that scraped away the steel beside it. The finer the abrasive used, the smaller the teeth that comprise the edge. Coarse-grit sharpening abrasives make relatively large, deep scratches on the steel's surface that translate to large, saw-like teeth at the edge. Those teeth will cut aggressively at first, but their sharp points are subject to the entire cutting force and will become dull sooner than smaller teeth. If the teeth are large enough, they can leave visible striations on the surface of the wood you're cutting. Continued honing with subsequently finer grit sizes reduces the size of the teeth along the edge and, as the size of the teeth decreases, the number of them along the edge increases. The concentration of force described above is in effect here: smaller teeth require less force to cut the wood and, with a greater number of them to share the overall cutting force, the teeth will tend to stay sharp longer, leaving a smoother surface behind.

Another reason sharper is better: a polished blade is smoother and slides through wood fibers with less effort, which translates to more control, resulting in a precise, satisfying cut. I have encountered a number of novice woodworkers who have never used a well-tuned plane that has been fitted with a sharp blade. Their only experience with hand planes was typified by the frustration of making a shaving with the neglected and dull bench plane from junior high woodshop. That plane hopped and chattered and instilled a sense that hand planes are horrible tools to use or that the student was not competent to use them. Both sad conclusions, to be sure. But hand these former shop students a tuned-up, plain-Jane #5 with a properly sharpened blade and they go slack-jawed with amazement. How easy to push, how thin the shaving, how smooth the surface just planed, and how very satisfying the experience. It can change lives.

Ommmmm.

Concentration of force: A simple illustration of the concentration of force. Or, which would you rather have step on your foot?

A properly sharpened edge eliminates one important variable when you're learning a new woodworking procedure. To flatten a board with hand planes is a task that incorporates a number of skills, tricks and metrics. If you haven't done it, it's not as easy as it seems, but there's plenty of help, including many excellent instructional media. Before you can begin to flatten a board, you must be confident that your plane is set up to function properly. It is not an exaggeration to say that all woodcutting operations start at the sharpening station and you cannot be sure of a plane's performance unless its blade is flat and sharp.

Though not as life-altering an observation as the first-time feel of a properly sharpened plane blade

LEFT A steel sample with both polished and rough surfaces that's been allowed to rust evenly. Which would you prefer on your plane blade?

Properly sharpened tools can make any task a pleasure; from rough timber work, to fine paring with a chisel.

pushing against a wooden surface, polished steel is less inclined to rust than rough steel is. Those water droplets and oxygen pests in the air look for surface imperfections in the steel to cling to and oxidize (rust!). Polishing your blade is by no means rust-proofing, but the shinier the steel surface, the less inclined it will be to rust. I'll talk more about rust and its prevention in Chapter Two: What is Steel?

Though it's my purely subjective opinion, I feel it important to mention at this point that sharp tools are better tools. There is nothing like the simple pleasure of using a properly sharpened tool. A chisel with a polished, properly shaped edge is more likely to cut exactly where you want it to cut. Hand planing is a delightfully sensuous experience when all aspects of the plane are working properly. The planing action is smooth and easy, there's a pleasing "shisss" as gossamer shavings are released to float to the floor, and

the surface left behind has a sheen that begs to be touched. The same satisfaction applies to paring with a chisel, bucking firewood with your chain saw, ripping on the table saw or carving your family's Thanksgiving turkey. Although a thorough discussion of sharpening can be a bewildering mix of physics, geometry and metallurgy, with a dizzying array of gadgets and methods, once you've achieved a basic understanding and mastered a few techniques, a perfect edge is easy and quick to create. The process itself is quite satisfying.

The small investment of time spent sharpening your tools makes a huge difference in how they perform – and that's really what it's all about for me. I truly enjoy using a sharp knife, chisel or saw and enjoy the sense that it's just me and the work – the tool acting as an extension of my arms and hands, a willing agent at its design best, collaborating with me on the work to be done.

2 What is Steel?

Steel Things (from top left):
1. Golden Gate Bridge
2. Paper Clips
3. Richard Serra's "Fulcrum" 1987, PHOTO 2004 BY ANDREW DUNN
4. USS Midway, September 1991, PHOTO BY PHC CAROLYN HARRIS
5. Railroad Yard, Chicago, IL, PHOTO 1942 BY JACK DELANO
6. US Steel Tower, Pittsburgh, PA, PHOTO 2007 BY DEREK JENSEN

IT'S ALL AROUND US IN OUR EVERYDAY LIVES, so much so that we tend to take steel for granted. It may hold up the building you work in. It allows so many things – from your car to your screwdriver – to be the shapes that they are. It's the hundreds of thousands of miles of railroad in this country and it's the spring in your ballpoint pen.

Amazing stuff, steel: it can be melted and cast or heated and forged into complex shapes; pulled through little holes to make wire; hot rolled into structural shapes, or cold rolled into sheets that are then bent, stamped, rolled or spun into ships, washing machines, the internal structure of your television or computer. In so many ways steel is more valuable to us than gold. Imagine if all the gold in the world suddenly disappeared: monetary disarray, yes; a bling crisis and dental problems, certainly. Now, imagine if steel disappeared. Think of all the things that rely on steel that would simply collapse or cease to exist. The skeleton holding up the man-made world is made of steel.

It's easy for any of us, woodworkers included, to take steel for granted. Think about it: much, if not most, of the actual work of woodworking depends on a piece of steel somewhere between you and the wood.

What is Steel?

Steel is a mixture – an alloy – of iron and carbon. Iron, without any alloying elements, needs help to make it truly useful in all the structural applications we ask of it. Though iron may have been a wonder during the ascent of man – harder and tougher than gold, copper or bronze – with the addition of very small quantities of carbon, as little as 0.2% (two tenths of a percent), the wonder that was iron turns into steel – a very different, incredibly strong yet malleable material. That little bit of carbon adds enough strength to make steel a suitable material for bridges, high-rise buildings, cars and refrigerators.

Most of the steel that we encounter is 0.2%, low-carbon, *mild steel* and is available in hot-rolled or cold-finished sheets, round bars, flat bars, I-beams, angles, etc. *Hot-rolled* steel is the most common structural steel and is used for building and bridge superstructures, big ships, and such; it's the rough and dirty workhorse of the steel industry with a layer

The top sample is hot rolled steel. The bottom is cold finished – or "cold rolled" steel.

of heat-induced iron oxide, called *scale,* over its entire surface. *Cold-finished* (also known as cold-rolled) steel with its smoother, more attractive surface, can be rolled to a more accurate thickness, or *gauge,* and boasts improved uniformity over the hot-rolled version. Cold rolling *work hardens* the steel, making it *tougher* – more resistant to deformation, harder to dent or bend – than hot rolled. With that added toughness and its smoother surface, cold-finished steel is used for car bodies, file cabinets and the like. By adding additional amounts of carbon beyond the 0.2% required to make steel from iron, we can change steel's physical properties, such as *hardness* – the resistance to compressive deformation and *tensile strength* – the resistance to elongation.

More to our interest in woodworking is the fact that, with about 0.8% or more carbon, steel is fully hardenable with heat treatment. Steel with the minimum amount of carbon necessary to be fully hardenable with heat treatment is called *eutectoid* steel. Steel with 0.8% or more carbon is commonly called *high-carbon* steel. Carbon content below 0.8% may allow the steel to partially harden with heat treatment but full hardness can only be achieved with a carbon content of 0.8% or greater. Adding yet more carbon allows the formation of iron and other carbides,

STEEL HISTORY

The discovery of King Tutankhamun's tomb was one of the greatest archeological finds of all time. The lavish riches that were buried with the young king included more gold than the Royal Bank of Egypt had on deposit when the discovery was made in 1922. Among the 107 objects discovered on Tutankhamun's body was an ornately decorated iron dagger that he carried on his belt. Presumably fashioned from meteoritic iron – very rare and much harder and tougher than other metals available at the time – his dagger was considered so precious that the king would certainly want it with him in the afterlife. In an age dominated by the smelting of copper and its stronger alloy, bronze, iron was immeasurably valuable – more so than gold.

While iron oxide makes up over 6% of the Earth's crust, it took a long time for mankind to figure out how to convert *dirt* into something as useful as steel. The first smelting of iron from ore was probably accidental when some iron-bearing ore was mixed in with the copper ore during the smelting of copper. Iron ore is composed mostly of various iron oxides which need to be reduced – have oxygen removed – to form metallic iron. The iron ore was mixed with charcoal, which is mostly carbon, and fired. The carbon dioxide produced by burning charcoal combines with the hot carbon in the charcoal, forming carbon monoxide. The hot carbon monoxide turns again to carbon dioxide by stealing oxygen from – reducing – the iron oxides, leaving metallic iron behind. But the heat needed for melting copper isn't nearly sufficient to melt the iron that may be present in the copper ore. The reaction from ore to iron occurs while in a solid state when the iron forms into a solid, ugly mass of spongy metal called a *bloom*. The bloom's cavities were full of slag (molten impurities from the smelting) that needed to be removed. Someone must have recognized the spongy mass as a metallic substance, probably by using appropriate scientific methodology such as hitting it with a rock. Eventually, the bloom was processed by heating

More valuable than gold? This photo of King Tutankhamen's iron dagger was taken by Harry Burton, the only photographer allowed to photograph inside the tomb discovered by Howard Carter in 1922. This is one of 1,400 photographs Burton took of the contents, their cataloging and removal to the Cairo Museum completed in 1932. PHOTO COPYRIGHT: GRIFFITH INSTITUTE, UNIVERSITY OF OXFORD

it to the slag's melting point and hammering on it until all of the slag had squirted out. This would be hard, dangerous and resource-intensive work as the iron was reheated and beaten over and over to produce wrought iron. This process was the way iron was made from late B.C. to early A.D.

Sometimes the bloom production could be managed so that it contained some carbon, and it is believed that the first steel was produced in East Africa as early as 1400 B.C. The Chinese melted wrought iron and cast iron together to make a middle-carbon steel. In the 1st century A.D, Wootz steel, also known as Damascus or pattern-welded steel, a layering of steels with different carbon contents, was being produced in India and Sri Lanka and was imported into China by the 5th century A.D. The Celts made steel from bars of wrought iron in about 200 A.D. by enclosing them in an iron container with bones or other carbonaceous materials and heating the whole thing over high heat for ten to twelve hours. With this process the iron absorbs the carbon and becomes steel that can be forge-welded and shaped to produce tools.

Modern steel production took a huge leap forward in 1855 when Henry Bessemer patented a process that removed impurities from iron by blowing air though the crucible of liquid metal. Fifteen tons or more of molten iron could be purified in twenty minutes by the Bessemer process, after which carbon and other alloying elements would be added in the desired proportions. Thus began the age of inexpensive, mass-produced steel.

ABOVE Carnegie Steel Co., Youngstown, Ohio, 1910.

LEFT Pattern-welded steel
PHOTO 2005 BY RALF PFEIFER

BELOW Bessemer converter at work in the Republic Steel Mill, Youngstown, Ohio, 1941.
PHOTO BY ALFRED T. PALMER

which improve the steel's hardness. Improved hardness increases the resistance to abrasion and is what makes the steel hold a cutting edge, and forms the foundation for most of the cutting tools in the woodshop. More carbon in the alloy can easily become too much and above about 1.5% the additional carbon only makes the steel brittle. With the addition of 2% or more of carbon, the metal is called *cast iron*.

The changes in the physical properties of steel that occur by adding more or less carbon are due to the formation of different steel crystal structures as well as the way carbon interacts with steel's iron atoms. Low carbon steel is mostly *ferrite*, the simplest iron crystal. Above 0.8% carbon, the steel will contain some amount of *cementite*, or iron carbide (Fe_3C). At 0.8% carbon, the steel is made of *pearlite*, which is a solid solution, a layered mixture of ferrite and cementite.

Let's look at a piece of eutectoid (0.8% carbon) steel. At room temperature, the iron crystal is made of pearlite. The ferrite component has a *body-centered cubic* (bcc) crystal structure, like a cube with nine iron atoms: one at each corner and one in the center. In this crystal configuration carbon atoms have to find room to hang out amongst the iron atoms comprising the cubic crystal structure, which have to deform a bit to accommodate the carbon atoms.

Pearlite crystals are formed of millions of iron atoms; a piece of steel is made of millions of crystals. When steel is bent these crystals slide on one another, squeezing closer, an action that bumps some of their atoms out of formation. These disruptions are known as *dislocations*, and as the surrounding matrix accommodates the atoms dislocated by the bending action, it becomes most stressed in the area where the steel is being bent. Due to this compression of crystals and the resultant dislocations, the area stressed by the bending will be harder. This action is known as *work hardening.** When the steel is bent again at the same place, the same sliding and squeezing occurs but now the neighborhood is less able to accommodate the dislocations and yet more stress is added. If the piece is bent back and forth enough times, the sliding crystals will have used up all their local goodwill and the piece will fracture at the bending site – like breaking a piece of wire by bending it back and forth, (instead of using wire cutters).

What makes one steel harder or stronger than another is the internal resistance to dislocation movement. The more you can restrict the dislocation movement, the harder it will be to bend or dent a piece of metal. The addition of alloying elements and the application of heat treatment are methods employed to inhibit dislocation movement and make the steel harder.

When heated to 1450° F (788° C), the *critical temperature* for simple, high carbon steels, the crystal structure *goes into solution*. It doesn't melt – it's not liquid – but the crystalline nature of the metal – ferrite, pearlite and cementite – reorganizes into a new non-magnetic** crystal called *austenite* while the carbon atoms are free to migrate as if in a liquid.

Work hardening also occurs when metal is hammered upon, creating stressful dislocations directly by impact.

STRENGTH OF STEEL

Chart (abridged) of steel strengths by carbon content from *Machinery's Handbook*: "While the ultimate strength and the yield point both increase as carbon content increases, the shear strength and modulus of elasticity remain the same."

| MATERIALS | Ultimate Strength | | | Modules of Elasticity |
	TENSION, THOUSANDS OF POUNDS PER SQUARE INCH, T	SHEAR IN TERMS OF T	YIELD POINT, THOUSANDS OF POUNDS PER SQUARE INCH	IN TENSION MILLONS OF PSI
Steel, SAE 950 (low alloy)	65 to 70	0.75T	45 to 50	30
1025 (low carbon)	60 to 103	0.75T	40 to 90	30
1045 (medium carbon)	80 to 182	0.75T	50 to 162	30
1950 (high carbon)	90 to 213	0.75T	20 to 150	30

Iron atoms line up in their body-centered ferrite crystal with the smaller carbon atoms squeezed in the spaces. Image created using PTC Pro/Desktop.

Austenite, named for the English metallurgist William Chandler Roberts-Austen (1843–1902), is a *face-centered cubic* (fcc) structured crystal with fourteen iron atoms: one on each corner and one in the center of each face of the cube, if you could isolate just one of the austenite crystals. In reality, the atoms are shared by the neighboring crystals so no one crystal has exclusive ownership of all its atoms. The roaming carbon atoms find a roomy, comfortable place to reside in the newly-vacated center of the austenite cube. The crystal change from a body-centered cubic (bcc) structure to a face-centered cubic (fcc) structure opened up room for the carbon atom's relocation into the center of the austenite cube where we want to trap it by rapidly cooling the hot steel and forcing yet another crystal transformation.

When austenite cools slowly, the crystal structure returns to pearlite and the carbon atoms will all wander back to the between-the-iron-atoms digs they occupied before the heating. The steel at that point will be *annealed* – soft, ductile, easily cut or machined. But if it is cooled quickly – *quenched* – in a liquid bath, austenite becomes yet another crystal called *martensite*, named for German metallurgist Adolph Martens (1850–1914). The martensite crystal is a very hard *body-centered tetragonal* structure, like the body-centered ferrite cube, but flattened so that one cross section is rectangular. It is martensite that gives heat-treated tool steels their hardness and wear-resistance. The carbon atoms that found new, comfortable places to reside in the austenite got trapped in the compressed martensitic structure when the steel was quenched. The captured carbon atoms stress the crystals and lock the structure together in a highly compressed state. The iron atoms deform considerably to accommodate the carbon atoms. In fact, the steel is so stressed that it will be brittle and can fracture very easily.

To reduce these embrittling stresses, the steel must be *tempered*. Tempering, or drawing – a term that probably comes from "drawing back the hardness" – is a low temperature re-heating that relieves some

of the stresses in the steel, making it less brittle by allowing some of the martensite to return to the less-stressed pearlitic structure. For knives, planes irons, chisels and such, simple high-carbon steel is tempered to approximately 325° to 400° F (160° to 205° C). The necessary temperature to achieve a specific hardness, based on the intended use of the steel, is a function of the exact alloy of steel being tempered. As tempering reduces stress and brittleness in the steel, it also reduces hardness and hence, edge life. So, determining the final hardness of a tool is a balance between brittleness and edge-holding ability. A tool that is intended only for paring soft, clear woods can be considerably harder than a tool that will be struck with a hammer or used for hard, knotty woods. The harder tool will hold its edge longer – its higher *compressive strength* gives greater resistance to abrasive pressure. But the softer tool will be tougher and better able to absorb impact and resist chipping – its higher *tensile strength* allows more deformation before failing).

The carbon atom resides comfortably in the hollow center of the austenite crystal. One of the iron atoms has been pulled away so we can see inside. Image created using PTC Pro/Desktop.

In martensite, the carbon atoms are compressed in the tighter tetragonal crystal. Image created using PTC Pro/Desktop.

The point at which steel loses its magnetism while being heated is called the Curie Point *after the discoverer, Madame Curie's husband, Pierre. In simple high carbon alloys, it conveniently indicates that the steel has reached its critical temperature; the transformation to austenite is complete.*

WATER-HARDENING STEELS

With a simple alloy of only iron and carbon, the quench must be very rapid to insure complete hardening. The heat must be removed from the metal with sufficient speed that the carbon atoms do not have time to migrate out of the center of the cubic austenite – they must get trapped or the resulting steel won't be hard. With such a simple alloy, the preferred medium for quenching would be water or salt brine, giving this class of steels the name *water-hardening* and the American Iron and Steel Institute (AISI) prefix of W as in W1 or W2, etc. Even with such a rapid quenchant as water, a thick piece of metal may not harden fully in the center. Sometimes this can be used to advantage as in a chisel where the unhardened core acts as a ductile shock absorber for hammer blows. But the rapid quench of water or brine causes such a thermal shock that the steel is more apt to warp, or even fracture as can a cold glass quickly filled with boiling water. In most cases a gentler quench would be desirable, which leads us to … oil-hardening steels.

OIL-HARDENING STEELS

A small addition of manganese (Mn) to our simple, high carbon alloy reduces the quench rate requirement such that oil can be used as a quenchant. Tool steels that are hardened in an oil quench are called *oil hardening* and designated AISI O1, O2, etc. Oil removes the heat from the steel more slowly, too slowly to be used as a quenchant for a W-series steel, but the manganese impedes the movement of the carbon and iron atoms in the "solution" and allows it to fully quench at oil's slower rate. These steels will distort less during heat treatment and can be hardened to a greater depth. This non-distorting characteristic is especially important with complex metal stamping punches and dies where the tool to be hardened may have many hours of highly skilled labor invested and where no one wants it to warp or move at all. The manganese addition has very little effect on the mechanical characteristics of the steel or the performance of a cutting edge, so these steels are an excellent choice for woodworking tools. They offer the sharpness advantage of fine-grain simplicity, yet are relatively inexpensive as well as being easy and predictable to harden with minimal distortion during heat treatment. Still, since oil hardening steels may

distort too much for some applications we may wish to consider … air-hardening steels.

AIR-HARDENING STEELS

As with water or brine, oil quenching may also cause problematic distortion of the steel due to thermal shock, so other elements are added to allow the steel to harden when quenched in the air. These additional alloying elements – chromium, silicon and others – increase the steel's critical temperature to as high as 2400° F (1315° C) depending on the mixture of alloying elements. Air quenching is very gentle, minimizing distortion in the finished piece. The piece is simply removed from the heat and, for thin pieces, left in still air to cool. Larger parts may require a blast of air from a fan or blower to adequately quench to full hardness. However, the additional alloying elements can create large carbide particles that may interfere with precision sharpening and the durability of a cutting edge. Once again, a balance must be struck, this time between hardening stability and a fine cutting edge. Common *air-hardening* steels are designated with an A for air hardening such as A2 and A10, but there are many other steel alloys that are quenched in air that are not designated with an "A", such as … high speed steels.

HIGH-SPEED STEELS

Some alloying elements affect the steel in other ways and are added to achieve certain specific characteristics in the steel. Elements like tungsten, vanadium, cobalt or molybdenum, added in various amounts, will allow the hardened steel to resist softening at very high working temperatures. The resulting steels are called "high-speed steel" for their ability to run at high speeds, usually while cutting metals, and some can be used even while glowing red-hot without losing their hardness and ability to cut. This is not a requirement in hand woodworking tools, but many power woodworking tools can generate heat in cutting edges well past the tempering temperature of our simple high carbon steel, so high-speed steels are recommended in these applications. High-speed steels are not recommended, however, for hand tool cutters due to the additional cost incurred by the inclusion of these expensive elements that contribute next to nothing to a hand tool's edge. And, the large carbide

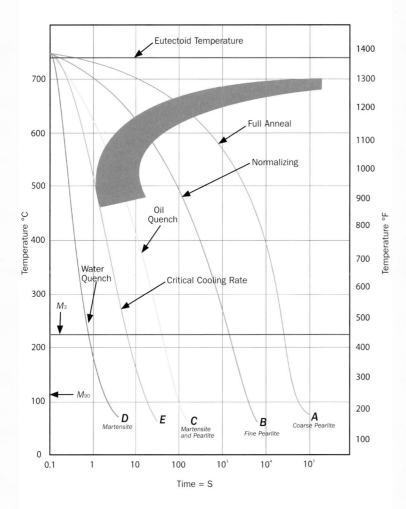

This chart shows the quench rate requirement for a simple steel – just iron with .7% carbon. Line E represents the slowest rate that will fully transform austenite to martensite. Line D represents the rate of water quench, which is faster than necessary to achieve full hardness. Line C represents the quench rate of an oil bath – oil removes heat more slowly than water – not fast enough for this steel. Some of line C goes through the shaded area in which austenite converts back to pearlite instead of being frozen into martensite. Lines A and B represent the very slow cooling rates required for *normalizing* (refining the grain size to normal after forging, etc.) and *annealing* (full softening of the metal).

particles that the exotic alloying elements create during heat treatment can also make them very difficult to sharpen (see Grain Size sidebar on page 20). High-speed steels are usually indicated with their primary alloying element: "T" for tungsten e.g. "M" for molybdenum.

CHROME-VANADIUM STEELS

Chromium is an element that is almost impervious to environmental corrosion. Many tool steels will have chromium contents in excess of 5%. With that much chromium the steel is somewhat resistant to corrosion but the cutting edge will tend to be a bit coarse and in the sharpening process may feel "gummy". The chromium carbides that form during heat treatment may resist wear well, though, so high chromium steels tend to hold their edges for a long time. This characteristic can be useful in, for instance, a scrub plane, where the surface finish left behind by the cutter is secondary to the need for rapid stock removal. However, a "stainless" quality can be an asset to the manufacturer since the blades made of chromium carbides like chrome-vanadium will stay bright and shiny longer, extending market shelf-life. And since these steels are mostly air-hardened post-heat treatment, grinding to remove distortion or warpage is minimized. Vanadium is added to steel to improve edge retention – vanadium carbides are small, hard, wear-resistant particles – and to minimize grain growth during heat treatment. Although we like vanadium in our woodworking tool steels, chromium tends to cause more problems than it solves.

STAINLESS STEEL

A steel is officially considered a stainless steel if its chromium content is in excess of 10.5%. However, in order

GRAIN SIZE

The amount of carbon in a tool steel recipe determines the degree of hardness and wear resistance the steel can achieve. Steel is fully hardenable with a carbon content of about 0.8%. Any extra carbon will combine with the iron atoms to form iron carbides – small, hard, wear-resistant granules interspersed in the steel – which add to the steel's edge-holding ability. Other alloying elements combine with carbon to form carbides of their own, so the amount of carbon must be increased to accommodate their carbide needs without starving the iron matrix of the carbon necessary to fully harden and form iron carbides. These other carbides: chromium carbide, vanadium carbide, etc., are hard and durable and aid in the quest for edge-retention. But some carbides are larger than may be desired – large enough to inhibit the sharp edge that is the hallmark of simpler alloys. These large carbide particles form during heat treatment. Careful, controlled hardening can minimize their growth so that their presence is beneficial. But some steels and some processes create very large carbide particles that will get in the way of a near-zero-radius perfect edge. In the photos the white spots are carbide particles. The O1 has no visible carbides, the A2 sample contains a few, well-dispersed carbides, while the D2 sample (with 13% chromium) contains many, very large carbide particles. The presence of carbides will help the steel hold an edge but make it difficult to sharpen and may prohibit a high degree of initial sharpness as the carbide particles are larger than the radius of the final polished edge. Sharpening abrasion reduces the size of the carbides but the bonds that hold carbide particles in place are weaker than the steel matrix, so when that surrounding martensitic structure is honed to a sharp edge, there is little to hold the carbides in place and they are easily dislodged, leaving a gap in the edge.

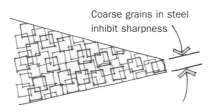

Coarse grains in steel inhibit sharpness

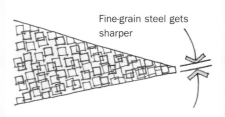

Fine-grain steel gets sharper

O1 sample prepared to show its crystal structure at 1000x magnification. There are no carbides visible in this image.

COURTESY TIMKEN-LATROBE STEEL

A2 sample prepared to show its crystal structure at 1000x magnification. A few of the carbide particles are identified and colored.

COURTESY TIMKEN-LATROBE STEEL

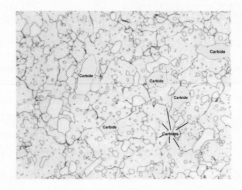

D2 sample prepared to show its crystal structure at 1000x magnification. Note the large size of the carbides identified and colored; the largest ones are probably chromium carbides.

COURTESY TIMKEN-LATROBE STEEL

to have truly stainless behavior, steels need higher chromium content and a significant nickel content. A popular composition is *18-8* (18% chromium with 8% nickel). With these high alloy contents the steel's crystal structure is no longer body-centered cubic (bcc) but remains as face-centered cubic (fcc), even at room temperature. Steels of this type are referred to as *austentic stainlesses* and are extremely resistant to corrosion, tarnishing and staining but have low hardness, low strength and are non-magnetic. 18-8 stainless steel is the type of material used in a stainless-steel eating utensils. But, this steel is too soft for even a table knife so the nickel content is usually reduced so the knife blades can be slightly hardened. Look at your stainless-steel flatware, the blades of the knives will tend to have more tarnish and stains than the forks or spoons as a result of their lower nickel content. If you check the magnetic behavior of your stainless-steel flatware, you will usually find that the spoons, forks and knife handles are non-magnetic (they are fcc) but that the knife blade is magnetic (they are bcc).

High-carbon stainless steels, like you see in kitchen knives, strike a compromise between being "stainless" (they're not, but they do resist corrosion well) and being good edge-tools. My experience with them has always been disappointing in the edge-tool category. Usually, they've been very difficult to sharpen and reluctant to take a keen edge though they tend to hold a less-than-perfect edge for a long time. Yet, high-quality, high-chromium-"stainless"-steel knives do have their place. Certainly putting "stainless" in any corrosive environment like a fishing tackle box or boat makes good sense, as it does in some commercial kitchen uses where easy cleaning and sanitizing is required.

Even though some high-quality tool bodies are made of stainless steel to minimize tarnish or rust, stainless steels are of no primary interest when it comes to blades and cutting edges for woodworking.

ALLOY STEELS

The American Iron and Steel Institute (AISI) has established standards for steel alloys and designates them with either a four digit number or a letter followed by a number. The four digit series are called alloy steels, the number indicating certain properties of the steel. The first two digits indicate the steel's grade, usually with its primary alloying element such as plain carbon (10xx), free cutting carbon (11xx), manganese steels (13xx), nickel steels (23xx) and so on. The second two digits indicate the percent of carbon so that "AISI 1095" would designate a plain carbon steel with 0.95% carbon. There can be a letter in between the two sets of digits indicating another alloying element (xxLxx). An additional digit may sometimes be added to the first two to indicate a further subclass of steel and an additional digit may be added to the last two if the amount of carbon exceeds 1.0%. The system has been in use for decades and has grown fairly complex but many of the original four digit designations are still in use today.

TOOL STEELS

The other class of alloy steels is the tool steels. Tool steels differ from the alloy steels in that they are more metallurgically pure and must be manufactured to closer tolerances for their alloy proportions. The AISI designates tool steels with a letter followed by one or two digits. There is some logic to the letters … up to a point. Some are designated according to the steel's quench medium: W1 is water hardening steel number one, O6 is the sixth of the oil hardening alloys and A10 is air hardening number 10. Others are classified by the work they do: D2 is the second of the die steels, H13 is used for hot work such as forging dies and the like because it can withstand extreme heat, S1 is a shock-resistant steel used in high impact applications. Some of the tool steels get their name from the predominant alloying element: T15 is a tungsten steel; M42 is a molybdenum steel (and both are high-speed steels.) It almost makes sense. Then there are all the proprietary grades of tool steels that have been formulated by one steel company or another such as 154CM, ATS-34 or CPM9V. It'll make your head spin.

There are many charts and discussions of blade steels on the internet. A search on "knife-blade steel" will yield many results – and many more opinions about which one is best for this or that application. The charts they offer tend to be accurate, in my limited searching around, but the opinions should be taken as just that. I've included the Advisor in Metals (AIM) Tool Steel Selector chart (on page 22) to show how the different tool steels relate to each other.

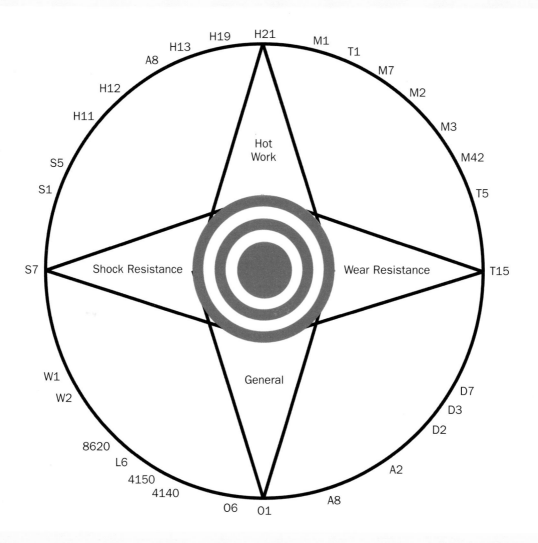

Taken from Heat Treatment, Selection and Application of Tool Steels by permission.

The steels that are used most commonly for hand woodworking are in an arc along the bottom of the circle. Woodworking steels are most commonly W1 (traditional chisels and plane irons), O1 (my favorite for plane irons and Hock Tools' choice for our high-carbon steel blades), A2 (gaining in user popularity – a great choice when extended edge-life is a primary consideration), as well as several of the high-speed steels in the upper right quadrant such as M2.

You might be tempted, after studying the chart, to say "hey, if A2 holds an edge better than O1, then D7 must be better still, right?" Well, yes and no. Die steels like D7 and the more commonly available D2 will hold an edge much longer but they're very difficult to sharpen and the enormous chromium carbide particles present in the hardened steel make it very

difficult to get an edge as sharp as you can get with a simpler alloy. D2, et al, are used mostly in punch-and-die metal stamping tools and are sharpened with bevel angles just barely less than 90° so the edge produced is quite strong and isn't bothered by the carbide size. So, okay, you say, how about going the other way and trying the S7? It's super shock resistant so it oughta be really tough so I can make a chisel out of it and beat on it all day, right? Again, yes and no. S7 is used for cold chisels and rock drills, things that don't need to hold a sharp edge; they only need to not fracture when banged on. So your chisel will hold up to abusive hammering without fracturing but it won't hold its edge very well at all.

I wish it were otherwise, but there is no free lunch. Everything boils down to finding a balance between these

AISI TOOL STEEL COMPOSITIONS

Composite Materials	W1	W2	O1	O6	A2	A6	A10	D2	D7	S1	S5	S7	H13	M2	M3	M4	M42	T1	T15	4140
Carbon (C)	1.00	.86	.95	1.45	1.00	.70	1.35	1.50	2.30	.50	.60	.50	.40	.80	1.05	1.30	1.10	.72	1.55	.40
Silicon (Si)	.20	.23	.25	1.20	.30	.30	1.20	.30	.40	.80	1.95	.25	1.10	.30	.30	.30	.30	.30	.30	.40
Manganese (Mn)	.25	.32	1.00	.80	.70	2.00	1.80	.35	.40	.25	.85	.50	.40	.30	.30	.30	.30	.30	.30	.90
Chromium (Cr)	.15	.15	.50	.20	5.20	1.00	–	12.0	12.5	1.25	.30	3.25	5.30	4.00	4.00	4.50	3.75	4.00	4.75	1.00
Nickel (Ni)	–	–	–	–	–	–	1.85	–	–	–	–	–	–	–	–	–	–	–	–	–
Molybdenum (Mo)	.10	.10	–	.25	1.10	1.35	1.50	.80	1.10	–	.45	1.45	1.40	5.00	6.25	4.50	9.50	–	1.00	.20
Tungsten (W)	.15	.15	.60	–	–	–	–	–	–	2.25	–	–	–	6.00	6.25	5.50	1.60	18.0	12.5	–
Cobalt (Co)	–	–	–	–	–	–	–	–	–	–	–	–	–	–	–	–	8.0	–	5.0	–
Vanadium (V)	1.00	.24	.25	–	.20	–	–	.60	4.00	.25	.20	.20	1.00	2.00	2.50	4.00	1.15	1.00	5.00	–

three features: edge holding, sharpenability (both ease of and how sharp it can get) and corrosion resistance – at the risk of oversimplifying, you can only have two of the three.

CARBIDE

When woodworkers hear about carbide tools, the material is usually *cemented tungsten carbide* (WC). Tungsten carbide is one of the hardest materials known and is used for its extreme wear resistance, its ability to withstand high temperatures in use and its resistance to corrosion. All of these attributes make it desirable for powered wood-cutting applications. The carbide production process begins with tungsten carbide powders in a variety of grain sizes from 0.5 micron (abbreviated μ, the Greek letter mu) to 50μ. Different grain sizes account for different properties (such as toughness) in the finished carbide parts and account for all the different carbide grades available. These powders are mixed with cobalt or nickel binders along with a bit of wax, to hold the powder mixture together, while being shaped into an enormous variety of near-final configurations. The "cemented" part of cemented carbide refers to the *sintering process* in which the shaped powder and wax parts are heated in a vacuum to 2,600° F (1,430° C). During sintering, the cobalt and nickel binders melt to fuse with and bind the particles of WC together into the final high-density, pore-free structure that is used for saw-tooth tips, router and shaper bits, etc.

Looking at the right-hand column of the chart on page 24 you can see that the same toughness vs. hardness trade-off exists with carbide as with tool steels,

where shock resistance is inversely proportional to wear resistance. For the most part, woodworkers don't have to choose carbide by grade; you can trust the cutter manufacturer to have done that for you.

So, you may ask, why don't we use carbide for all of our woodworking tools? Three reasons: one, it's very expensive and is only economical in the small bits and inserts that are available; two, it is so very difficult to sharpen; and three, it is very brittle compared to steel and won't hold up when shaped to the small edge angles required for hand wood cutting operations. Take a look at one of your carbide tools and you'll see that the cutting angles are very large to support the wear-resistant but fragile cutting edge.

POWDER METALS

When I fell into the world of woodworking tools, the state of the art in tool steel was pretty much chrome-vanadium steel. There were high carbon stainless steels being used in mediocre kitchen knives and some pioneering custom knife makers were using A2, D2 along with O1, and old car springs and that was about as exotic as things got way back in the Reagan years.

Woodworkers were looking for something better and who could blame them? James Krenov was setting up shop here in Fort Bragg at the College of the Redwoods and teaching, among the rest of his philosophy and techniques, the joys and pleasures of using wooden planes of one's own making. So his students would traipse down to the local hardware store to buy cheap chrome-vanadium (Cr-V) block plane replacement blades to build their planes around. Chip

CARBIDE GRADE CHART

Industry Code	Approximate Binder %	Hardness Rockwell "A"	Hardness Rockwell "C"	Transverse Rupture PSI	Compressive Strength PSI	Grain Size
C3 C4	3	92.5–93.0	80–82	225,000	660,000	Fine
C1 C2 C9	6	91.0–92.0	79–81	275,000	700,000	Fine
C10	9	90.0–91.0	77–79	350,000	600,000	Fine
C11	13	88.5–89.5	73–75	370,000	600,000	Fine
C12	14	88.0–89.0	72–74	385,000	575,000	Fine
C13	15	87.5–88.5	71–73	400,000	560,000	Fine
C14	20	84.0–85.0	65–67	450,000	530,000	Coarse
C17	22	81.5–83.0	60–62	350,000	480,000	Extra Coarse

Ridge TS2000 Carbide-Tipped Saw Blade

PHOTO COURTESY WOODPECKERS, (WWW.WOODPECK.COM)

breakers posed an altogether different problem that required some metalworking. And being woodworkers, well, you should have seen some of the creative ways they managed to clobber together chip breakers. I was making knives at the time, and they heard about me and asked if I could make some blades for their planes. One batch led to another and I quit making knives a short time after that to concentrate on making blades for planes. When I came along with a blade that was better than the mediocre Cr-V replacements they were using, (trust me, it wasn't that hard to do – I was definitely in the right place at the right time) these woodworkers were quite pleased with what I did. But some of them realized that maybe, just maybe, there was a yet superior steel out there, waiting for someone to try it out.

Over the years, I've noticed a longing on the part of hand tool users for better blades, as well as a suspicion that there must be something better "out there." I've always replied to the query with something to the effect of, "How much better would you want it?" and "Better in which way?" Usually, woodworkers want something that will stay sharp longer. Okay, A2 does that with little compromise (but still no free lunch, remember?) So, now we basically have two steels doing most of the hand tool work: O1 and A2. Current metallurgical constraints limit the chances for another alloy to improve the situation. Some people spend their money on expensive, high-speed steel alloys for hand tools, yet, I continue to believe they are spending a lot for little or no improvement over what we already have available.

Powder metal technology has been around a long time and is used for all kinds of things. Oil-impregnated bronze bearings, for example, are a powder metal product; the powder metal process, in this case, leaves the bearing porous and it can be loaded with oil for a self-lubricating bearing. And, powdered metal can be pressed into a three-dimensional shape and sintered to yield a like-cast part for a fraction of the cost of a casting.

Here's where it gets interesting for us. Vanadium is a desirable alloying metal for tool steels. Vanadium carbide particles are very small and very wear-resistant. Many alloys have some amount of vanadium in them, for a variety of reasons, but if the metallurgists could add more, they probably would. The problem is, vanadium tends to fall out of suspension as the molten batch of steel cools into an ingot, so there can't be as much of it in the alloy as we might want. To solve this problem molten high-vanadium steel is sprayed through a very small nozzle into a vacuum chamber to cool into a fine powder with a particle size of about 3μ. This powder still has all the vanadium mixed in. The high-vanadium powder is then compressed and sintered and rolled into sheets like any other steel. But, it now contains as much as 10% vanadium because the vanadium never got the chance to settle out. Because the atomized particle size is smaller than the steel's normal grain structure, the resulting product is an incredibly fine-grained, highly wear-resistant steel that will take a keen edge and hold it.

Where is it, you ask? Where can I get some? There are a few powder metal turning tools on the market that are gaining in popularity. And, some plane blade makers are currently experimenting with it, but the raw metal stock is very expensive, difficult to work with and to heat treat, and the hardened steel is extremely difficult to sharpen. Some grades are similar to sharpening carbide, but unlike carbide, the powder metal can be used with a small bevel angle. The issue of sharpening difficulty is not as great for woodturners because power grinders are generally chosen for this particular job.

With these powder metals I do see something truly new in the steel arena for the first time in a long time, and thought I'd share my view with you that there may be something new on the horizon. Stay tuned.

Heat Treating

It's not magic that you can change something as fundamental as the very hardness of steel by heating and cooling it. Of course, you must follow a procedure, but even after all these years, I find it wonderful, and a bit magical, that it can be done at all.

Though each steel alloy has a different procedure for hardening by heat treatment, the basic procedure is similar for all. I'll cover the two most popular steels for woodworking hand tools such as chisels and plane irons: AISI O1 and A2.

Basically, the steel must be heated to its critical temperature (see the preceding section) and held there while the ferrite crystal structure transforms to austenite. It is during this phase that the iron and carbon are "in solution". Remember that this does not mean the steel is a liquid, only that the iron atoms are able to re-arrange themselves into austenite and that the carbon atoms can migrate about in the new austenitic crystal structure. More complex alloys will require more heat and a longer time to accomplish this, but for a common, oil hardening steel such as O1, the required critical temperature is between 1,450° and 1,500° F (790° to 815° C).

Care must be taken to prevent the loss of carbon to the atmosphere while it roams freely throughout the steel. If carbon migrates to a surface in an atmosphere that includes oxygen, it will combine with the oxygen and depart forever. Commercial heat treaters use several methods to prevent contact with air. These include: molten salt baths; vacuum furnaces; atmosphere-controlled furnaces where the chamber of the oven is purged with an inert gas such as nitrogen or argon;

A rack of HOCK blades being removed from the furnace.
PHOTO COURTESY EDWARDS HEAT TREATING SERVICE.

TEMPERATURE GUIDE

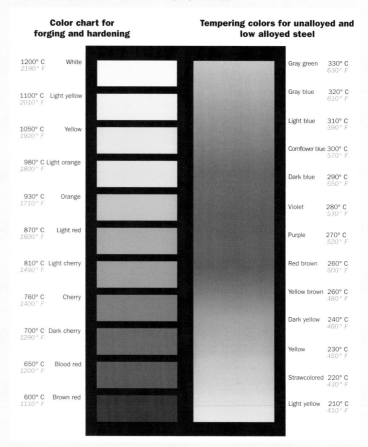

Color chart for forging and hardening		Tempering colors for unalloyed and low alloyed steel	
1200° C / 2190° F	White	Gray green	330° C / 630° F
1100° C / 2010° F	Light yellow	Gray blue	320° C / 610° F
1050° C / 1920° F	Yellow	Light blue	310° C / 590° F
980° C / 1800° F	Light orange	Cornflower blue	300° C / 570° F
930° C / 1710° F	Orange	Dark blue	290° C / 550° F
870° C / 1600° F	Light red	Violet	280° C / 530° F
810° C / 1490° F	Light cherry	Purple	270° C / 520° F
760° C / 1400° F	Cherry	Red brown	260° C / 500° F
700° C / 1290° F	Dark cherry	Yellow brown	260° C / 480° F
650° C / 1200° F	Blood red	Dark yellow	240° C / 460° F
600° C / 1110° F	Brown red	Yellow	230° C / 450° F
		Strawcolored	220° C / 430° F
		Light yellow	210° C / 410° F

This color chart should be viewed in normal, diffused daylight and not in sunlight or artivicial light. Colors assigned to a tempereing time of 30 minutes. The colors should be viewed on a polished piece of steel.
CHART COURTESY OF UDDEHOLM TOOLING AB, WWW.UDDEHOLM.COM.

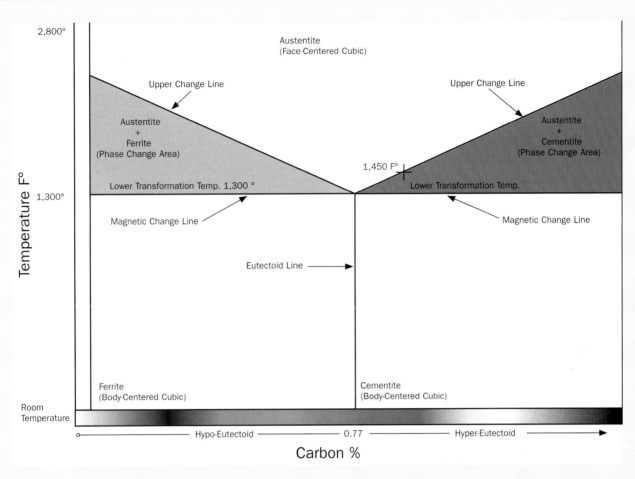

This diagram shows the phases at different temperatures relative to the carbon content of the steel. Low carbon steels are to the left of the eutectoid line while high carbon steels are to the right. The line at 1,300° F is the "carbon line," indicating the temperature when carbon goes into solution. Steel with 0.77% carbon will convert entirely to austenite above 1300° F. If the steel has more or less carbon than that, the conversion temperature will be higher. Our oil hardening AISI O1 has 0.95% carbon and converts to austenite at 1,450° F.

an atmosphere of natural gas, containing sufficient carbon to balance the carbon in the steel so that no carbon will be given up or absorbed by the steel during heat treatment.

Atmosphere control is especially important during the heat treatment of A2. Carbon begins moving about in the steel at about 1,300° F (700° C). A2's critical temperature is 1,775° F (970° C), which means that it will take longer to reach its critical temperature, increasing the risk of carbon burnout.

When the steel has reached critical temperature, it should be allowed to soak for 20 minutes per inch of cross section to allow for complete crystal transformation. Care must be taken that the steel not exceed the critical temperature. Overheating encourages the growth of large grains that weaken the hardened steel. The steel is then quenched – O1 in a bath of oil, A2 is simply removed to still air – to trap the carbon atoms

in their new locations and convert the austenite crystals to hard, wear-resistant martensite. Tempering is done as soon as the piece reaches room temperature, otherwise, there is a risk of fracturing as the internal and external dimensions change with the transformation of austenite into martensite. With some thick pieces of steel, uneven dimensional changes can crack the outer surface, as the transformation continues for some time after the piece has cooled.

The final, usable hardness is determined by the tempering temperature. Again, the alloy used dictates the exact temperatures. The O1 example should have an as-quenched hardness approaching Rc66 (that's very hard and brittle, like a file) and will temper to Rc63 at 300° F (150° C), Rc60 at 400° F (205° C), Rc57 at 500° F (260° C), etc. A2 should quench at about Rc64 and tempers to 63 at 300° F (150° C), Rc61 at 400° F (205° C), Rc60 at 500° F (260° C).

Our WWII-vintage hardness tester with a spokeshave blade being tested.

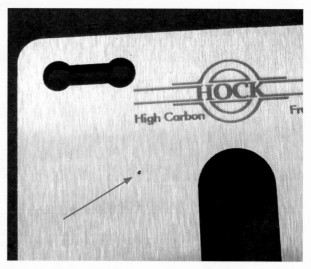

The hardness test leaves a small dent in the part. It measures the depth of the dent to determine the hardness of the sample.

HARDNESS

The Rockwell scale is an arbitrary scale developed to quantify the hardness of materials. Hardness is defined as "resistance to indentation" so the Rockwell hardness test uses indentation to measure hardness. A diamond stylus of a precisely prescribed conical shape is pressed into the surface of the test material with a measured and repeatable amount of pressure. The depth of penetration is measured and translated to the Rockwell scale. There are different Rockwell scales, A, B, C, etc., with the C scale applicable to hard materials like hardened tool steel. For reference, a metal-cutting file should be very hard, Rc65 for instance, a plane iron or chisel should be Rc62, while a saw is usually in the mid 40's to low 50's. You can estimate hardness by using a file to "cut" a bit of the steel in question. A file is usually harder than any sample you'd want to test so the harder the metal, the less the file will "bite." By comparing the "bite" of a variety of tools you can develop your own scale for relative hardness.

DIY TECHNIQUES

You can successfully harden your own tools with a little knowledge, some heat and a known alloy of steel. That's often the hardest part: what steel have I got here? And, which quenchant do I use? The steel used in any given tool is not an easy thing to determine. A metallurgical laboratory charges a fair amount of money to test for alloy and there is no surefire home test that I know of. Also, there is some risk in quenching, say, an oil hardening steel in water. It could warp like crazy or, worse, it could fracture. The old-timers "sparked" steels to tell what was in them. The sparks generated from a grinder will burn with different visual characteristics depending on the alloying elements (like the different mineral colorants in fireworks.) So you can grind a corner of the piece in question, observe the sparks, then grind a known steel and try to compare the little spark-flares for shape, brightness, complexity, etc. and then attempt a match.

For the do-it-yourselfer, the most common issue will be whether a piece of steel (car spring, old saw, whatever) is oil or water hardening. It is safer to quench an unknown, perhaps water hardening steel in oil than vice versa. The water hardening steel may not fully harden in the oil and if that is the case, the chemistry and physics let you try again in water. I know this sounds cautionary and that's because it is. Although I am wary of giving false hope to do-it-yourselfers, I also know it is possible to harden steels on your own. When I was making knives from saw blades, I cobbled together a high-temperature oven and an oil bath (like a deep fryer) for hardening and tempering on a very tight budget and managed to do a respectable job of heat treating over a thousand knives. I learned a lot about the process through trial and error, building and rebuilding and fine-tuning the gear. I still keep my hand in, for simple, small jobs in the shop and for curiosity testing on a small scale, but I now let the pro's handle our production heat treating. With our current batch sizes, they do a much more consistent, uniform job than I could with my shoestring setup.

The first step is to get the metal to its critical temperature, which with good old O1 (the oil hardening stuff) is 1,450°–1,500° F (790°–815° C). Got a good pyrometer? No problem. Two events signal the transformation of pearlite (the low-temperature iron crystal) to austenite. One is a sudden leap in the color

of the red-hot steel. As the piece approaches critical temperature, the red glow that starts at around 1,200° F (650° C) [photo 1] will visibly brighten until the piece approaches 1,400° F (760° C) [photo 2]. It will then remain at that color while the pearlite converts to austenite. Once that transformation is complete, the color suddenly jumps to a much brighter orange (photo 3). Recognizing that color change can take some experience, though, it may not be that obvious to the novice. Lucky for you, austenite is not magnetic. The point at which plain high-carbon steel ceases to be magnetic is its critical temperature. Because of

this handy fact of physics, you can simply heat the metal until a magnet is no longer attracted to it, then quench it in oil. There are commercially available quench oils but, for simplicity's sake, I use peanut oil. Peanut oil has a very high flash point that reduces the risk of fire (see Fire Danger Alert! on page 31) and it smells nicer than a petroleum oil when it smokes.

How to get the blade to the Curie point is probably the biggest problem for the do-it-yourselfer. As the metal passes 1,300° F (700° C) or so, the carbon behaves as if it's in a liquid and can therefore migrate around as it pleases. This is necessary for the hard-

FIRE DANGER ALERT! SAFETY FIRST

The risk of fire here is very real. Flames + Red-Hot Metal + Hot Oil = Danger! Be prepared: use long tongs to handle the work, wear gloves and eye/face protection. Bring your most alert brain with you, along with a fire extinguisher, when you're heat-treating. If you're doing this in the shop or garage, turn on a fan and don't be surprised when the smoke alarm sounds off. Don't heat the oil over an open flame! An electric fryer used outdoors is recommended. If you're doing this in the house, call a divorce attorney. Be careful!

ening to occur but near the surface of the metal those carbon atoms become fickle and would just as soon run off with any available oxygen atoms they encounter, lost forever to their new relationship as atmospheric carbon dioxide. We attempt to prevent this decarburization of the steel by heating the metal in an inert (oxygen-free) atmosphere, or by severely limiting the time at red-heat. An oxy-acetylene torch, which is often the heat source of choice for the do-it-yourselfer, makes the former impossible and the latter very difficult. It's a real challenge to heat something as large as a plane blade evenly with a small torch-generated spot of heat. A forge fire is better than a torch because of its uniformity, and it can be starved for air just a bit to decrease the oxygen in the immediate vicinity. A small lab-type test oven or a kiln used for ceramic glaze tests works quite well, though you may not be able to observe the color changes as the steel is heating. Toss in a charcoal briquette to scavenge some of the oxygen from inside the oven while the steel is in it. The best solution to the carbon burnout problem for the DIY heat treater is to coat the steel with an occlusive powder coating (see resources). The powder is applied to the part that's been preheated to 450° F (230° C). The part is then returned to the heat to finish the process. The coating washes off with water after quenching.

Even though the official instructions say to allow a piece to soak at critical temperature for 20 minutes per inch of cross section, for most backyard work with a thin section, such as a knife, as soon as you're sure it has reached critical temperature (photo 4) you can remove the piece from the heat and quickly dunk it into a sufficient quantity of room-temperature oil (photo 5). Be prepared for the oil to catch fire – don't hold the blade in such a way that your hand (or your face) is directly above it (photo 6). For uniform cooling, move the piece up and down in the oil. If you swirl it around, there is a risk that it will cool faster on one side which could lead to warpage. The piece should be tempered as soon as it has cooled to about 150° F (65° C). Without tempering it will be very hard and too brittle to use. You can check for hardness with a file. There will probably be a thin, soft skin on the piece due to decarburization, so the file may grab that decarburized skin, which is soft. Push a little harder on the file to get through that skin and you should find hard, non-fileable steel beneath that the file will simply skid across.

Temper immediately after quenching to avoid the risk of damage mentioned above. The goal is simple: heat the part to the desired tempering temperature (see the chart), hold it there for twenty minutes per inch of cross section and you're done. Knowing

The familiar rainbow of colors that indicate surface temperatures. The light "straw" on the right shows up at about 400° F (200° C) the dark brown at about 500°F (260° C), pale blue about 600° F (315° C) and light blue 640° F (340° C).

whether or not you've reached the right temperature may pose a problem. If you have a very accurate oven in the kitchen, and when your spouse is out of the house for the day, just dial in the target temperature and heat your blade in the oven for the time required. An accurate deep fryer will accomplish the same result and tempering in an oil bath (see Fire Danger Alert! on page 31) works well. Always use a reliable thermometer to double check the oven or deep fryer's thermostat. There is no need to quench at this step (although you can), just be sure the blade has thoroughly reached the intended temperature without exceeding that temperature.

Without accurate temperature control, you'll have to use the surface oxide colors to know when enough is enough. The as-quenched piece will be black and scaly, so first, if you're tempering with a torch, use a piece of sandpaper to clean some part of the blade until it's bright metal again. When heated, that spot will change colors (you've seen the rainbow of colors that appears when steel heats) starting with a very faint yellow, called light straw, and progressing through a striking vermilion to teal blue and gray. Hock Tools' high-carbon plane blades are tempered to 325° F (163° C) for a hardness of Rc62. I recommend this hardness, it has worked well for us for decades, but it presents a conundrum for the DIY heat treater because the first, faint hint of color will appear at a temperature just slightly higher than 325° F (163° C). It's like telling a fellow passenger on the bus, "Get out at the stop right before mine." So my best advice is to overheat slightly to the first sign of color, the faintest of the light straw, and stop there. Your finished part may not be quite as hard as Rc62 but it will be very close and should perform well. Tempering "by the colors" may be an old romantic blacksmith's tradition

but it is not as effective as an oven or oil bath that allows the steel to soak for the optimal time to allow full transformation.

Start heating away from the cutting edge, apply the torch flame sparingly and allow the colors to run to the edge. You may have to quench the piece to arrest any further increase in temperature. Any color beyond the faintest straw is too much. (The blade will still work – it just won't hold its edge as long as you may like.) Also, be overly cautious with tempering. You can always re-temper a too-hard blade, but if you go too far and soften it too much, you have to re-harden it all over again. If a blade seems too hard, you can always toss it back in the oven and let it go 25° F (13° C) hotter, holding it there for a few minutes before removing it from the heat.

If you are using the oil-bath, "deep-fryer" method for tempering, the blade won't present the tempering colors because the oil prevents oxygen from creating the colorful oxides on the steel surface. Trust the thermometer and the method, then remove the blade from the oil or just turn off the heat and let it cool.

You're done! If the blade looks awful, you can sandblast or grind it pretty but it should work well regardless. If you've made a plane iron or a chisel, be sure to grind back the bevel a bit before honing. Without protective coating or atmosphere control, that thin edge probably received more than its fair share of carbon burnout abuse and you need to get down to the good steel (the decarburized layer may be as thick as 0.025" (0.6mm)). The same goes for the back: careful honing of the back is at least, if not more, important than honing the bevel. A little extra elbow grease will remove the de-carbed layer and expose the hardened steel. Don't forget, the back is the cutting edge. Think about it: if the back hasn't

One of the computer-controlled cryogenic "freezers" made by, and in use at, Cryogenics International in Scottsdale, Arizona. This is not your mother's freezer!

been honed deeply enough, the blade will never work as well as it should.

CRYOGENIC TREATMENT

In the last twenty-five years, much has been claimed about the effects that extreme cold or *cryogenic treatment* can have on metals (and almost everything else, it seems.) Some of the claims sound outrageous and others just sound silly, but after all this time some truths are emerging from the claims. The companies that perform the cryogenic treatments claim that metalworking cutters can last ten times longer without sharpening, that stamping dies enjoy similar increases in run-times between sharpenings, that treated gun barrels shoot more accurately and treated engine parts last longer. Brass musical instruments sound better, guitar strings sound brighter and last longer,

even golf balls fly farther and panty hose resist runs longer. Wow!

When high carbon steel is quenched, austenite is converted to martensite in the hardened piece. With simple high carbon steels and careful heat-treating, the conversion is complete in any practical sense. With more complex steels, especially ones that air harden, there can be, and often is, some retained austenite after the quench. The conversion to martensite takes longer than the quench cycle and some of the retained austenite may or may not convert over hours, days, months or even years. Cryogenic treatment allows very nearly all of the retained austenite to convert to martensite. It's as if the piece is finally, fully quenched. Cryogenic treatment improves toughness with little, if any, change in hardness. The improvement possible in any given piece will depend on how much retained austenite it contains and that depends on how carefully it was heat-treated in the first place.

There are other factors at play during deep cryogenic treatment that improve edge retention as well. Deep cryogenic treatment, at -320° F (-195° C), is instrumental in the formation of very small (as small as 0.1µ), very hard carbide particles called *eta-carbides* (or η-carbides, "η" being the Greek letter eta) dispersed throughout the iron matrix. The conversion of retained austenite to martensite can be completed at "shallow" cryogenic temperatures of -120° F (-85° C), much higher than the deep cryogenic temperatures, but the dramatic improvements in wear resistance are realized only with deep cryogenics and the formation of η-carbides. It is also claimed that the stresses in the matrix that are relieved by the cryogenic treatment contribute to some degree of corrosion resistance. All in all, it's easy to make the case for cryogenic treatment of tool steels.

Even bamboo fly-rod makers benefit from cryogenic blade treatment.
PHOTO COURTESY OF JIM LOWE

The commercial cryogenic treatment process is performed in computer-controlled "freezers" that take the items down very slowly to -320° F (-195° C) using liquid nitrogen as a coolant. The process takes about 40 hours all together for the system to cool down, soak or "dwell" for the prescribed time and warm back up, all at a specified rate of cooling and re-warming. Cryogenic treating can be performed at any time during the life of the object and lasts for the rest of its life (or until the steel is re-heat-treated). It is not a simple surface treatment, but the dénouement of the heat treatment drama.

Many years ago I had a large sample of a variety of woodworking tools cryogenically treated and found the results inconclusive. But these were all simple alloys of high-carbon steel that had been heat-treated with the utmost care in the first place. They apparently contained very little, if any, retained austenite, hence, the lack of noticeable improvement. When Hock Tools started offering blades made from A2

tool steel, we insisted on cryogenic treatment for them because A2 is an air hardening alloy, prone to austenite retention, and the potential for improved edge-retention by the cryogenic treatment was too great to ignore. The blades' performance is bearing this out through satisfied feedback from our customers. Bamboo fly-rod makers are especially enthusiastic about the ability of A2 blades to hold an edge while planing bamboo, a species that contains a large amount of abrasive silica famous for quickly dulling a sharp edge.

Rust

Any discussion about steel is incomplete without mentioning rust. Rust is the product of the oxidation of iron. Iron and oxygen are eager to combine and make rust, but for this to occur iron must be in contact with water and oxygen. Air contains both of these, depending on the relative humidity. Water in the air is readily absorbed by a speck of dust on the surface of one of your tools to form a droplet. That tiny water droplet on the iron surface is all it takes to provide the electrolyte necessary to allow oxygen to combine with the iron and water, creating an iron hydroxide molecule ($Fe(OH)x$). Additional oxygen in the water combines with the iron hydroxide to form hydrated iron oxide ($Fe_2O_3.H_2O$), which we know so well as brown rust: a porous, absorbent coating that encourages yet more rust. The rust molecule is physically larger than iron alone, so rust literally grows as oxidation continues deeper into the iron. The larger iron hydroxide and iron oxide molecules push each other out of the way causing scales and flakes of rust to detach from the iron's surface. Under the right conditions, at least as far as rust is concerned, the surface coating of brown rust will continue until all the iron is converted to its oxide and there is nothing left but a pile of rust. Musician Neil Young got it right: "Rust Never Sleeps."

Iron is so reactive with oxygen that the only samples of pure metallic iron available on Earth are nodules buried so deep in the crust that they have yet to encounter any of oxygen's efforts. It has been said that for every pound of iron or steel produced in a year, one-quarter pound of previously produced iron or steel is lost to rust! The National Association of Corrosion Engineers (NACE) did a study in 2002 to determine what corrosion costs the United States and estimates it to be a staggering $276 billion dollars each year. That accounts for 3.1% of our Gross Domestic Product and comes down to $970 per person in direct costs. If you include indirect costs of corrosion, such as lost productivity due to failures, outages, delays, and litigation, the per-person tab would be about twice that amount. So those pesky oxygen atoms, the same ones that rob carbon from our tool steels during heat treatment, are also hell-bent on ruining our tools after hardening through a direct assault on the very iron these tools are made from.

THE CHEMISTRY OF RUST

The corrosion of iron into rust is a much more complex process than it appears. Seems simple to me: iron atom gets attacked by oxygen atom and together form a new compound, rust. Yet, it's just not that straightforward.

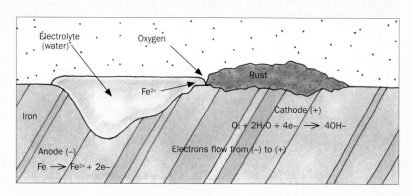

Iron atoms are exceptionally willing to give up an electron or two at the drop of a hat. Or rather, to a drop of water. The iron atom is now positively charged (giving up electrons will do that) and will quite agreeably bond with other atoms that are negatively charged. Water absorbs oxygen from the air and our droplet has some extra electrons (from the iron atoms) that produce hydroxyl ions in the water. These negatively charged hydroxyl ions combine with the positively charged iron ions and form iron hydroxide. Because water dissolves oxygen, there is usually an excess of oxygen available to combine with the iron hydroxide to form hydrated iron oxide: red rust.

I'm not qualified to explain all the chemical reactions that occur during the creation of rust so I'm grateful to corrosion engineer Katherine Cockey for this contribution:

Rust is the corrosion product of an electrochemical action. Electric potential differences exist over the surface of the steel leading to numerous galvanic cells, i.e. many minute batteries. In this case, the process begins with the transfer of electrons from iron to oxygen. The cell electrode where the loss of electrons occurs through an oxidation reaction is called the anode. Iron gives up electrons to the water:

$$Fe \rightarrow Fe^{2+} + 2e^-$$

The other electrode in the cell, called the cathode, is where a reduction reaction occurs. Oxygen gains the electrons and hydroxide ions are formed:

$$O_2 + 4e^- + 2H_2O \rightarrow 4OH^-$$

Crucial to the formation of rust is the accompanying reduction/oxidation (redox) reaction between iron and oxygen in the presence of water.

$$4Fe^{2+} + O_2 \rightarrow 4Fe^{3+} + 2O_2^-$$

Just like cholesterol, iron forms "good" and "bad" oxides. The ferrous (Fe^{2+}) oxide adheres to the iron surface to form a protective layer – good. The ferric (Fe^{3+}) oxide tends not to adhere and to flake off – bad. In the iron-oxygen-water microcosm, the corrosion product is governed by the availability of oxygen and water. Limit the dissolved oxygen and this favors the ferrous (FeO) oxide in the following balance:

$$Fe^{2+} + 2H_2O \leftrightarrow Fe(OH)_2 + 2H^-$$
$$Fe(OH)_2 \leftrightarrow FeO + H_2O$$

Increase the oxygen concentration and the ferric (Fe_2O_3) oxide wins out:

$$Fe^{3+} + 3H_2O \leftrightarrow Fe(OH)_3 + 3H^-$$
$$Fe(OH)_3 \leftrightarrow FeO(OH) + H_2O$$
$$2FeO(OH) \leftrightarrow Fe_2O_3 + H_2O$$

The world is still balanced but the result is undesirable red rust and more the norm.

The point to all this anode/cathode talk is that the rust that grows on the surface may not be at the same location as the iron atoms that gave up the electrons which started the whole reaction. That's how rust can spread under paint or plating. A pinhole in the coating can allow water to contact metal and rust will spread from there. Sneaky, rust.

This special "see-through" paint pot allows you to see the canning jar inside that has a blade in it. By evacuating the paint pot, you remove the air from the canning jar as well and the lid seals via atmospheric pressure when the vacuum is removed from the pot. No air in the jar means no water to start rust.

RUST PREVENTION

What are we to do? Well, there are two basic approaches to rust prevention: prevent water and oxygen from coming in contact with the iron, or convert the iron into another compound that is better able to resist oxygen's efforts.

DESICCATION

The simplest way to keep rust from eating your tools is to keep them in a place that is too dry to allow the rust reaction to get started. Woodworkers living in dry climates expend far less time and effort defeating rust than those of us in a moisture-enhanced environment. You can keep your tools in a vacuum, or a sealed container purged with nitrogen or containing a desiccant of some kind to absorb all the moisture. Okay, not too practical, but here at Hock Tools, less than two miles from the Pacific Ocean, we often store small parts in canning jars that we've pulled a vacuum on. Parts are placed into a canning jar with the lid screwed on securely but not too tight. The jar is then placed into a paint pot that's attached to an old refrigerator compressor via the intake tube and the air is pumped out of the paint pot. The canning jar lids allow the air inside to escape but seal tightly when atmosphere is restored to the paint pot and the small blades or screws are stored in a near-total vacuum that, in one test, has held for over eight years. Not bad. Some people use a low-wattage heater, a small light bulb or moisture-absorbing products in their toolbox to keep it warm and/or dry.

A common rust-promoting condition that we often see is the condensation that forms when metal parts are moved from a cold place to a warm one. Warm air holds more moisture than cold air. That moisture can condense on the surface of the cold

This piece of steel was half-polished and half-sandblasted then placed in and removed from the freezer several times. The moisture that condenses during the exposure of cold metal to warm air is a sure way to create rust. The sandblasted side provided the texture that corrosion needs to get started.

steel, forming myriad beads of "sweat" as you see on your glass of iced tea in the warm air of summer. Each of those beads is a new electrolytic cell corroding the steel beneath. Condensation can even occur when the atmosphere warms up faster than the steel parts. A chilly spring morning can warm up quickly enough to cause metal in the shop to sweat. Circulating the air can help avoid condensation but a moisture-resistant coating may be necessary.

Similar to simply keeping tools away from moisture, keeping them polished can help prevent rust by eliminating surface imperfections that can trap a droplet of water that allows rust to get started. Polished steel is not rustproof – it still needs rust avoidance and protection measures – but shiny, polished steel tends to stay that way longer than the rough stuff.

OCCLUSION

Other methods used to prevent rust include the various things we do all the time to keep oxygen from attacking anything we care about. We apply barrier films including plating steel with other, less reactive metals such as brass, zinc or chromium, or the barrier can be the paint film that protects our cars from damaging oxidization. These measures work well, but as we know from experience, the slightest breach in the integrity of the film will allow rust to get started. And once it starts, it spreads quickly under the chrome or the paint until the coating flakes off and you have nothing left but rust.

With edged tools, we can't tolerate a film on the cutting edge, yet that's the part we most care about protecting: a bit of a conundrum.

A film that's blocking the air and moisture from the steel, however, can be made from things other than paint or plating. Wax, grease, oil, etc. can all become part of the armory we enlist in the defense of

our tools. The market has many products to offer and most work well, keeping in mind that some are better suited than others to one application or another.

Generally, and with little effort, an edged tool can be oiled after, and wiped off before, each use. A protective wax coating on a machine table can also perform the double duty of keeping out moisture and allowing things to slide easily over it. The downside for these specific applications is that wax and oil require frequent maintenance and recoating. In neither of these situations would we want a coating of heavy grease, even though grease may be indicated for certain long-term storage needs. The market also offers certain oil-type products that do a good job of displacing water on a metal surface – a real plus because rust may continue its attack if you applied oil over water. Water-displacing oils are formulated to drive away any moisture that may be on the surface they are coating, thus improving the protective effect.

I do not recommend silicone-based products. They work well for rust prevention and general lubrication but can be vexing in the woodshop. Silicone seems to find its way onto everything in the shop either by contact with fingers or other carriers, or by atomization when sprayed. And, because nothing likes to stick to silicone, it will interfere with glue adhesion and finish application when and where you least expect it. (So called "fisheyes" in a paint or varnish surface can be caused by a number of contaminants. Chief among them? Silicone droplets.) The safest solution is strict avoidance: do not allow silicone in your shop in the first place. Ever. Period.

CONVERSION

The conversion defense against rust is not as simple as rust-preventative coatings; however, there are a number of rust-conversion chemicals that can be applied to iron or steel that convert any iron oxide present (and

These are just a few of the readily available products for preventing and converting rust. There are dozens more: waxes, greases, oils, phosphating compounds and vapor phase inhibitors.

it's there even if you can't see it) into a stable, firmly adhering layer of iron phosphate or iron tannate. These chemical converters can be painted or wiped on and some form a film that acts as a primer for additional coats of paint. It is important to note that any chemical converters that create a film are usually disqualified from edged-tool protection tasks because any coating would coat the sharp parts of our tools.

Gun bluing and Parkerizing are surface treatments that are used to rustproof firearms. Bluing is a controlled oxidation of the iron on the surface, converting iron to a black form of iron oxide, which is a more stable molecule that occupies the same volume as the un-oxidized iron, forming a protective coating on the steel surface. Parkerizing was a brand-name electrochemical phosphate conversion coating popular until the 1940s that has been replaced by other phosphate conversion processes. Blued and Parkerized surfaces are still somewhat porous, and will only prevent rust if the surfaces are kept oiled. Consequently, we'd best call these conversion defense methods "rust-resistant."

In addition to chemical solutions that coat and convert a surface, there are a number of vapor phase inhibitors or volatile corrosion inhibitors (VCI) that are dry chemicals that vaporize very slowly. These chemical vapors neutralize the available ions on the steel's surface, which prevents the interaction of oxy-

gen with the metal, which then inhibits rust formation. VCIs are commonly available in rust preventative wrapping papers or small containers that can be placed inside tool chests, etc. The protection is only a molecule or two thick but that's enough to help prevent rust in enclosed, storage-type situations. When the toolbox is opened, the vapors escape of course, but they refill the space as soon as they're closed back up again. Volatile corrosion inhibitors will eventually evaporate, so it is important to follow the manufacturer's recommendations for periodic replacement to insure ongoing protection.

Enclosed spaces such as toolboxes have historically been rustproofed by the addition of camphor blocks or naphthalene mothballs. These are oil-based, solid products that sublimate (vaporize without going through the liquid phase) at low temperatures and permeate the enclosed space depositing a thin layer on the tools, which in turn protects the tools from contact with air and moisture (if you can stand the odor).

Basically, rust prevention is achieved by either keeping your steel dry, preventing water and oxygen from contacting the tool you wish to preserve, or by changing the iron to something that reacts less readily with oxygen. You can turn the iron into iron phosphate, or coat it with plating, paint, grease, wax or oil. Or, knowing that rust never sleeps – you can maintain the vigilance required to keep your tools scrupulously dry, avoiding the frustrating and time-consuming problem of rust and corrosion. Your rust-prevention efforts are part of an age-old continuum of defense against oxygen's evil efforts to ruin our stuff – you are a member of an ancient battalion for the forces of good.

RUST REMOVAL

Once rust has occurred, the evil forces of oxidation have stolen some of your iron and you can never have it back – the iron atoms that have been oxidized are no longer available to you – you cannot undo the rust and put the iron atoms back into the tool's surface from whence they came. So there will be a pit, at the very least, in the surface. If that pit is at or near a cutting edge, you'll need to abrade the surrounding surface down to the level of the bottom of the pit and just a molecule beyond because you want to be sure to remove all of the rust or it may continue to eat your steel. Anytime you expose fresh metal, it, too, will need to be protected from further rusting.

Some oxidation is really not material. The blue-gray patina that develops on carbon-steel kitchen knives does little damage, and is just a fact of having and using fine knives (I think carbon-steel knives are vastly superior to so-called "stainless-steel" ones). Sometimes they get a little too motley for my taste

and I'll gently and carefully scrub them back to uniform gray with steel wool. But aggressive red rust is nasty and must be dealt with before too much damage is done. Light sanding and oiling will suffice for some tools – a hammerhead or wrench – but cutting edges should be cared for preventatively by one or more of the methods described above.

It is possible to remove rust by chemical or electrolytic action. Citric acid is acclaimed for its ability to dissolve rust much faster than it dissolves the underlying steel and is often used to de-rust tools. Recipes or mixture recommendations vary from 1 to 2 ounces of citric acid crystals to 32 ounces of water. Disassemble the tool and immerse the rusty steel parts only. Check on the progress and brush off the loosened rust every few minutes. Treatment with fresh solution can take as little as 20 minutes depending on solution concentration, temperature and agitation. You should experiment to find the technique that works best for you. The acid will eventually attack the steel so don't leave it in longer than necessary to dissolve the rust. Be sure to rinse the treated parts thoroughly and immediately apply new rust protection.

The electrolytic method is quite simple and, if done properly, will not harm the iron substrate at all. Here's what works for me: start with a 5-gallon (20-liter) plastic bucket, or similar container, almost filled with water, into which you've added a handful (1.2 metric handfuls) of baking soda to make the electrolyte. For

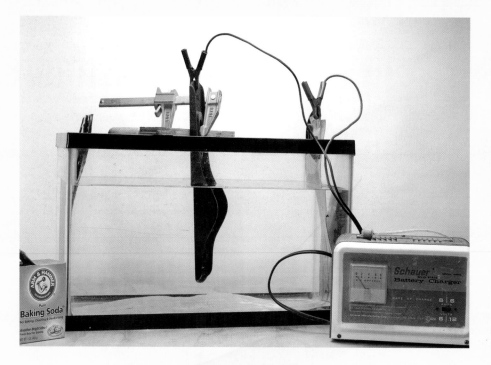

I'm using an aquarium for visibility while de-rusting a #5 plane body. I have it only partially in the water/baking soda bath to best illustrate what's going on. Notice the negative (black) lead from the battery charger is connected to the plane body (the cathode) and the positive (red) lead connects to a piece of stainless steel (the anode) roughly bent to the shape of the tank to provide maximal exposure of the cathode to the anode.

the anode, I prefer something stainless steel – a vegetable steamer or cheese grater. Some stainless steel wires in the bottom of the container will suffice. Stainless lasts longer as an anode – you can use any iron or steel as an anode but it will be consumed by the process. Disassemble as much as you can (some "impossible" screws may loosen in the process) and remove anything that isn't steel. Suspend the rusty thing, the workpiece, in the solution being very careful that it does not touch the anode at all. The action is "line-of-sight" between the rusty thing and the anode, so you may need to reposition the workpiece or wrap the anode in order to surround it for complete coverage.

Connect a battery charger's positive lead to the anode and the negative lead to the rusty workpiece. Let me say this again: Positive to Anode, Negative to Workpiece. Don't mix them up because the anode is sacrificed in this reaction and you only want to dissolve the rust, not your rusty thing. You'll see bubbles rising in the solution as soon as the battery charger is switched on. Through the magic of chemistry the iron oxide that you want to remove is converted back into metallic iron and falls to the bottom of the bucket. It will not re-deposit itself where it came from. The rust will be removed; however, the pitted surface will still be pitted. De-rusting can take a few minutes or a few days depending on the amount of rust and the amperage available from the charger, etc. Be patient and check the piece occasionally. Bubbles will continue to rise from the piece even after all the rust is gone but don't worry, at that point you're just splitting the water into its component oxygen and hydrogen. The resulting de-rusted surface will have a black layer on it that you'll probably want to wash/wipe off. Dry it thoroughly in an oven, with compressed air or a hair dryer. Rust prevention measures should be applied immediately upon drying the piece or it will rust again in minutes.

The rust has been converted to a chalky black surface coating that should now be wire-brushed or sanded off. The clean and rust-free surface will begin to oxidize immediately; don't delay in applying rust prevention measures.

3 Abrasives

ZION CANYON IN SOUTH-western Utah is one of the most strikingly beautiful places I've ever had the pleasure to visit. 150 million years of sedimentary layers were slowly lifted to over 10,000 feet (3,000m) to form what we now refer to as the Colorado Plateau. This gradual elevation change accelerated rivers into fast-moving, stone-cutting water-saws that channeled through the layers of sedimentary rock by carrying silt, sand and rocks downstream – all the while wearing their courses deeper and wider by abrasion. The north fork of the Virgin River wore down the plateau to create Zion Canyon and every year carries three million tons of rock and sand through this spectacular canyon, carving it a little bit deeper year after year. I sometimes think about this when I'm sharpening.

The Virgin River does its honing with whatever it carries along with the flow; debris made mostly of grit

Wall Street, Zion Narrows, Zion National Park, 2006.
PHOTO BY JON SULLIVAN

composed of silicon dioxide (sand). We can take a much more aggressive approach to abrading steel than the Virgin River does to the Colorado Plateau by selecting the hardest, sharpest grit particles available. We are able to select the best-suited abrasive for the job. Numerous compounds are used as abrasives: garnet; cerium oxide; cubic boron nitride; chromium oxide; iron oxide; zirconium dioxide; etc. However the ones we use for sharpening – whether as loose grains or as sandpaper, bench stones or grinding wheels – in the vast majority are some form of silicon dioxide, silicon carbide, aluminum oxide or diamond. Sharpening hardened tool steel requires grit particles that are harder than the steel and sharp enough to dig in and scratch away a bit of the steel.

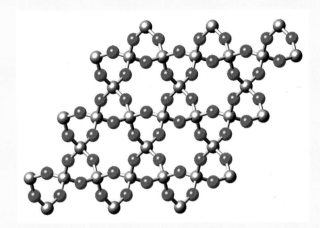

Silicon Dioxide, SiO₂. IMAGE COURTESY BEN MILLS

Silicon Dioxide SiO₂

Silicon dioxide (SiO₂) is the most abundant mineral in the Earth's crust. Silicon dioxide has a Knoop hardness of about 820. Tool steel (at Rc62) has a Knoop hardness of about 780. The difference in those hardnesses, though not huge, is sufficient to allow SiO₂ to be used as a honing medium. Included among its many forms are sand, flint, quartz, chert and the less abundant form we're most interested in: *novaculite*. Novaculite is a sedimentary rock mainly composed of microcrystalline quartz, and is a recrystallized variety of chert. The crystal structure of novaculite determines its abrasive aggressiveness, with the harder forms tending to be composed of finer grits. Novaculite's density and hardness make it an excellent candidate for sharpening, a trait that has been recognized for centuries.

The best novaculite is quarried from the Ouachita (pronounced "Washita") Mountains near Hot Springs, Arkansas. Commonly known as Washita stone, Arkansas stone, etc., these are the naturally occurring *oilstones* that were the standard sharpening media until man-made stones became popular over the last few decades. More about using oilstones shortly.

Silicon dioxide is also the abrasive grit in natural waterstones. Where novaculite is a crystallized formation, natural *waterstones* are composed primarily of silicon dioxide particles suspended in a clay matrix.

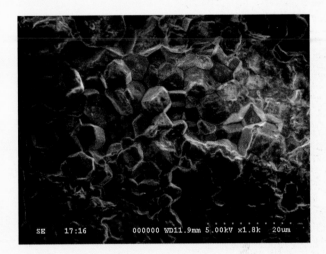

Hard Arkansas stone at 1800x magnification.

The average size of the particles in the stone determines coarse (arato), medium (nakato), and fine (shiageto). As with natural Arkansas oilstones, natural waterstones are becoming rare as the highest quality deposits are being mined out. Unlike Arkansas stones, natural waterstones are *friable* – fragile, they break down under pressure – the clay matrix being softer than novaculite. This friability allows the stone to wear with use, exposing fresh grit as dull grains are dislodged by honing pressure.

Silicon Carbide
SiC

Silicon carbide (SiC) occurs naturally, but rarely in the clear crystals known as moissanite that are sometimes passed off as diamonds to unsuspecting jewelry buyers. In 1893, Edward Goodrich Acheson (1856–1931) invented and patented a method for manufacturing silicon carbide. The story has it that Mr. Acheson's attempt to create a new compound by dissolving carbon in molten aluminum oxide produced sparkly black crystals that he called *Carborundum* – "carbon + corundum" – assuming he had succeeded. He hadn't. But he did make silicon carbide. His process led to large-scale production of SiC for abrasives. Silicon carbide is also used in semiconductor applications, astronomical mirrors and extreme-heat structural applications.

SiC is the abrasive applied to the ubiquitous black wet-or-dry sandpaper, as well as sharpening stones, including the Crystolon brand. Our interest in SiC concerns its hardness and the sharpness of its crystals. SiC grains are very sharp and hard with a Mohs hardness of 9 to 9.5 (Knoop hardness of 2480), but are very friable. This fragility is both good and bad: good because as the grains break down under grinding pressure, they expose new, sharp points. Bad because, with hard steel, they break down too easily and stop cutting too soon. SiC is not recommended for wood either, as wood is not hard enough to crush the SiC grains. If you use SiC on wood, it tends to load up and quit cutting before it gets dull (hence, the wet-or-dry feature; wet sanding helps to avoid the loading and clogging problem when sanding soft surfaces, such as wood, or paint – the automotive paint industry is the largest consumer of wet-or-dry sandpaper.)

Loose silicon carbide grains can come in handy for lapping sharpening stones when used on a surface such as cast iron, copper or plastic, that is softer than that which you are lapping. A soft surface allows the grains to embed in it, immobilizing them while grinding the stone flat.

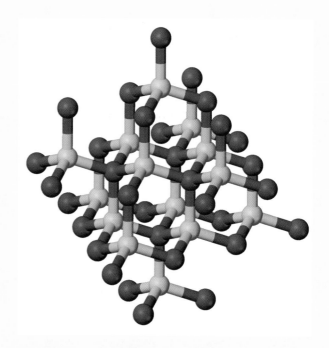

Silicon Carbide, SiC. IMAGE COURTESY BEN MILLS

15 micron Silicon Carbide grains at 1000x magnification.

SiC grinding wheels are used for soft metals like brass and aluminum; the abrasive particles are sharp enough to cut softer metals. And, due to both its sharpness and hardness, SiC is used in specially formulated grinding wheels for grinding carbide.

Aluminum Oxide
Al₂O₃

Alumina – *aluminum oxide* (Al₂O₃, often abbreviated as simply AO) – comprises over 15% of the earth's crust (compared to about 6% iron oxides). Sixty-five million tons of it are mined each year as the aluminum-bearing ore *bauxite* with 90% of that being used to make aluminum metal. The pure, natural form of aluminum oxide is a white compound called *corundum,* which, when contaminated with about 2.5% chromic oxide becomes a *ruby*. If contaminated with other elements such as iron, titanium and chromium, corundum is called *sapphire* which, while most commonly blue, can be almost any color but red (which is exclusive to rubies).

Alumina is also the major component of *emery*, a natural compound and one of the most commonly available abrasives until man-made aluminum oxide and silicon carbide abrasives of greater purity and uniformity were developed. There are eight or so different crystalline forms of AO manufactured today, each with different degrees of friability. AO easily passes the primary test of an abrasive: it is hard and sharp. While not as hard as silicon carbide, with a Mohs hardness of 9 (Knoop 2100), AO is one of the hardest substances around. However, not all of the crystal forms of aluminum oxide have silicon carbide's friability to refresh its sharp points. Aluminum oxide is tougher – harder to crush – than SiC, but it will eventually dull. The tendency of AO to dull is usually addressed by formulating grinding wheels with the AO grains in a *friable bond*. As a grain dulls, pressure against it increases until the grain breaks free of the bond, which exposes a new, sharp grain that continues cutting. Friable grinding media are truly self-sharpening.

AO crystals with a greater friability, which allows them to crush to new sharpness, are also employed

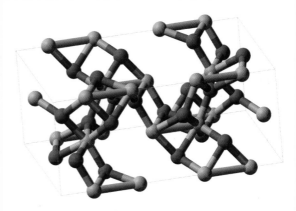

Aluminum Oxide, Al₂O₃. IMAGE COURTESY BEN MILLS

15 micron Aluminum Oxide grains at 1000x magnification.

and available in the marketplace. Norton makes a *seeded gel* grinding wheel with friable AO grains and 3M offers their *sol-gel* to the same end. Specific grain sizes of AO are usually obtained by crushing larger chunks into smaller ones, while the seeded-gel and sol-gel grains are literally grown from seed crystals until they become the desired size.

Aluminum oxide is the work horse of the tool-sharpening industry. The large majority of abrasive media in use daily throughout the world is made from one form or another of aluminum oxide.

Superabrasives

DIAMOND

Prior to the 1870s, *diamonds* were rare precious stones mostly from India and Brazil. In 1870, large quantities of diamonds were discovered near the Orange River in South Africa, spawning a boom of diamond mines. These new mines flooded the market with so many diamonds that the producers (and their investors) feared diamonds would lose their luster, so to speak, and be downgraded to mere semiprecious stones. To prevent this, the diamond mining companies merged in 1888 to form perhaps the most successful cartel in history, De Beers Consolidated Mines, Ltd. With near-complete control over supply, De Beers decided in 1938 to control demand as well. It hired a New York advertising agency to instill in the public the notion that diamonds should be the only choice for engagement and wedding rings. With a clever campaign – *Diamonds are Forever* – that featured product placements in Hollywood movies, publicized celebrity weddings with press releases to the society pages that made certain to mention the ever-important wedding ring, De Beers successfully established the diamond as the premier icon of romance. All the while, De Beers carefully controlled supply by hording the vast majority of the world's diamonds to maintain artificially high prices.

What does this have to do with us? Well, if not for De Beers, there would not likely have been the impetus for research and development that led to the creation of artificial diamonds in the 1950s. Most of the current emphasis in diamond manufacturing is focused on making diamond semiconductors for the electronics industry (your next computer may well have a "Diamond-Pentium" processor). As time and entrepreneurism have marched on, several techniques for producing diamonds have been developed, dramatically reducing the price for diamond abrasives. Virtually all of the diamond abrasive products available today use "synthetic" manufactured diamonds. Natural diamonds may be a "girl's best friend" but man-made diamonds are among woodworkers' best buddies.

The two predominant technologies in the diamond manufacturing tool kit produce diamonds with differing properties that are significant to the tool-sharpener. Having been used for at least a half-century, the

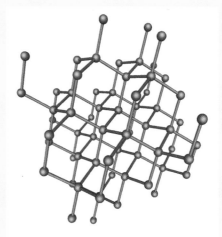

Diamond. BY MICHAEL STRÖCK

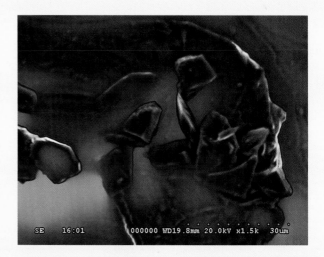

Diamonds in nickel matrix, 1500x magnification.

high-pressure high-temperature (HPHT) method has earned its place as the "traditional" method of making diamonds. In a box the size of a washing machine, HPHT replicates the hot, high-pressure geologic conditions that form diamonds deep inside our lovely planet. These conditions coax a carbonaceous batter to grow a new diamond around a small seed-crystal of natural diamond. At 2,700° F (1,500° C) and 850,000psi (58,000atm), a gem-quality 2.8 carat diamond will grow in about 3 days. Take that, De Beers!

The second, newer method is a *chemical vapor deposition* (CVD) method that heats a carbon-rich gas to a plasma state in a low-pressure chamber that precipitates onto a polished seed diamond. This method holds the greatest hope for the semiconductor industry as the diamonds it generates can be pure carbon while the HPHT method imparts impurities from the necessary catalysts used in the mix. And with CVD, other elements, like boron, can be added to the gas in precise concentrations to make a diamond with specific properties desired for electrical semiconductivity.

"So what", you say? The HPHT method produces a *monocrystalline* diamond while CVD produces a *polycrystalline* diamond. The difference for sharpeners is particularly significant. A monocrystalline diamond is a single crystal composed entirely of the incredibly strong carbon bonds that give diamonds their unique strength. Polycrystalline diamonds have many crystals of diamonds attached to each other via carbon bonds that are weaker than the monocrystalline diamond's bonds. Those weaker bonds will cause the polycrystalline diamond particles that you may be using for sharpening to break apart more easily than particles of monocrystalline diamonds. Bottom line: poly-crystalline diamonds are well suited for loose-grain (or paste) lapping compounds. They'll crush as they wear and resharpen themselves. Monocrystalline diamonds are recommended for bench "stones" or hones where the diamond grit is fixed in place (usually in a layer of plated-on nickel). In that application you want the crystals to stay put, and not crush, so they will continue to cut efficiently as long as possible.

Carbon is one of the elements that can exist in different forms, or *allotropes*. Diamonds are an allotrope of carbon – carbon atoms in a tetrahedral arrangement. (Graphite is another well known allotrope of carbon where the carbon atoms are arranged in platelets that slide against each other.) Due to the fact that diamonds are entirely carbon, they cannot be used for powered grinding of steel where the temperature of the steel may become high enough that the carbon dissolves into the steel. Wearing dull is one thing; dissolving into the tool is entirely unacceptable. Hand-sharpening, *si* – power-grinding, *no*.

With a Mohs hardness of 10 (Knoop 7000), diamond is the hardest material known (except for other

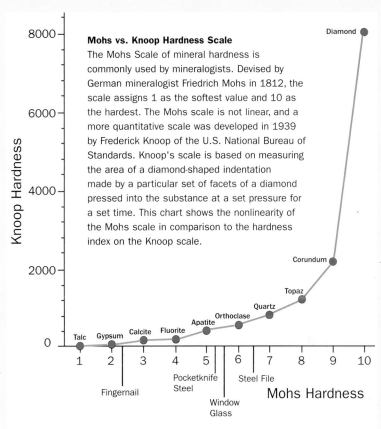

Mohs vs. Knoop Hardness Scale
The Mohs Scale of mineral hardness is commonly used by mineralogists. Devised by German mineralogist Friedrich Mohs in 1812, the scale assigns 1 as the softest value and 10 as the hardest. The Mohs scale is not linear, and a more quantitative scale was developed in 1939 by Frederick Knoop of the U.S. National Bureau of Standards. Knoop's scale is based on measuring the area of a diamond-shaped indentation made by a particular set of facets of a diamond pressed into the substance at a set pressure for a set time. This chart shows the nonlinearity of the Mohs scale in comparison to the hardness index on the Knoop scale.

Chart and information modified from *Some Fundamentals of Mineralogy and Geochemistry* by L. Bruce Railsback of the Department of Geology of the University of Georgia.

forms of diamond – do a web search for *fullerene*). That, and the fact that diamond crystals are sharp, means they can be called upon for sharpening duty. Diamond crystals do wear out eventually but the lifespan of diamond abrasive in most applications is long enough to justify their expense (one caveat: in spite of their manufactured abundance, diamond abrasives are still pricey when compared to the other commonly available abrasives).

CUBIC BORON NITRIDE (cBN)

Along with diamonds, *cubic boron nitride* (cBN) is considered a *superabrasive* – a small category of the hardest and toughest abrasives. CBN has a similar structure to diamond and is almost as hard. With no carbon, cBN can be used to cut steel at high temperatures where the carbon in diamond would be dissolved into the steel. CBN's usefulness to us is limited, therefore, and because it is almost as expensive as diamond, there are few applications where it is used for sharpening.

CHROMIUM OXIDE (Cr₂O₃)

Often used for charging a strop or a buffing wheel, *chromium oxide* is also known as viridian, a beautiful green pigment used in inks and paints. It is available in a green crayon-like stick that can be applied to a felt or muslin wheel, or simply rubbed on a leather, felt, cardboard or wooden strop. I keep a waxy-greasy "brick" of it in the shop for the buffing wheels that I buy from a gunsmith supply. It is sold sometimes as "knife-maker's green" as it is popular with that industry for its ability to final-polish hardened steel to a mirror finish.

Chromium oxide grains at 1500x magnification.

POLISHING COMPOUNDS

If a *polishing compound* is being sold as a sharpening aid, odds are good that it will contain aluminum oxide (if it's white), chromium oxide (if it's dark green), or both (if it's light green). Some compounds of other colors are simply aluminum oxide with colorant added to differentiate them. Manufacturers tend to be reluctant to reveal the ingredients in their compounds, so my advice is to ask other woodworkers, read the postings on the various forums and listen to others' experiences to make an informed choice. Most of these compounds are quite affordable, so direct experimentation contains little risk.

It never hurts to try something new or different and if you like the way it works, please spread the word. But some compounds are formulated for polishing materials that are softer than hardened tool steel and, while they may eventually work on your blade, it'll tend to be very slow going.

A custom-made stropping bat made by JRE Industries (www.jreindustries.com). Four-sided comes preloaded: (one side each) with black, green and white compound, and one natural leather.

STROPS

Strops are usually a strip of leather charged with an abrasive compound used as a final, finest-grit polishing and deburring step. As with most everything in woodworking and sharpening, there is controversy surrounding the use of strops. Aside from a strop's inherent risk of rounding-over an edge, there are those who claim that the strop actually degrades an edge that's been honed with the finest abrasives. The rounding-over fear is legitimate when using a leather strop as leather is a resilient surface that compresses slightly when you press the tool to it. Even using minimal pressure, that compression and rebound may tend to round the edge slightly and for some (and some tools) any rounding is too much.

As for the edge degradation with stropping, the only evidence that my time with the *Scanning Electron Microscope* (see Appendix) exposed was some hint that the stropping compounds that I used may have a range of grit sizes in them. But all in all, I think stropping does provide a last, super-fine polish and burr removal. Although your mileage may vary, it certainly does not entail a large investment to try it out. You can buy a strop or make one from almost any piece of leather and use it on a bench top or fasten it to a like-sized board. You can also use a flattened piece of wood as the strop itself and avoid the rebound issue entirely. Other strops I've seen have been made from paper, boxboard, MDF and canvas, or other fabric.

This traditional honing system for carvers and whittlers is from Woodcraft (www.woodcraft.com). Easy to use, just prime the leather with the appropriate compound and hone your tool with a lapping "barber's" stroke. PHOTO COURTESY OF WOODCRAFT

GRIT SIZE COMPARISON CHART

Micron average	ANSI/CAMI (USA)	FEPA (Europe)	JIS (Japan)	Stones (Approx.)
0.5			30000	Green Chromium Oxide Compound
0.9			16000	
1.2		F2000	8000	
2		F1500	6000	
3		F1200	4000	
4			3000	
4.5		F1000		
5.5	1200		2500	
6				Hard Black or Translucent Arkansas
6.5		F800	2000	
7	1000			
8		P2500	1500	
9	900			
9.5		F600	1200	
10		P2000		
11.5			1000	Hard White Arkansas
12	800			
13		F500/P1500		
14	700		800	
15		P1200		
17		F400	700	
18	600	P1000		
19	500			
22	400	P800		Soft Arkansas/X-fine India
23		F360		
25			500	
26		P600		
29		F320		
30		P500	400	
31	320			
35		P400	360	Washita/Fine India
36.5		F280		
39	280			
40		P360	320	
44.5		F240		Fine Crystolon
46		P320		
48			280	
50	240			
53		F230/P280		Medium India
57			240	
58.5		P240/F220		
63	220			
69		F180		
76	180			Medium Crystolon
89	150	F150		
102	120	F120		Coarse India
122	100	F100		Coase Crystolon
165	80			
254	60	F60		
269		P60		
336		P50		
438		F40		
483	36			
538		P36		

GRIT SIZE

The size of the grains used in any abrasive configuration – loose grains, sandpaper, stones and wheels – is described by several standards. Most commonly used is a screen size which refers to the number of holes per inch in a screen through which the abrasive grains are sifted. Sieves with successively finer screens catch the particles that can't get through and are then named for the screen they just passed through. This method is used for granules up to about 220-grit (about 60µ). Straightforward enough; but with finer particles a variety of clever methods are used. Sorting by *sedimentation* mixes the grains with water and allows them to settle for a specified amount of time; the larger particles settling fastest. The unsettled mixture is drawn off and allowed to settle again, etc. Sorting or classifying by air means that air blows the particles across a series of holes, the larger, heavier particles settling first.

Using a process called *elutriation*, a particle of a given size and weight will fall through a liquid or gas of a given viscosity at a given rate (look up *Stokes' Law* for the formula). If all variables are known but the size of the particle, it can be calculated from the other values.

The problem for us regarding the sizing of abrasive grains is that it is very difficult to segregate any one size of grain from all the others. Even something as straightforward as the sieve method will result in the capture of a range of grit sizes. Grit grains are not spheres (or they wouldn't work well as abrasives) so whether or not they pass through or get caught by a screen depends on the orientation of the particle. Imagine grains of rice being sieved. Some may pass through long-wise while a sideways presentation to the screen will prevent the grain from passing through. If the abrasive grains all looked like rice, your sheet of sandpaper would have a range of grit sizes that would include the width and length of the grains and all orientations in between.

From here, the issue of abrasive grain size designation just gets Byzantine. There are standards for abrasive sizing issued by ANSI (the American National Standards Institute), FEPA (the Federation of European Producers of Abrasives) and JIS (the Japanese Standardization Organization). The standards are different for *bonded* (stones and wheels), *coated* (sandpaper) and *loose* abrasives (blasting media) and differ between the different standards organizations as well. The Unified Abrasives Manufacturers' Association explains quite well how confusing this all can get:

ANSI B74.18-1996, currently under revision, covers coated abrasives. These sizing requirements are quite different from those for bonded and loose abrasives. (For brevity, the differing standards will be referred to as "bonded" and "coated.") In general, it is entirely possible that any particular abrasive that meets the requirements for a coated size will meet the requirements for the same bonded size (that is, an ANSI bonded 180 may also be acceptable as an ANSI coated 180), and vice-versa. It is also entirely possible that a FEPA F120 (bonded) will not meet the requirements of a FEPA P120 (coated), and vice-versa. This is because the standards specify different sieve sizes to be used for testing, allow or require different percentages of retained material on the various sieves, and, in general, state the requirements in a manner which frustrates direct comparison of the sizes.

Without entering into a detailed comparison of the standards, which the interested user is encouraged to do, one example will hopefully suffice. For FEPA P80 (coated), FEPA GB43-1991 requires all of the material to pass through a 355-micron sieve, and a maximum of 3% be retained on a 255-micron sieve. For FEPA F80 (bonded), FEPA 42GB-1984R1993 requires all the material

to pass through a 300-micron sieve. There is no requirement with regard to a 255-micron sieve, and up to 25% of the material may be retained on a 212-micron sieve. Clearly, a single abrasive with no particles over 255 microns would meet both these standards. But an abrasive with no particles over 355 microns, 1% from 300 to 355 microns, and 2% from 255 to 300 microns would meet the coated standard and fail the bonded one. An abrasive with no particles over 300 microns but 4% from 255 to 300 microns would meet the bonded standard and fail the coated one. (Source: www.uama.org.)

Got it? Me neither. Suffice it to say that if you suspect that your 8000-grit Norton waterstone behaves differently from your friend's 8000-grit Shapton stone, you are undoubtedly correct. The grains may be of different crystalline composition, may have a larger or smaller range of sizes included in the mix, and may use a different standard for grading the grains or a different method for segregating them. I am not saying that one is better or worse, only that if they seem somehow different, don't be surprised. And this doesn't even touch on the different bonds and manufacturing methods used by the various brands.

Four sandpaper grits (from left to right) 60 grit (coarse); 100 grit (medium); 150 grit (fine) and 220 grit (very fine).

BENCH STONES

While the type of abrasive used on sandpapers and grinding wheels is clearly marked on the product or packaging, that's not always the case with *bench stones*. Sandpapers and grinding wheels may be called upon to sand or grind all manner of substances such as wood, paint, plastics, etc. and their selection is based on the application. But bench stones exist to sharpen tool steel only, so the manufacturers don't feel any need to disclose those specifics. The exact composition is often a blend of two or more abrasives with the details guarded as trade secrets. Rest assured, however, that if it's being sold as a vehicle for sharpening tool steel, it will most likely perform that function to some degree of satisfaction and knowing the precise mixture or crystal structure of the abrasives is not necessary in making a selection.

The hardness/friability range of bench stones is panoramic and extends from very soft waterstones at one extreme to steel-plate diamond "stones" at the other. Except for the diamond-on-steel honing plates, bench stones consist of abrasive grains bound together in some sort of matrix bond – resin, shellac, ceramic or the geologic glue of sedimentation and crystallization – hence the term *bonded abrasives* includes grinding wheels and bench stones (as opposed to coated abrasives such as sandpaper). The hardness of the stone is a function of its binder –

ceramic and traditional oilstones reside on the "hard" end of the scale and waterstones on the "soft" side. It's the softness of waterstones that lets them cut steel so quickly. The surface is constantly being worn away by the sharpening activity and this constant ablation exposes fresh, sharp grit particles. Harder stones don't wear as quickly, so you have to rely on the hardness of the particles that are there from the beginning to do their job for a long time. Of course, there's a trade-off in that you will wear a depression in the center of softer waterstones, which need frequent flattening (remember, one of the keys to successfully sharpening chisels, plane irons, etc. is a flat stone). Soft stones are high-maintenance and require such to perform at their best. Ceramic stones on the other hand, and according to the manufacturer, just need an occasional cleaning – throw them in the dishwasher (no kidding!) – to unclog their pores and they're back in action. Same for oilstones – an infrequent cleaning with a solvent or kerosene is all they need for years of service (okay, they wear in the center, too, though much more slowly. And they do get dull – flattening with a diamond plate or sandpaper solves both problems). The trade-off here is that these harder stones cut more slowly and your sharpening experience may be more "meditative" than you'd like. Oilstones can be used with soapy water instead of oil, though waterstones should only be used with water; no oil

ever. If you don't like water slopping around the shop, oilstones may be for you. On the other hand, if you're nervous about oil getting onto your woodwork, or want stones that cut faster, waterstones may be what you're looking for.

In the middle of the spectrum are the *ceramic waterstones*, such as *Shapton* and Naniwa's *Superstones*. Ceramic waterstones utilize a harder compound than natural or man-made waterstones, which are meant to wear longer while maintaining the ability to cut quickly. Though often not as soft as waterstones, ceramic waterstones still require frequent flattening. One of the experienced sharpeners I talked to prefers Shapton stones because the *Norton* waterstones wore down too quickly while another of my expert sharpening friends thinks the Shapton stones glaze too easily and prefers Naniwa Superstones. Meanwhile, many of the students at the College of the Redwoods Fine Woodworking program swear by Norton stones exclusively. If you are ever at a loss for something to talk about with a woodworker, just start talking about sharpening. It's a conversation that can go on and on.

The diamond-plate "stones" offer an ideal solution in that they require no flattening and can just be rinsed after using to keep them clean. But they're expensive. And, though it takes quite a while, the diamond particles do eventually wear down; typically

in the center of the plate, which may effect uniform honing of wider blades.

Confused? Me too. Each of the sharpening stones available today has fans (that's short for "fanatic," don't forget) as well as detractors. The very fact that a large number of woodworkers recommend a stone indicates that it must work well. I'd recommend trying out as many stones as you can beg or borrow. Haunt the tool retailers and try out the demo models, or ask the members of your local woodworking club to bring in their sharpening gear for a show-and-tell meeting.

Joel Moskowitz at Tools for Working Wood (.com) compares the selection of a sharpening stone to the selection of wine for a meal. It's a matter of personal preference and taste combined with the task – or meal – that's being considered; something like "wine and food pairing." There are times when a fast-cutting stone is desired in spite of the maintenance required while other times the slower, more careful action of an oil- or ceramic stone may be preferred. May I suggest a Zinfandel with your filet mignon?

Larry Williams (of Clark & Williams – (www.planemaker.com) says: *I use three stones in sharpening: a medium India, a Translucent Hard Arkansas and a coarse diamond stone that's only used to maintain the other two. The two oilstones, contrary to what people say, do wear but they also get dull. Very brief use of the coarse diamond stone on both oilstones before each sharpening keeps the oilstones flat and fast cutting. Everyone talks about flat in sharpening but no one ever says why. What we look for in flat is repeatability. If the stones are uniformly flat, you don't have to make a tool conform to a different topography each time you change grits. I used to waste most of my honing time making tools conform to the out-of-flat shape of my stones. I don't do that anymore; when I switch between stones, they cut in the same locations. First dress the fine hard Arkansas then the coarser India stone. Leave the resulting slurry on the stones; it makes them cut faster. I also use a leather strop to remove the final wire edge.*

Left to right, softer to harder: King, Norton, Superstone, Shapton, Guangxi Polishing, Soft Arkansas, Medium Spyderco, Black, Transluscent, Combo India, Fine Spiderco, DMT diamond plate.

LOOSE ABRASIVE GRAINS

The abrasives mentioned earlier are available as size-graded *loose grains* and can be used that way. *Lapping* in the metal-working world refers to any process that rubs two pieces together with abrasive in between them. This is usually done to flatten and polish an item to an extreme level of both flatness and polish. Most commonly, lapping is done with one of the surfaces being softer than the piece being flattened; cast iron is a common lap material, so that the abrasive grains embed in the soft surface and stay put. Veritas' Stone Pond includes a piece of tempered glass to act as the flat part and it also includes a like-sized sheet of adhesive-backed plastic that you stick to the glass. The plastic allows 90-grit silicon carbide grains (also included) to embed so the carbide grains can grind the stone that you're flattening. If you simply sprinkled the grains on the glass, without the plastic, they would move around with the lapping action and abrade the glass as well as (or perhaps more so than) the stone.

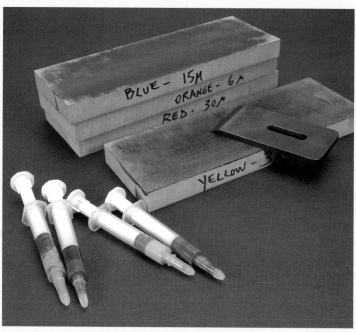

Norton diamond paste kit.

There are cast iron lapping plates available from machine shop suppliers that are precision-ground flat. They are used with loose abrasives for lapping as well as sharpening. But lapping as a sharpening method entails its own learning curve and has never been very popular, though there are, of course, those who swear by it. Some claim that when using silicon carbide grains, they need only start with a single application of coarse grains – say 90-grit for initial grinding and flattening – and, as the grains crush smaller, the finish gets finer until they're very small and polishing the blade. This assumes that each grain has been successfully crushed to the same size and there are no residual large grains lurking on the surface somewhere waiting to damage that shiny, flat surface you just created. However, if lapping-plate honing is done properly, the surface is always flat and, if you add successively smaller grains instead of simply crushing the larger ones as you go, you always have a fresh, sharp abrasive doing the work. Rinsing well at grit changes is imperative to avoid contamination. Lapping-plate honing has the advantage of being a one-tool sharpening kit, with inexpensive, loose abrasives the only expendables and the only expense beyond the initial lapping plate purchase. If you want to try lapping, you may use many surfaces as a substrate for the loose grains. While the formal, precision-ground cast iron plate is the standard, I've heard of people using plastic on glass, like what Veritas' Stone Pond offers, copper or brass plates from salvage yards, even CD/DVD's for small work; anything softer than the blade should work to immobilize the grains. It's sort of like you're making your own sandpaper as you go.

Diamonds are also available as loose, graded-grains, though more commonly they're mixed into a paste. Norton's diamond paste honing kit comes with four syringes with 5 grams each of different grit-size diamond paste, color-coded so you know at a glance which size is which. The kit includes four pieces of MDF to be used as the embeddable substrate, one for each grit size. Once applied, the diamonds in the paste should last a long time, though in reality, they do crush and will need to be refreshed with an occasional drop of paste. I recommend you keep each in its own plastic bag to avoid contamination. Unlike other bench stones, you cannot just rinse off the MDF if it gets dirty, or you'll wash off your investment in diamonds and be forced to reapply.

SANDPAPERS AND BELTS

Sandpapers and sanding belts all fall under the category of *coated abrasives*. There are many products in the marketplace that may be called "sandpaper" but sand is rarely used and paper is not the best backing for a sharpening medium. I've used basic hardware store wet-or-dry paper for sharpening with reasonably good results; however, the silicon carbide abrasive wears down very quickly. Don Naples of Wood Artistry (www.woodartistry.com), makers of the Lap-Sharp Sharpening System says: *Silicon carbide is a sharp abrasive but breaks down very quickly. It then burnishes the tool rather than abrading it. This is easily demonstrated with two progressively*

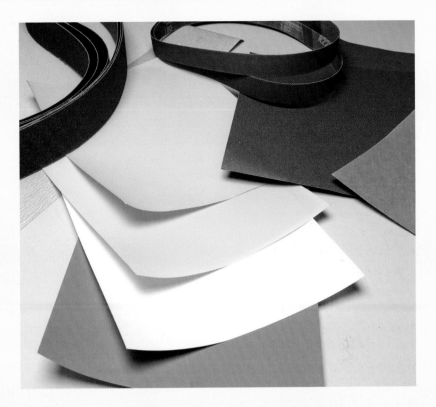

smaller silicon carbide abrasive sheets. Rub a steel tool on a piece of this abrasive paper, such as 400-grit. After working the tool for a short time, the tool will begin to shine. Next, rub the same tool area once or twice on a new piece of 500-grit paper. Note the scratches on the area that had been shining. The fresh but finer grit was abrading the area that had been burnished by the previous grit. A sharp tool is created by abrading the meeting edges of a tool to finely finished surfaces, not by buffing them till they are shiny. Silicon carbide abrasive does not hold up as well as aluminum oxide.

The aluminum oxide sandpapers sold at the hardware store are *open-coat*, which means there are sizeable gaps in the grit coverage on the paper. This helps keep the sandpaper from clogging with wood or paint swarf and is a desirable attribute in those applications. Even though open-coat papers will work if you have nothing else at hand, sandpaper with better coverage works better for sharpening.

The world of coated abrasives recently became a bit more high-tech with the availability of honing films – thin Mylar sheets *closed-coated* with a high concentration of uniform size grains of aluminum oxide grit (the manufacturers claim that 90% of the grains on a sheet are the stated size). These sheets are available in a variety of sizes, both plain and pressure

sensitive adhesive (PSA) backed for peel-and-stick convenience when applied to a piece of glass, granite, or whatever flat substrate you use. They are waterproof and remarkably long-lasting; the PSA-backed sheets stay stuck down and flat and for a modest investment you can have an impressive range of grits from 180μ (approximately 80 grit) to 0.3μ (consider that an 8000-grit waterstone has an average particle size of about 2μ) in your sharpening kit.

Belts for belt sanders (in the metalworking world we call them belt-grinders) are usually made from a woven fabric coated with grit. Once again, aluminum oxide is the most common grit for metalworking and belts coated with it will perform well for wood and for other sanding/grinding jobs, too. Zirconium oxide and some other high-performance minerals are also available on belts and, while they cost more, they do last longer and provide a high rate of stock removal. For the average woodworker doing some sharpening on a small bench belt sander, the readily available aluminum oxide belts will suffice. That being said, I would encourage you to try out whatever you can find. The cost per belt is not high and it never hurts to experiment.

WHEELS

After the confusion and uncertainty about bench stones and grit sizes, grinding wheels will seem simple. There is an industry-standard marking system for grinding wheels that covers the entire spectrum of wheels from machine-shop surface grinders, auto-body angle-head grinders to the 6- or 8-inch bench grinder you may have in your shop. The standard marking system looks like this: *A60-I8-V,* where *A* stands for aluminum oxide grit (by far the most common abrasive for grinding wheels, *C* stands for silicon carbide (but a manufacturer may use a letter-code such as *PA* to designate Pink Aluminum oxide, etc.), *60* is the grit size, *I* is the hardness grade of the bond (for tool steels you want a softer/weaker bond grade – harder material, softer wheel – *A* is the softest, *Z* is the hardest; for sharpening you want to shop in the *H-K* range), *8* refers to the spacing of the grits in the bond (from *4* to *15*) and the *V* indicates the wheel is held together with a Vitrified bond (the most common kind – others are *B* for resin bond, *R* for rubber, *E* for shellac and *P* for epoxy).

All of this information may be academic, however, because for the most part, the grinding wheels that are readily available will fall into the most common categories, and you may not have a large selection. Woodworking suppliers may offer only one or two types of aluminum oxide in one or two hardness grades (maybe I or J) with two or three grit sizes to choose from. Though it sounds like they're restricting your ability to make an informed choice, the wheels they offer tend to be the ones needed for sharpening tool steel. The real decision will be between the basic, hardware-store gray wheel, the more expensive and more friable white wheels that cut a bit cooler, and the yet-more-expensive blue Norton Seeded Gel wheels that cut cooler still.

When sharpening is the goal, a cooler cutting action is a desirable characteristic in a grinding wheel. If the piece of metal you're grinding can be allowed to heat up (i.e. *not* hardened steel), you'd want the toughest, longest lasting wheel available. But when the piece needs to be kept below its tempering temperature, a friable wheel will keep things cooler. There are two kinds of friability offered. With the more economical gray wheels, as the grains of aluminum oxide dull, the pressure on them increases until they break free of the bond to expose a new, sharp grain. The dull grain generates heat before it breaks loose, however, which is to be carefully avoided. The more friable white wheels are made from a purer, sharper form of aluminum oxide that cuts with less pressure and breaks free more easily to stay sharp and keep their cool. You can still burn a tool, though, and care must always be exercised. The blue-seeded gel wheels are a ceramic-alumina grit that repeatedly fractures into smaller, sharp grains before finally breaking free from the bond. All that fracturing keeps the wheel sharp to reduce heat. Again, you can still burn a tool with these wheels, but they do reduce the risk.

Kevin Glen Drake (www.Glen-Drake.com) says: *For my turning tools I use the wheels that come with the grinder until they're used up, and then I go buy new ones as needed off the hook at the hardware store. Just the standard gray kind of the right grit. But I only grind bench tools, like plane irons and chisels, with a hand grinder and a white wheel. I then hone my bench tools but not my turning tools.*

GRINDING WHEEL SAFETY TIPS

As far as I'm concerned, any tool driven by a motor can be dangerous. So can the hand-powered ones, but power tools demand safety considerations that hand tools don't. Power tools should never be used when you're tired, distracted, stupid, stoned or with a blood alcohol level above zero percent. Okay?

Before mounting any grinding wheel on the grinder, check that your grinder doesn't exceed the wheel's rated speed. Then perform a simple "ring test" (OSHA #1910.215(d)(1), honest) to be sure it isn't cracked. Support the wheel, new or old, on a screwdriver shaft and tap it gently at a few points around the wheel with the wooden handle of a hammer. It should ring clearly (okay, it's not a bell, but try it and you'll hear what I mean). If it sounds dull or dead, it's most likely cracked and should not be used. A wheel that fractures at speed can explode into shrapnel at ballistic speeds putting you and anyone nearby at extreme risk. Use all the proper washers, flanges, etc. that came with your grinder and your wheel. Oh, and while you're at it, put the guards back on the grinder!

Next, put on your eye/face protection (never cheat!). Tuck in your shirttails, apron strings, ponytail, necktie, etc. Set the grinder table/tool rest close to the wheel so nothing can get pulled down in between the tool rest and the wheel. Never grind on the side of a wheel. I've seen this advocated as a sharpening technique, but bench grinder wheels are not made to withstand side pressure and could fracture with catastrophic results. Don't risk it.

Stand to one side when you turn on the grinder with a new wheel and let it run for a full minute at least before standing in its way. C'mon, what's a minute or two for safety's sake?

4 How Wood is Cut

TO GET THE MOST FROM YOUR SHARPENING efforts, you will be well served by knowing how a blade cuts wood. Because so much of woodworking is about cutting wood, it can't help but improve your relationship with the wood itself if you develop a clear understanding of the cutting action – how a tool severs wood fibers. For some, the cutting is the woodworking, as any carver or turner can tell you. That understanding goes hand-in-hand with sharpening. Knowing how the fibers react to a sharp edge will remove some of the mystery about sharpening that edge. It's all of a piece: if you don't know the basics of edge geometry and its relationship to the cutting action, some amount of your woodworking effort

That's me amongst the Redwoods (Sequoia sempervirens) at Montgomery Woods State Natural Reserve in Mendocino County, California, August 6, 2007.

will simply be hit-and-miss, and you may find yourself wondering why your efforts result in something other than you intended. For example, understanding the relationship between cutting edges and wood will help you prevent tear-out during handplaning. Eventually, you won't even think about it. You will easily know which chisel to choose for paring and which to use for chopping, and you will understand why. Furthermore, a better understanding of something as basic as the difference in the cutting action between a ripsaw and a crosscut saw will improve both your power-saw and hand-saw skills. It is the knowing that underlies the artfulness of it all.

Much of the information that follows was also presented in 1980 by Bruce Hoadley in his excellent book *Understanding Wood – A Craftsman's Guide to Wood Technology*. Mr. Hoadley's chapter on wood machining goes into considerably more detail than I do here, and I urge anyone interested to refer to his work for a greater depth of knowledge. Wood machining is a complex subject and Mr. Hoadley does a more thorough job of explaining it than I have room for.

All woodcutting involves "chip formation"; sawing, planing, whittling, even scraping and sanding, all are about removing some wood from a larger piece and the piece removed – chunk, sliver, shaving or dust – is referred to as the *chip*. Chips are formed by cutting them from the stock, or workpiece, by a sharp edge. The edge wedges its way either between or through wood fibers, shearing them from themselves and their neighbors. The cutting action is a result of the stress applied via the cutting edge to the wood and the strain caused by that stress in the wood compresses the fibers, eventually resulting in a failure, which is what we want. No matter what the bevel angle or how sharp the edge, the blade must compress wood fibers before cutting them, before they fail. A primary goal of all sharpness and edge geometry considerations is to minimize the compression that occurs in advance of the failure. We want the bonds that hold the wood together to fail and we want them to fail predictably.

Edges

There are distinct parameters for what a cutting edge can be: it must be harder than the wood fibers and hard enough to retain its shape (its sharpness) for as long as possible while doing the work required. That hardness is often a compromise between longevity and fragility. Usually, the harder the blade, the longer-lasting the edge, but with increased hardness comes an increase in brittleness. With soft, knot-free woods, that extra brittleness is not such a big factor, and the added longevity that a harder blade's edge offers is a real bonus. But if the edge is too brittle, it may break down by small fractures and lose its sharpness when cutting harder, more difficult woods.

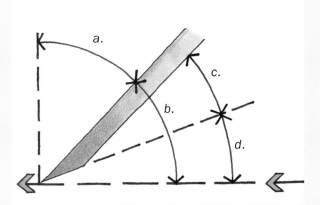

To efficiently cut wood fibers a blade must enter the wood at an effective *angle of attack* or *rake angle* (*a.* or *b.* in this illustration, depending on whether you measure from vertical or horizontal), using an appropriate angle at the cutting edge (*c.* depicts the *sharpness* or *bevel angle*) combined with sufficient *clearance* or *relief* (*d.*).

Other parameters include edge shape, angle of attack and clearance angle – all factors in the blade's ability to separate a chip from the workpiece.

Cutting edges encounter wood fibers at either adjustable or fixed angles of attack. The difference between these is the difference between the way a knife or chisel is used and the way a plane iron or saw tooth approaches a cut. A knife or chisel's angle of attack can be varied by the woodworker before and during the cut to optimize the effort and the result, whereas a plane blade or sawtooth is typically set to travel on a fixed path through the cut.

When using a knife or chisel, a smaller, more acute *bevel angle* on the edge will make it easier to cut wood fibers. An acute bevel angle minimizes the compression of the fibers being cut. If the bevel is too acute, the thin edge may be too weak to withstand the forces demanded of it and will break down too rapidly to be useable. A razor blade may shear hairs easily, but such a thin edge won't hold up to the twisting, levering motions needed for, say, a carving chisel. If you increase the bevel angle to strengthen the edge, you'll also increase the compression of the wood fibers and hence, the resistance to cutting. Therefore, the effort required to push the chisel through the wood will increase. If you continue to increase the bevel angle, at some point, due to the increase in wood fiber compression, the resistance to the forward advance of the blade will affect the quality of the cut. With too much

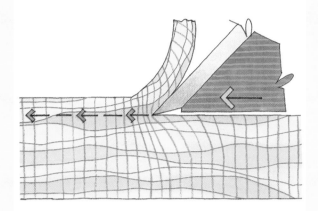

Cutting action compresses wood fibers before they fail. A sharper blade compresses them less resulting in a smoother surface left behind.

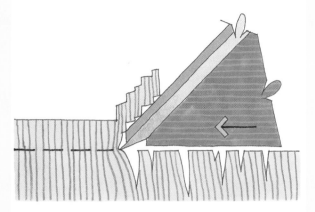

End grain being cut with a blade at too steep an angle or with a dull blade. The force compresses the fibers until they are torn rather than severed.

resistance, the blade cannot sever the fibers cleanly, and a rough surface will result as the fibers are smashed and torn away. An increase in the bevel angle is also a way to describe an edge that is wearing and getting dull. A dull edge compresses fibers more than a sharp one and eventually becomes too dull to use. An edge that is too dull leaves the same results as does a too-large bevel angle: smashed and torn fibers.

These angle-of-attack parameters also apply in similar ways to fixed-angle applications such as planes and saws. However, *bed angle* for plane applications and *tooth-rake angle* for saw applications take precedent over the *bevel angle*. With fixed-angle tools the bed- and rake-angles are essentially non-adjustable at the time of use and are not affected by changes to the bevel angles – as long as a proper *clearance angle* is maintained (see Chapter Six: Plane Irons).

A low angle plane cuts end grain more easily than one with a higher bed angle – it acts more like an acute angle knife. But a low-angle plane may tend, during with-the-grain planing, to lift some fibers ahead of the blade before shearing them, resulting in tear-out. This is particularly problematic when the grain is inconsistent, such that you are sometimes planing "uphill" or against the grain. Consequently, a higher angle plane (45° is the standard, such as the Stanley-style bench plane bed angle, but some planes have bed angles as high as 65°) is preferred for with-the-grain planing, as a higher bed angle can reduce the chance of tear-out.

Knives and chisels have variable angles of attack that can be adjusted during a cut. Planes and saws have fixed angles of attack.

As a plane's bed angle increases, the blade is forced to push the fibers forward as it cuts them. The fibers are compressed against their neighbors before being cut free. For this reason, high-angle planing requires more push force. This compression of the fibers being planed does not take place in the chip alone. The blade compresses fibers in an arc ahead of its path, both in the chip *and* below the line of cut into the substrate. As the chip is released, the newly exposed surface will decompress and spring back a bit. Hence, the need for the clearance angle shown on page 59. If the clearance angle is too small, the heel of the bevel will rub against the rebounding surface and lift the edge enough to make the blade stop cutting.

One of the things to check when troubleshooting poor plane performance is that the blade's bevel angle is providing sufficient clearance behind the edge. A popular sharpening shortcut for plane blades is to simply lift the blade a few degrees while honing the bevel. This speeds honing by concentrating the abrasive effort to a narrow strip right along the cutting edge, creating a *microbevel* at a slightly larger angle. There is nothing wrong with doing this. In fact, I recommend it in most cases, but you must beware that if you continue to do this sharpening after sharpening, you'll increase the bevel angle to the point where you'll have created a zero or negative clearance angle and your plane will stop cutting properly. At that point, you have to regrind the bevel back to the optimum specification and start the microbevel procession over again.

RIGHT Without enough clearance or relief behind the blade, the rebound from the compression of the fibers after being cut can lift the edge enough to prevent it from cutting.

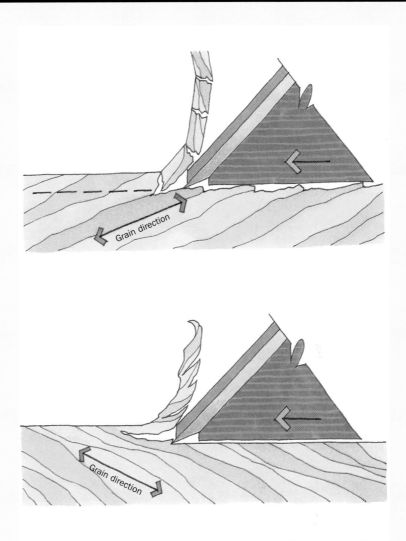

It is difficult to avoid tear-out when planing against the grain, or *uphill*. Planing *downhill* – with the grain – creates a smoother surface.

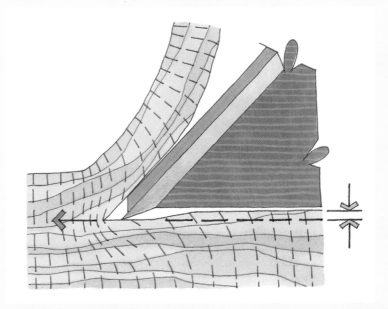

Cut Orientation

Cutting edges can be oriented relative to wood grain in one or more of three basic ways. Using planing action to illustrate: 1) Planing with the grain, like edge-planing a board, 2) Across the end grain, 3) Across the flat grain, like planing a tenon cheek with a shoulder plane. Rip sawing, lathe turning and other tools can incorporate more than one of these cutting actions in the same operation.

WITH GRAIN

Planing more or less in the direction of the grain is *with-grain* planing. Wood fibers rarely run perfectly parallel to the surface being planed however, so there is a real risk that the fibers, as they run up the ramp of the blade, will lift a chip that extends ahead of the cutting edge, sometimes deeply into the wood surface (this is what Hoadley calls a *Type I* chip). In fact, many woodcarvers have suffered stab-wounds in the heel of their chisel-holding hand when a long, sharp chip suddenly pops free while momentum carries the vulnerable hand into it.

Planing a surface smooth requires cutting thin shavings without levering up large chips. While a chisel is not the tool for that job, a plane is. A plane is actually just a holder for a blade and replaces the chisel in the previous example. The advantage that a plane brings to this application is that it holds the blade at a fixed angle relative to the workpiece *and* provides a pressure bar across the front of the mouth that holds the shaving down while it is being cut. This pressure bar, the leading edge of the mouth, teams up with the chip breaker to fracture the chip before it can lever up and tear out ahead of the blade (Hoadley's *Type II* chip). The "chip breaker" is called that because its function is to break the fibers in the shaving, thus preventing them from having enough strength to lift and tear ahead of the blade. You don't want the chips to create the surface of the workpiece; you want the blade that you've so carefully sharpened to create that surface, leaving a satiny finish behind.

A fine plane-mouth aperture mated with a sharp blade set to take a thin shaving is the best combination to produce a smooth surface, free of tear-out. Most fine woodworkers take such very thin shavings with their well-tuned planes that the chip breaker

With-grain planing. Bocote plane by James Krenov

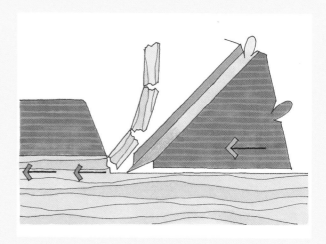

The leading edge of the mouth acts as a pressure bar to hold down the shaving as it is being sheared by the blade. This helps reduce tearout by preventing the levering up of fibers ahead of the blade.

does very little actual chip breaking. Thin, translucent shavings, like those that are produced with finish planing, are weak as tissue paper – their fibers don't have enough strength to cause any tear-out. For some difficult woods or for aggressive planing, increased tear-out prevention (or is it avoidance?) can be achieved by changing to a plane with a different angle of attack. However, few boards will have the perfect grain pattern for planing and sooner or later you'll be faced with having to smooth a board with grain that reverses direction, sometimes more than once and sometimes every fraction of an inch (quilted maple, for instance). Even the best plane – tight, crisp mouth, sharp blade – will experience trouble with some woods. If this is the case, it may be time to change tools.

Planing with the grain leaves a beautiful, satiny surface. Notice how the grain rises up in the direction of the cut.

Planing against the grain may lead to tear-out and a rough, chipped surface. The grain here rises up into the cut and gets caught and torn by the advancing blade.

I mentioned above the effects of an increased bevel angle (on page 60): that it increases the amount of force required to cut the fibers due to the increased compression of those fibers ahead of the cut. You can take advantage of that compression to improve your ability to plane difficult woods. As those fibers are compressed they are weakened, so much so that, with the correct blade angle and a shallow cut, a crushed, lacy shaving will be scraped off the surface (Hoadley's *Type III* chip). The mangling of the shaving weakens it as it is being cut, preventing it from lifting up in front of the blade, and is often your best chance for against-the-grain cutting without tear-out. However, as with so many things, there is a trade-off. Due to the greater compression of the fibers while this type of chip is being cut, the surface won't usually acquire the satiny surface that can be the result of a lower-angle shearing cut. The resulting surface will be smooth (if everything is tuned right and the wood spirits are on your side) but may need sanding to become the surface you want.

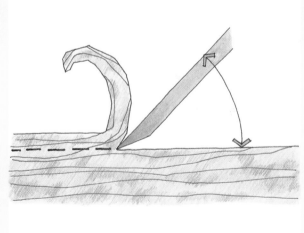

While a shearing cut severs fibers cleanly, a scraping cut mashes them until they fail and are scraped off the surface.

END GRAIN

Shearing *end grain* is more difficult than with-grain cutting. It takes more stress to cause a fiber to fail straight across than it does to shear it obliquely and lift it from its neighborhood. You need to minimize the forward fiber compression by keeping the edge sharp and by using a low cutting angle. If the edge is dull it compresses the fibers until, with enough effort, the fibers break off and rip out, instead of being sheared straight across. With a lower angle of attack and a smaller bevel angle, within the limits of the blade's edge geometry and metallurgy discussed ear-lier, cutting end grain will be easier. The chip that is formed when cutting end grain with a suitably sharp blade will tend to look stair-stepped, as small blocks of fibers pop loose off the blade. And, the chip will be very fragile, as the bonds holding the short fibers together are comparatively weak.

CROSS GRAIN

When cutting across flat grain – *cross-grain* cutting – the fibers release from one another and roll-up, out of the path of the cut as if they were a bamboo shade. Without shearing the fibers at each side of the cut, the fibers tear out of the walls of the cut, leaving a rough, mangled finish on the wall. Many shoulder planes incorporate a small nicker blade to shear the fibers ahead of and at the side of the flat, cross-grain cut. The nicker is engaged in an end-grain action because it is cutting the shoulder's end-grain fibers.

Most wood cutting involves compromises and combinations of the three basic cutting orientations: with-grain, end-grain and cross-grain. The dynamics of each hold true regardless of whether the cutting is being done with hand or power tools.

As an example: the action of rip sawing often includes with-grain cutting and end-grain cutting depending on the blade's angle of attack. On a table saw, the height of the blade can change the rip cut from with-grain to end-grain, and because the blade is circular, both actions can occur in the same cut. An examination of the chips created while ripping con-firms which style of cutting was taking place: a blade set low, relative to the board, will produce the long, stringy shavings typical of with-grain cutting, while a blade set higher will make the coarse, pellet-like chips that are the result of cutting end grain.

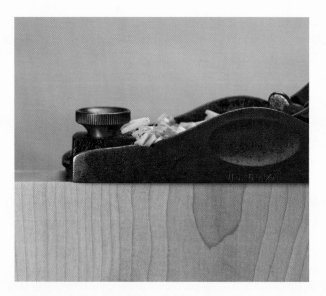

Here's my old #60½ planing end-grain maple. But you don't need a "low angle" plane to work end grain. A sharp blade in a standard pitch (45°) plane can easily do the job.

This beautiful Lie-Nielsen shoulder plane cuts cross grain right up to the shoulder.

To further complicate things, imagine boring a hole in a board with an auger bit. The bit has four cutting edges, two on each side. The spurs define the hole and the lips cut the bottom of the hole. Each spur will switch from with-grain to end-grain cutting while the lips switch from with-grain to cross-grain twice each revolution.

Woodturning and woodcarving can and often do involve all three types of cutting, changing from one to another to yet another, with each subtle move per-formed by the craftsman.

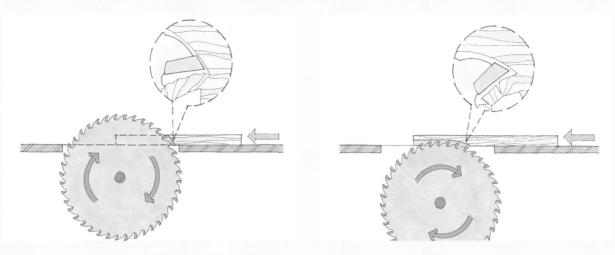

During a rip-cut on a table saw with the blade adjusted high, a saw tooth will cut more end grain. With the blade set low, the cut will be more with-grain.

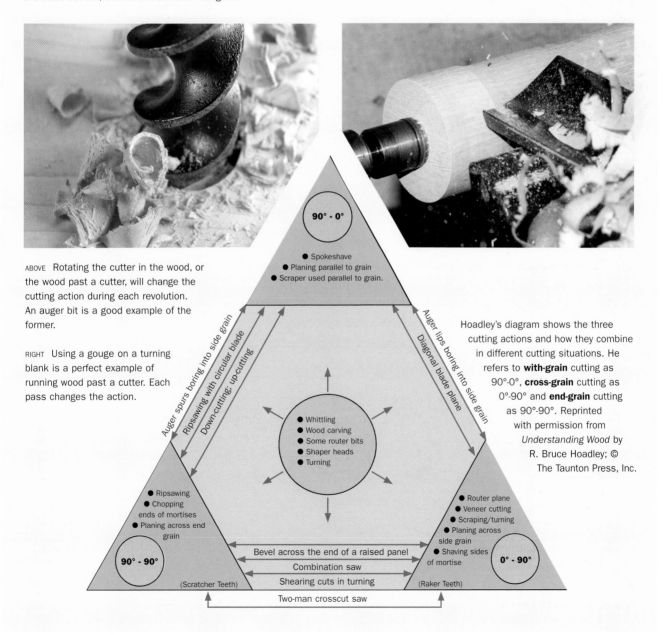

ABOVE Rotating the cutter in the wood, or the wood past a cutter, will change the cutting action during each revolution. An auger bit is a good example of the former.

RIGHT Using a gouge on a turning blank is a perfect example of running wood past a cutter. Each pass changes the action.

Hoadley's diagram shows the three cutting actions and how they combine in different cutting situations. He refers to **with-grain** cutting as 90°-0°, **cross-grain** cutting as 0°-90° and **end-grain** cutting as 90°-90°. Reprinted with permission from *Understanding Wood* by R. Bruce Hoadley; © The Taunton Press, Inc.

90° - 0°
● Spokeshave
● Planing parallel to grain
● Scraper used parallel to grain.

Auger spurs boring into side grain
Ripsawing with circular blade
Down-cutting: up-cutting

Auger lips boring into side grain
Diagonal blade plane

● Whittling
● Wood carving
● Some router bits
● Shaper heads
● Turning

● Ripsawing
● Chopping ends of mortises
● Planing across end grain

90° - 90°
(Scratcher Teeth)

● Router plane
● Veneer cutting
● Scraping/turning
● Planing across side grain
● Shaving sides of mortise

0° - 90°
(Raker Teeth)

Bevel across the end of a raised panel
Combination saw
Shearing cuts in turning
Two-man crosscut saw

5 The Fundamentals

SOME SHARPENING FUNDAMENTALS APPLY TO all tools, all grits, all gizmos and gadgets. I touched on them earlier and will expand on them now, before getting into how-to descriptions for specific tools. For the most part, when I use the term "grinding" I am referring to the process of reshaping an edge either by hand on a coarse abrasive stone or paper, or with a powered grinder. "Honing" refers to refining a dull edge that is the correct shape through successively finer-grit media. "Polishing" is the final, near-mirror finishing with the finest abrasive, and I use "sharpening" to refer to any or all of the whole shebang.

Bevel Angle

Your first consideration is the angle of the bevel, or bevels. (For an overview of bevel angles for woodworker considerations, see Chapter Four: How Wood is Cut.) I own a beautiful antique straight razor with an edge so thin you can easily distort it just by pushing on it with a fingernail. An edge like that will shave hairs with little effort but do not chop kindling with it – an edge that fine will not withstand such punishment without damage. By the same token, the hatchet you use for making kindling, honed shaving-sharp, would require more effort to cut whiskers due to its larger bevel angle.

For whatever reason, we have, over time, collected words and phrases that mean the same thing. A brief glossary might be helpful: a plane's *bed angle* is also called its *pitch* (the angle of the blade on the ramp in the plane). What I call *angle of attack* is also called *cutting angle* (the angle from horizontal at which the edge enters the wood). *Relief* and *clearance* are, in this case, the same thing (the angle of the edge that rises up and away from the wood and also allows the edge to enter the wood). Some sources describe the *cutting angle, hook angle* or *chip angle* as the angle back from vertical but I prefer to call that the *rake angle*. What some call the *sharpness angle*, I refer to as the *bevel angle*, meaning the angle at which the two surfaces meet to form the cutting edge. A *microbevel* is sometimes added to the bevel of single-bevel tools like chisels. A *back-bevel* is sometimes added to the back of plane irons. Knives and similar double-beveled tools often have large primary bevels and much smaller secondary bevels that are also sometimes called microbevels. More details about all these angles can be found in the specific tool chapters.

When sharpening a tool like an axe, you rarely need to abrade the entire primary bevel; sharpening the small, secondary bevel will do. That secondary bevel angle needs to be fairly large to support a cutting edge that must withstand the impact forces sustained in use by a tool such as an axe. The range of tools called "chisels" offers some good illustrations of bevel angle requirements: mortising, butt, paring, etc. Each chisel may need a different bevel because each may be used so differently. Mortising and paring chisels are probably as different as they can be.

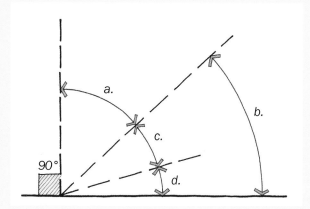

a. Rake Angle
b. Angle of Attack
c. Bevel Angle
d. Clearance Angle

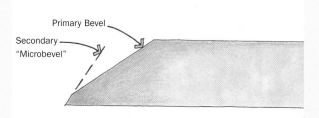

Primary Bevel
Secondary "Microbevel"

Mortising is a muscular chopping and prying action that demands a lot of strength from the tool and from its edge (not to mention the woodworker!) A paring chisel requires great control to perform its duty of making precise, thin-as-onionskin shavings. Never struck, but always pushed by hand, the paring chisel can be used with a bevel angle as low and fragile as 15°, while a chisel used for mortising hardwoods, struck hard to cut end-grain and levered against to break loose the chip, may have an angle as high as 35°. I'll get to detailed bevel angle specifications in the specific tool chapters.

A microbevel is a very narrow extra bevel near the cutting edge. This extra bevel is a couple of degrees larger than the main bevel and is easily obtained by simply tilting the blade up a few degrees during final honing. The main arguments in favor of microbevels are that they add strength to the cutting edge and they require much less time and effort to hone. You first establish your primary bevel with a coarse grit. Rather than proceeding to each successively finer grit on the whole bevel, just tilt the blade a bit and hone a small stripe, which is quick and easy. Keep in mind,

Different cutting tools (a straight razor on the left, and an ax on the right) require very different bevel angles on their edge.

though, once you have established the microbevel, if you continue to tilt each time you hone a little more, you will be adding a few degrees, which means that after a few sharpenings you'll have made the cutting angle too large. If you get to that point, you'll need to re-establish the primary bevel and start again with the microbevel progression.

A honing guide can avoid this microbevel progression by allowing you to re-hone your microbevel at the same angle each time. In this case, the microbevel simply grows larger with each honing until it accretes the entire bevel. At that point, it is time to regrind the bevel and start the microbevel honing anew.

On some tools the bevel angle can be adjusted to accommodate whatever it is you need to cut. A chisel can be sharpened for a specific job, such as a larger, and therefore stronger, bevel for hardwoods. A bevel-down bench plane, however, has a fixed angle of attack – the bed angle – so the blade bevel provides the relief angle behind the cutting edge. A relief, or clearance, angle behind the cutting edge allows room for the wood fibers to rebound after being compressed while being cut. Because a certain amount of relief is essential to a plane's performance, there is less latitude in the bevel angle specification. A bevel angle that's too large won't allow the necessary relief.

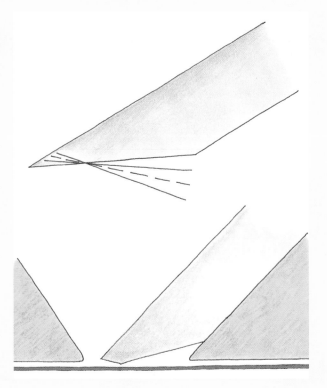

If you add a couple of degrees each time you sharpen by hand, you'll eventually create a bevel with an angle that's too steep. If this is a bevel-down plane blade, you'll lose the blade's clearance angle. Either way, you'll have to reshape the bevel and start the microbevel progression again. An accurately set honing guide can help avoid this by helping you re-hone the microbevel to the same angle each time.

Western-style kitchen knives, such as the ubiquitous "French chef's" knife (above, top), almost always incorporate a secondary microbevel because it is so time consuming to hone the entire flat bevel of the knife. By contrast, however, a Japanese chef's knife such as a willow-leaf sashimi knife (above, lower), is sharpened by honing the entire bevel to the cutting edge. The edge is very thin and fragile and is intended only for slicing raw fish. There are a number of specialty knives made and used for one function only. This is true of some woodworking tools as well.

Zero-Radius

When sharpening anything, the goal is to bring the edge as close as can be to *zero-radius*. You do this by removing metal from one or both of the faces that meet to form the edge.

This is achieved with abrasives made from various hard, sharp particles; grains of grit dig–in to scrape away a small amount of metal. With enough particles performing this ablation, the metal's surface wears away sufficiently to intersect the plane on the

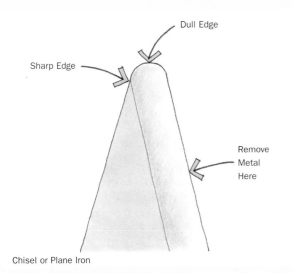

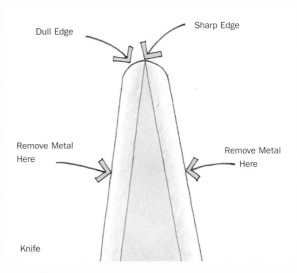

A double-beveled knife is sharpened equally on both bevels while a single-beveled blade, such as a chisel, is sharpened by removing metal on the bevel only.

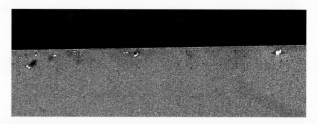

Raggedy edge seen at 200x magnification formed with a 325-grit diamond hone.

Same edge after honing through successive grits to 8000-grit diamond hone.

This edge was polished on a Shapton 16000-grit stone and is shown here at about 200x magnification. While there is some dust on the sample, the edge is, for any of my purposes, perfect, and will easily pass any of the sharpness tests described in this book.

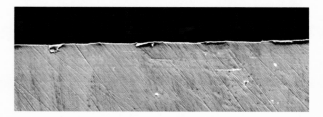

Burr at 300x magnification.

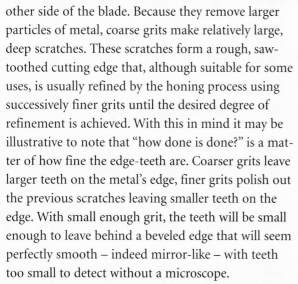

Photo of scratch pattern.

other side of the blade. Because they remove larger particles of metal, coarse grits make relatively large, deep scratches. These scratches form a rough, saw-toothed cutting edge that, although suitable for some uses, is usually refined by the honing process using successively finer grits until the desired degree of refinement is achieved. With this in mind it may be illustrative to note that "how done is done?" is a matter of how fine the edge-teeth are. Coarser grits leave larger teeth on the metal's edge, finer grits polish out the previous scratches leaving smaller teeth on the edge. With small enough grit, the teeth will be small enough to leave behind a beveled edge that will seem perfectly smooth – indeed mirror-like – with teeth too small to detect without a microscope.

Most of the little bits of metal being scraped away combine with the spent grit grains and are brushed away or carried away by the water or oil used as a honing lubricant. (This mixture of sharpening waste is called *swarf*.) But as the zero-radius intersection is approached, some of the shredded metal bits cling to the edge instead of breaking free. They form a thin, ragged fringe called a *burr* or *wire edge*. Each successively finer grit removes the burr formed by the previous grit and leaves its own, smaller burr. When using coarse abrasives, this burr is quite obvious. As finer grits are employed the burr gets very small and sometimes difficult to see. However, you must be sure it is there. If not, the bevel has not been honed enough to reach zero-radius and your work at that grit-size is not finished. Once you've raised a burr using whichever grit you start with, you can switch to a finer grit. The burr should be detectable with a scrape of a fingernail, or you can use a magnifier to see it. You might be tempted, when using the coarser

grits, to break the burr off by rubbing and bending it back and forth but that action may cause the burr "wires" to break off deeper than the edge. This creates something like a reverse saw tooth – a crevice or void in the edge that, in order to repair, will have to be honed away. It's best to simply hone the burr off with successively finer grits.

Depending on the blade you are sharpening, you may be able to change the honing angle as you progress to finer grit abrasives. If honing the back of a chisel, skew the blade on the stone at, say, a 30° angle. When changing grits, skew the blade to the other side. Your first few passes on the new grit will leave a crosshatch pattern of old and new scratches on the back. As you progress, the old scratches will fade away, being replaced by the ones made by the new grit. When all the old scratches are gone and there is a burr at the edge, it's time to switch to the next grit. (See Chapter Six: Plane Irons.)

Keep Flat

This step is not as important when sharpening tools with shaped edges, such as gouges, but for chisels and plane irons maintaining a flat abrasive surface is crucial. Steel diamond plates and honing films on glass do not need flattening but stones do – some more than others. If one of your stones is dished, the blade will follow that concavity and become slightly convex. When you switch to a finer stone that *is* flat, the blade will not sit flat on it. If a dished stone creates a convexity on the back of the blade that runs front-to-back, the edge will curve up when sitting on a flat abrasive surface making it very difficult to hone away the burr. If the hollowed stone creates a convexity in the blade from side-to-side, it can be very difficult to remove that hump, as any rocking of the blade during honing will tend to accentuate the convexity. The same problems accompany honing bevels as well. Following the stone's concavity will tend to round the edge to a subtle radius. While this may be desir-

able for some plane irons, there are more controllable ways to achieve it. And a radiused edge is not at all recommended for chisels.

Stones don't usually become convex with wear but such a condition would make the blade difficult to control as it rocks on the hump. Take care when flattening a convex stone that you don't simply rock the stone on the flattening surface and make it worse.

Some of the softer waterstones may require flattening *during* a sharpening step. (This is especially so with the coarser grits; in my experience they tend to wear more quickly than the finer ones.) If one of your stones needs re-flattening while sharpening a blade, it may be too fine. This forces you to work too long on that stone, honing out the previous grit's scratches. This extra wear on the stone results in its out-of-flat condition and necessitates the mid-sharpening re-flattening.

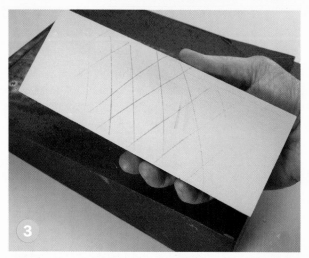

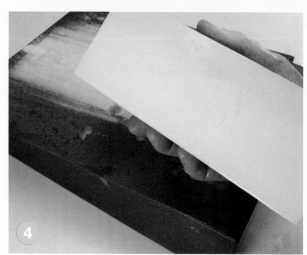

The solution is an intermediate grit – a half-step stone – added to your sharpening kit or procedure.

Shapton makes a diamond flattening plate that is itself flat to +/-5μ. A few passes with this over the stone (or the stone over it) and your stone will be as flat as the flattening plate. Norton makes a more affordable coarse stone for flattening that works quickly and efficiently; however, the Norton stone needs flattening once in a while, too. This is done by rubbing the stone on a piece of abrasive film or silicon carbide paper (220-grit or so) backed by a piece of glass or other flat surface. Flat surfaces for attaching paper or film are as simple as a piece of quarter-inch glass and as fancy as a granite surface plate intended for tool-and-die inspection and layout. Of course, waterstones can be flattened directly on the same sandpaper without an intermediary stone. I've even heard of woodworkers who flatten their water-stones on the sidewalk in front of their shop or on the side of a cinder block.

To flatten a stone, draw a crosshatch pattern with a pencil on the surface that you want to flatten (photo 1, above). Rub the stone against the flattening grit – whichever one you choose – and you'll see the pencil lines disappear as you go (photos 2 & 3, above). When the lines are gone, your stone is flat (photo 4, above). Check it with a straightedge to be sure, and repeat as necessary. An efficient practice is to flatten your waterstones after every use so they're always flat and ready to use.

Oilstones require less flattening because they are harder and wear more slowly than waterstones. The trade-off (again with the trade-offs!) is that they cut steel more slowly. See the quote from Larry Williams on page (Chapter Three, page 53) for his oilstone maintenance tricks.

Keep Wet

Oilstones need oil to work properly, although they can be used with slightly soapy water instead. Honing oil lore is rife with tales of creative "solutions," from diesel and baby oil to non-drying vegetable oils, paint thinner and mixtures thereof. I use a light hydraulic oil because it's clean, clear, odorless and I happen to have it around. Brand-name honing oils are a sure bet – readily available, a small quantity will last a long time and you can avoid yet another learning curve. You also have the assurance of the formulator that the oil will give you the best performance from your stones. No argument here. Period-furniture craftsperson Adam Cherubini uses soapy water instead of oil and recommends it as an effective *surfactant* even if you've already oiled your stones. A surfactant makes water "wetter" by breaking down surface tension and dispersing the swarf's insoluble particles. He says to just clean the oilstones well (run them through the dishwasher once or twice when your spouse is away) and liberally apply a weak solution of Ivory soap and

water during honing. He swears by it for keeping his sharpening area cleaner than it was when he used oil.

Follow the manufacturer's instruction for the care of your waterstones. Some waterstones need to be soaked thoroughly before use. The coarser stones fill with water quickly (in a few minutes), but the finer grits may take 15 or 20 minutes to saturate enough to use. Add water onto the surface often as the slurry dries and thickens. Some stones can be stored in water to keep them ready to use. Change the water frequently to avoid the pond-life scenario, and if you live where it's cold, do not let your stone pond freeze or you may thaw out a couple of pounds of expensive gravel.

Ceramic waterstones, like Shapton and Naniwa Superstones, should not be stored in water, or soaked. Simply wet the surface thoroughly before and during use, then rinse them off and let them dry. Diamond plates and hard ceramic stones can be used dry, but a little water helps carry the swarf away and prevents them from loading with metal particles. A shot of water with a drop of detergent can be helpful.

NAGURA STONE

An accessory for waterstones called a nagura stone is a hard, chalk-like stone used with the finest polishing stones to create a lubricating slurry on the surface of the stone. It's claimed that this slurry increases the abrasive's ability to polish to the highest level. Fine, natural waterstones are quite a bit harder than their manufactured counterparts and require this step to loosen some of the abrasive from the stone into a surface paste, rich in fine abrasive particles. It is my opinion that the slurry created by the nagura on a manufactured waterstone holds the blade off of the stone surface so that only the highest points of the stone are in contact with the blade. This reduces the effective grit-size of the stone, producing the desired high polish. Harrelson Stanley, of Japanesetools.com says: *I don't think there is any appreciable abrasive quality to nagura. I think of nagura as lubricant. It helps with really hard natural stones. I'm not a big fan of a slurry on waterstones because you're putting something else between the tool and the stone surface so there is less contact. Even if it has an abrasive quality it is not quantified, so its action is only subjective. My goal*

in sharpening is consistency above all else. I don't want unquantifiable variables. This is why I think we have to use man-made stones for serious sharpening. It's the only way to control and quantify variables.

Joel Moskowitz, of Toolsforworkingwood.com, adds: *Toshio Odate, in his classic book* Japanese Woodworking Tools, *says that if, on a hard finishing stone, your tool slips rather than abrades on the stone, creating a little slurry will stop the slippage. At the same time, letting the water on the finishing stone dry out lets the abrasive in the slurry break down and you have an effectively finer abrasive surface. The main thought here is that for faster honing, clean, sharp abrasive is better. For final polishing, a slurry is better. So adding slurry using a nagura before you start sharpening on a particular grit makes little sense to me, especially on coarser grits. On harder, finer stones, starting on a clean stone makes sense to me. Then as you work the stone, using a nagura to create more slurry, which you let dry, also makes logical sense. Although, if the stone is softer so that a good slurry develops anyway, why bother with the nagura?*

Keep Clean

As your sharpening progresses from coarse to finer and ever finer grits, be careful to avoid bringing any of the previous grit grains with you at each step. Rinse, wipe, brush, blow or vacuum away all remnants of the previous grit. Clean the surrounding area as needed, and don't forget your hands, apron and the tool itself. For me, sharpening is only "kinda fun;" I enjoy the process when it goes according to plan. If something goes awry, like a particle of 220-grit abrasive leaving deep tracks in the 8000-grit mirror that I've been creating, the whole process becomes, rather suddenly, a lot less fun.

Keep Cool

The edge, that is. When establishing the bevel with a powered grinder, be careful not to allow the steel to overheat. Depending on the tempering temperature used by the manufacturer, too-hot can be as low as 300° F (150° C), which is reached even before any of the surface-oxide, temperature-indicating colors will appear. I call those colors the "Oh, $%#@!" Colors," as that's the cry so often heard when that pretty rainbow appears while grinding a precious edge. This phase transformation happens very quickly and is irrevocable. The portion of the blade that is subjected to, and colored from, overheating will be softer and will not hold its sharpness as long as the rest. Once it happens the only solutions are: grind all the colored part away and re-shape the edge, or, re-harden the whole blade from scratch. Unfortunately, like so many other things in the world of craft, the closer you are to being finished, the easier it is to screw things up. You may be able to fix a burnt edge, and you should, by grinding it back past the burn and regrinding the edge anew. It won't take all that long. If the tool was worth sharpening in the first place, it will be worth the time to remediate a mistake. I wish I could say otherwise, but I have made this mistake and it is now part of my learning curve. Make the doing part of learning. Learn it well and you'll probably use that particular tool all the more often because the two of you have bonded at the grinder. The lesson here is: grind *slowly*, a little at a time. Dip the tool in water often and, when the residual droplets near the edge

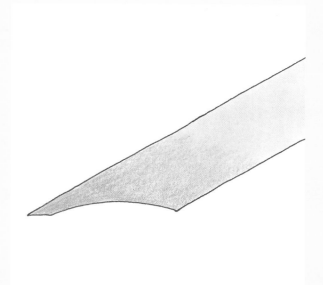

With a not-too-dull edge you can save some time by grinding the bevel just shy of the edge. It is often easier to resharpen the dull edge than it is to hone a just-ground edge.

start to boil, dip again.* Make it a Zen thing. Your patience will be rewarded with an edge that will be as hard as intended and that will stay sharp as long as possible.

One other grinder tip that's worth adding: if the edge is straight and intact, not chipped or out of square (just dull), do not grind all the way to the edge. Leave a thin stripe of unground bevel just behind the edge. It usually takes less effort to resharpen the old edge than it does to remove all the coarse scratches from the just-ground edge. Careful grinding in this manner can restore the hollow-ground bevel for easier handheld honing of the edge.

Keep At It

It's always best to resharpen an edge just before it really needs it. Okay, that's impossible, but you will do less sharpening and more woodworking if you stop to resharpen at the first indication that it is needed.

Concerns about the edge of the tool fracturing from the thermal shock of dipping it in water are unfounded. Cooling from <300° F (150° C) to room temperature represents a very small temperature differential compared to the quench the steel endured during hardening. So don't worry; if it didn't crack then, it won't now.

Keep Practicing

No one was born knowing all of this. Every craftsperson learned his or her skills by practicing them. Kevin Drake (musician, woodworker and tool-maker at Glen-Drake Tools) reminded me that professional musicians spend many more hours practicing than they do performing. Sharpening is a skill that you have to learn how to do. So give yourself a break and make some time to practice the skills that will make you a better woodworker – including sharpening. When you need to sharpen your new Lie-Nielsen blade for the first time, find an old chrome-vanadium blade that's been kicking around the shop and sharpen it first to get your chops down. You know that new chisel that you finally broke down and paid more for than you'd want your spouse to know? My advice is to practice on the POS chisel that someone used to dig out dandelions. When you set up to sharpen anything, look around for anything else that could use it. Make sharpening something that you do routinely and often enough that it's no big deal to do. A dedicated sharpening station in the shop can help, but even if it's just a dedicated place on a shelf to store all the sharpening gear, do what you can to make it happen with as little fuss and muss as possible, then your tools will be sharp when you need them. If you let dull edges pile up, waiting until you get some time, sharpening will become a big chore instead of the easy, routine task that it should be. And you may be tempted to use tools from the dull-pile, to the detriment of your work.

Practice and you will get better – at anything. Your tools will get sharper and they (and you), will work better as you understand them better. Your sharpening kit will become more refined as you streamline your techniques. And your sharpening routine will become … routine. Hey, they don't call it "honing your skills" for nothing!

Edge Testing
LOW-TECH, TOUCH-FEELY EDGE TESTING

Your blade is dull when too much effort is required to push a blade through material, or your edge is leaving behind a rough surface. A dull blade can be an educational opportunity, however, and with a bit of study, perhaps a magnifying glass or loupe, you can learn a lot about how to test for sharpness.

Know anyone with self-inflicted bald patches on their forearms? They're all woodworkers, right? This phenomenon relates directly to the most popular technique in determining sharpness: whether or not the edge shaves hair. The shaving test provides revealing data on how sharp an edge is by how it cuts hair and by how the blade feels to the skin underneath while the test is performed. If the edge presses the hairs against the skin, not cutting them at all but trapping them and then scraping along until the hairs slowly give way to being cut – that blade is not so sharp. If the edge snaps off hair with little or no pressure applied, it's sharp! Shaving hair off your forearm provides a relative scale based on empirical evidence and it is a traditionally straightforward, handy and useful test for many of today's (and yesterday's) woodworkers.

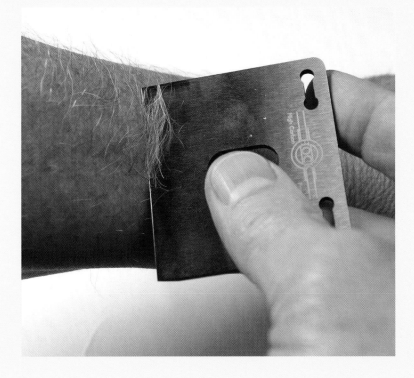

I know people who call the result of frequent edge testing Galoot Pattern Baldness.

The Thumbnail Test: Using *very light pressure* on the top of the nail, the blade should catch if sharp.

Again, *very light pressure* while sliding the edge along the nail will reveal every imperfection.

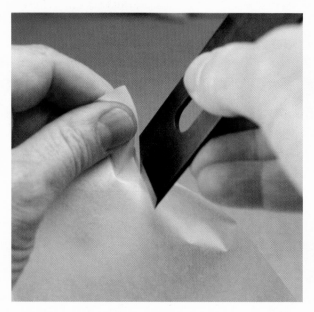

The Paper Trick: Dull ...

... and sharp.

I find it easy and quick to gently apply the blade's edge to the top of my thumbnail. I use just the lightest pressure; not trying to cut into the fingernail even a little. If the blade catches with no sliding at all, it's sharp! An edge that's dull will skid on the nail without that telling catch. If you're squeamish, use a ballpoint pen barrel instead of a thumbnail. You can also test the edge for uniformity by sliding the edge of the blade along the edge of a thumbnail (or pen barrel) as if to cut it but, again, with only the lightest pres-

sure. Even the slightest imperfection or roughness will telegraph clearly and tactilely. You'll know without a doubt whether or not you have more work to do on that edge. If the edge is sharp along all of its length, it will glide smoothly on your nail's edge, with no discernable vibration to indicate a rough spot.

Then there's always the paper-cutting trick. A sharp edge will slice a sheet of paper easily and cleanly, without catching, pulling or tearing.

Light reflects off a dull edge.

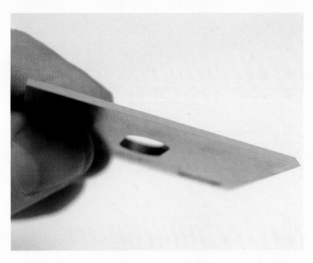

A sharp edge won't reflect light.

The fourth, handy, low-tech sharpness test is to simply look closely at the blade's edge to see if it reflects light. The closer an edge is to zero-radius the smaller that edge is; therefore, the less it reflects. When properly sharp, it won't reflect at all. You'll need to get the light at the proper angle – a magnifier helps – but it's not at all difficult to do. A couple of tries and you will clearly see that a dull edge reflects light while a sharp edge does not. Try this method with that blade that isn't cutting well. In fact, that dull blade offers a good opportunity to try all these simple tests and to get a feel for each of them. Then, when the edge has been sharpened, try them again to feel and see the difference. I mostly use the thumbnail test because it's so quick to do, but I have a few bald patches on my arm as well. At least with the latter two methods, you won't need to wear a long-sleeve shirt.

Gadgets

HOW MANY WAYS CAN YOU SKIN A CAT?

The need for accurate bevel angles combined with the trepidation of newbie sharpeners has created a boom market for accessories that assist in the sharpening process. Sometimes you need to sharpen to a specific angle for some specific cutting task. Sometimes you just need some training wheels. A honing guide can help. By locking the blade into a device at the proper angle, you then need only to run the blade/guide assembly over the abrasive and the bevel will be ground to the selected angle.

Here follows an incomplete list of honing guides and accessories for sharpening (mostly) chisels and plane irons by hand on stones or honing film. These are readily available now and represent the current design trends. There are other guides and systems out there, and something new will always be hitting the market. Great information, instruction and advice about woodworking tools and techniques can be had at your local woodworking club, school or retail outlet. Ask around to learn where local woodworkers congregate for classes or buy their tools and supplies. Could be that the local community college has classes – the students and instructors there can be a font of knowledge and experience you can dip into. And, of course, the internet provides a wealth of information about anything you can think of (and many you don't want to) but woodworking is very well represented through online forums, listserves, blogs, woodworking magazine sites and usenet newsgroups such as rec.woodworking. If there is something new that you need to know about, you can learn about it if, once in a while, you check in with your favorite online forum. And if you ask online for an opinion, I guarantee you'll get at least one.

There are many other accessories for sharpening other tools that will be covered in the sections on those specific tools. But so much woodshop time seems to be spent sharpening chisels and plane irons that I've dedicated this section to their specific honing guides.

The Eclipse Honing Guide that I've owned for over 20 years.

SIDE-CLAMPING STYLE

For chisels and plane irons, the simplest of the honing guides is a side-clamping model that used to be the Eclipse. While the Eclipse brand has been discontinued, clones are being made and are available today (try www.lie-nielsen.com). This honing guide was the standard for many years, is inexpensive, easy to use, and still works quite well. You set your bevel angle by adjusting the extension of the blade from the guide. Though the guide has blade extensions for different angles cast right into the side, a simple extension-setting fixture can easily be made and will ensure a quick setup for the same angle every time.

Side-clamping guides utilizes a small center wheel that rolls on your abrasive surface while honing your blade. Plane irons are clamped into it on the upper surface while chisels are gripped in a second jaw below. Chisels are not always parallel in thickness across the width. If you reference from the top surface, your edge will be skewed by the same angle that it is out-of-parallel with the back. To prevent this, all chisel-honing guides must be set using the back of the chisel as the reference surface to hold the edge parallel to the axle of the wheel. When using a side-clamping guide to sharpen a chisel, clamp it in the secondary jaws to keep the edge square.

A variation on the Eclipse design is a two-wheeled model by Richard Kell (richardkell.co.uk). Easily set and smooth as silk to use, the Kell guides employ two self-lubricating low-friction Ertalite TX outboard rollers. Three "blade guides" reference the flat as the back of the tool against the underside of the location rods, or brass plate. Kell offers three guides, one with a capacity of 0-1", a larger version that can hold

In the lower jaw, the chisel back is held parallel to the axle.

As beautiful as they are precise, these Kell guides are a silky smooth pleasure to use.

blades up to 2⅝" wide, while another can be adjusted to accommodate skew-edge blades. These well-made devices can be used with very narrow chisels or gravers and also easily accommodate short spokeshave-like blades. Because of the outboard wheels, a guide with a wide blade may be too wide for your sharpening stones. You can solve that with wooden "outriggers" approximately the same thickness as your stones for the wheels to ride on.

VERITAS MK.II™

Similar in function, yet an evolutionary step forward, is the Veritas Mk. II honing guide (leevalley.com). For greater stability, the Veritas roller is wider than the one used on the Eclipse, and it has an eccentric axle with an adjuster that allows you to tilt the blade in three small increments for adding microbevels. The upper part holds the blade, clamping from below so the back of the blade is always the reference surface (thus, avoiding the need for two clamping jaws like the Eclipse uses). This upper portion can be set in three positions relative to the roller to allow a good range of bevel angles from 15° to 54° and back bevels from 10° to 20°. The lower portion, with the roller, can be replaced with an optional barrel-shaped roller assembly that allows the side-to-side tilt some woodworkers employ to add a slight *camber* – a shallow radius (see page 109) – to the edge of their plane iron. The roller, while barrel-shaped, has a straight, cylindrical center section so you can easily feel when the blade is in the center position.

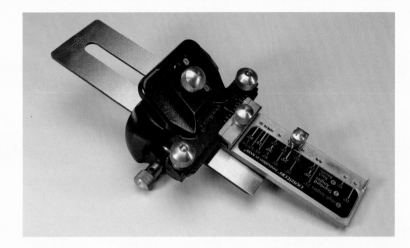

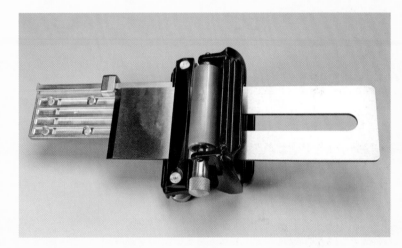

Use the blade registration jig, shown attached to the Veritas Mk.II Honing Guide (top, view from above; above, view from below) to set the bevel angle.

The Veritas Mk. II also comes with a blade extension jig for setting the bevel angle. It includes an integral fence to keep the blade square in the jig and pre-set extensions for a number of bevel angles on square-edge blades. A skew registration jig is an available option that is used in place of the square-edge registration jig. You use it to set the skew angle, as well as the extension angle for skew-edge blades.

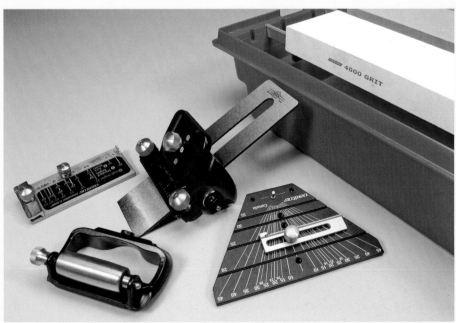

Mk.II Honing Guide with Registration Jig, optional Skew Registration Jig, Camber Roller and Stone Pond.

BURNS DOUBLE-BEVEL SHARPENING KIT

Brian Burns is a guitar maker and tool designer who offers a sharpening system that allows for bevel angles from 0° to 90° by using a stack of shims to adjust the level of the rollers attached to the bottom of the jig. Adding or removing shims allows for very fine adjustment of the bevel angle. The Burns Stone Box (available from lmii.com) includes seven ¾" shims and seven ⅛" shims, but you can add anything as a shim – boxboard, laminate or even sheets of paper – to set any angle (or fraction of one) you may want. The stones are set in the top of a box with the shims stacked in front at the base of the box. The Double Bevel Sharpening Kit includes a magnetic angle indicator and an angular steel jig with wheels and blade-clamp that allows you to bear down hard with great control to remove a lot of metal quickly.

This system was designed to facilitate the back-bevel sharpening method that Burns advocates in his book *Double Bevel Sharpening*. This system allows you to use angles as small as zero for flattening the back. Cambering of an edge can be accomplished by simply leaning on one corner of the blade then the other to impart the desired amount of camber.

Burns' Double-Bevel Sharpening Kit is available in two parts: The all-metal Honing Jig comes with the magnetic angle finder, and the Stone Box (sold separately) comes with the seven ¾" shims and seven ⅛" shims that allow very fine, repeatable bevel angle adjustments.

The Pinnacle Honing Guide with Honing Plate and attached abrasive film.

PINNACLE™

The Pinnacle Honing guide includes a set of extruded channel-rails that attach to your stone and a sled that holds the blade. The blade is clamped into the sled at one of six primary bevel angles, 15° through 40°, and can be tilted slightly for a microbevel by resetting the angle adjustment to one of the six secondary +2° bevel positions. The sled then rides the rails to sharpen the blade at the given angle.

The honing guides described previously all roll on a wheel or wheels while the blade contacts the stone, pivoting from the axle at an angle determined by the geometric relationship of the edge to the axle and to the surface of the stone. With those systems it is possible to grind the edge past the desired angle. With the Pinnacle, however, the blade is set at a desired angle in the sled. The sled rides on skids almost 4 inches long, so there is no pivoting and the grinding simply stops when the desired amount of blade has been ground away. Basically, you get everything set, slide the sled back and forth on the rails until the stone stops cutting, attach the next stone to the rails and continue on.

The Pinnacle system (woodcraft.com) is available with a honing plate for use with 8" *PSA*-backed (pressure sensitive adhesive) honing film strips. An optional kit includes longer rails along with a longer honing plate to use with their extra-long 14" honing film.

LAP-SHARP H-100™

One accessory available for The Lap-Sharp system (see below) is the H-100 honing guide that can be used on one of the Lap-Sharp machine's guide bars or on its own with your bench stones or sandpaper (woodartistry.com). The clamping mechanism holds the blade so that the flat back is parallel to the axle. It is spring-snap adjustable in 5° increments from 20° to 47.5°. A removable set-up reference block has a rab-bet machined in it so that when you flip it over, it re-registers the edge on the other surface of the rabbet for a 2.5° higher half-step of adjustability. The unique feature about the H-100 (other than it's compatibility with the Lap-Sharp machine) is that the wide roller is in front of the edge. When using this wide roller with a loose sheet of abrasive film, the roller holds down the film ahead of the edge, avoiding the "wave" of paper that can bunch up as the edge is pushed forward.

The Lap-Sharp H-100 honing guide has a removable U-shaped bar for setting the edge extension.

The H-100 can be used as a stand-alone honing guide on stones. It also slides onto an accessory cross-rod on the Lap Sharp machine.

To set the bevel angle, measure the blade extension from the SharpSkate or use the optional Angle Dock which sets that angle from the heel of the bevel.

PHOTO COURTESY HARRELSON STANLEY

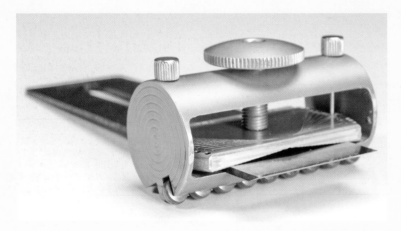

The SharpSkate with a plane iron. Note how close the edge is to the wheels. This provides for a lot of control and makes it easier to use more of the stone's surface, reducing wear in the center.

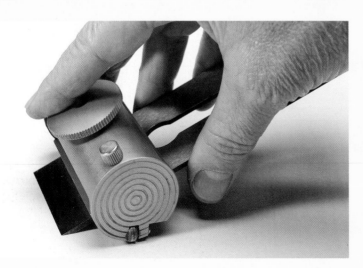

SHARPSKATE™

Harrelson Stanley has developed the SharpSkate (GetSharper.com) to hold chisels and plane blades for side-to-side sharpening which he calls "side sharpening." While most honing guides use a back-and-forth, to-and-fro motion, the SharpSkate's wheels roll the jig side-to-side which, Stanley claims, creates a stronger edge than obtained with back-and-forth sharpening. At normal bevel angles, the nine steel wheels of the SharpSkate are very close to the cutting edge – less than half the width of a standard stone – allowing you to use the whole stone while sharpening. This reduces the wear on the center of the stone, saving time from flattening it.

Also, the SharpSkate holds very narrow tools securely, allowing you to hone them more easily than if you tried to hold them by hand.

The blade extension is set using the optional Angle Dock accessory – a small platform with fine ridges that holds the SharpSkate. The ridges allow you to set the blade for the desired honing angle by registering the heel of the bevel against the appropriate ridge. Development of the Angle Dock is still in progress, but Mr. Stanley sent a photo and it looks promising.

The SharpSkate guide makes side sharpening easy.

STONE PONDS

Both Veritas (leevalley.com) and Shapton (shapton-stones.com) offer a solution to the mess presented by waterstones. Shapton provides a tray made of heavy rubber that is molded around a glass plate. The glass offers a flat surface to work on and the rubber perimeter contains the excess water while providing a skid-resistant base that sits securely on your bench. Add the Shapton Sharpening Stone Holder, another rubber-molded-around-glass creation that securely holds the Shapton stones up off the table or pond surface, and you're all set for tidy, skid-free sharpening.

While many woodworkers store their waterstones in a plastic food storage container, Veritas has raised that bar considerably with their stone pond. The Veritas Stone Pond goes beyond just storing stones under water: this box has formed-in recesses at the ends that accept aluminum struts with sliding clamps, which then hold the stones for use above the pond. When you're finished honing, the stones go back into the water and are held above the sludge at the bottom by integral ribs. Along with nonskid rubber strips that adhere to the bottom, the kit includes a plastic lid to keep the pond clean and the water from evaporating. It also includes a rectangular plate of tempered glass onto which is adhered a sheet of PSA-backed plastic. This is used with the included 90-grit silicon carbide abrasive powder as a lapping plate for flattening your waterstones. The glass provides the flatness and the replaceable plastic layer allows the abrasive grains to embed in the surface, immobilizing them so they'll cut instead of rolling around on the glass.

For oilstone fans, there are a number of stone holders, often holding them in a triangular configuration so that one stone is flat on top for use while the other two stones, on the other two sides of the triangle, are suspended in the oil bath.

The Shapton Stone Pond supplies a flat, nonskid, waterproof tray for no-mess sharpening with waterstones.

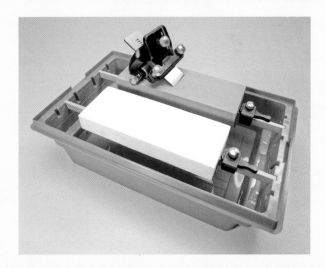

The Veritas Stone Pond helps tame some of the messiness of using waterstones while offering a container for soaking and storing your waterstones.

The Norton IM313 (nortonstones.com) system keeps three oilstones ready for use. The two that are not being used are rotated into the oil reservoir.

PHOTO COURTESY OF SAINT-GOBAIN ABRASIVES, INC. 2008

HANDS AND STONES

Need I say more? No – I'll let Joel do it:

Most sharpening lessons deal with the technology and sharpening sequence and leave out the technique for holding and moving a tool on a stone. But free-holding a tool consistently and comfortably is the key to sharpening easily and well. It's not that difficult at all. There are a tremendous number of products on the market designed to hold a blade at a consistent angle to a honing stone. However, almost all of them share two important flaws: The jigs allow you to repeat a motion but always in the same part of the stone. For waterstones, this means the stones will wear in certain spots faster and require more maintenance. The second problem with honing guides is more subtle: The first time you sharpen you establish some sort of bevel. The second time you sharpen you need to maintain the same exact bevel; the important word here is "exact;" If it's not exact, you tend to create a secondary and then tertiary bevel at each attempt at sharpening. This makes for much more work. Even if you can get really, really close to getting the same bevel, set-ting a tool in a jig exactly is tedious and difficult to get perfect. And, it takes time. You'll find it a great pleasure to be able to just take a tool and immediately put it onto a stone without having to worry about setting up a jig.

That being said, jigs and guides do have a place. I do use jigs for holding tools when we grind them and for especially rough honing where a grinder is not available and I have to remove a lot of metal using a coarse stone. Therefore, please realize I am not trying to present a "religious" argument but simply trying to show you how I make honing easier. An argument made against hand tools is that it's hard to make them work. A hundred years ago and more, people made hand tools work. They had no choice: they didn't have power tools. Woodworkers were able to be productive by having the right tool and developing the skill to maintain and use it properly. If you can duplicate that skill, you can be just as productive.

– Joel Moskowitz, Tools for Working Wood
(www.toolsforworkingwood.com)

Machines

All sharpening, like all woodworking, can be accomplished with hand tools and muscle power. But, as in woodworking, the power of electromagnetism can be useful for some sharpening processes. A blade used in the normal course of woodworking should never require more than the occasional reshaping of a bevel that's been honed to a different angle. Sometimes there may be a need for the removal of a nick and the subsequent re-establishment of the edge or the repair of larger damage caused by an unforeseen nail or mixture of gravity and concrete. This occasional need for larger reshaping can be done with hand tools and coarse grits, but precious time can be saved with the judicious application of electrical power.

BENCH GRINDER

A basic bench grinder comes in very handy in any shop. Seems there's always some metal thing that needs a bit of itself removed and a grinder is often the perfect tool for the job. When it comes to sharpening, the bench grinder can be your best friend – and

A simple bench grinder comes in very handy for all sorts of shop needs. We keep a wire-wheel brush on one end for rust-and-crust cleaning jobs. This machine is mounted to a plywood base that allows it to move around in the shop, clamped to whatever bench needs it nearby. And the base is drilled to receive the Veritas tool rest when needed.

Oh, $%#@!

In addition to their sliding fixture for grinding turning tools (top), Oneway's Wolverine Grinding Jig comes with a sturdy, adjustable-angle platform that has a 3" x 5" working area.

worst enemy. The friendly part happens when the machine is adjusted properly and used appropriately. The enemy shows up when you're in a hurry or not paying close attention, most likely when you're using the grinder for a task better performed by other tools in your arsenal, or when you're simply trying to take off too much material too quickly. The corners and thin edge of a blade will heat the fastest and often the warning signs of impending overheat*ing* will turn to full-blown overheat*ed* in a split second. Take your time, exercise some patience. Like I've said, the closer you get to finishing something, the easier it is to mess it up.

Bench grinders of varying quality are available everywhere in 6" (150mm) or 8" (200mm) sizes (that's wheel diameter). The more-expensive, name-brand grinders are a good investment that will last a lifetime, while the less-expensive ones, while functional, will require some tuning, especially in the tool-rest area. The high-end models will come with a heavy-duty, accurate tool rest while the others often come with a flimsy, stamped tool rest that is really not up to the demands of precision sharpening. After-market tool rests are available or you can clobber up a suitable substitute from metal, as a replacement for the one that came with the machine, or from wood that fastens to the bench below the wheel. Six inch or 8" wheels are the standard offerings with the motor turning at 3450rpm. There are slower grinders that turn 1725rpm that are well suited for sharpening (they'll tend to generate less heat or, at least, generate heat more slowly due to their slower speed). When

considering a grinder, remember that the surface speed of the wheel is what the tool's edge sees and that's a function of rpms and wheel diameter. A 6"-diameter wheel's surface speed, when spinning at 3450rpm, is roughly 90 ft/sec. An 8" wheel's surface speed is 120 ft/sec. The surface speed is halved when the wheel spins at 1725rpm.

Again, *technique is more important than tools* – you *can* learn to use the grinder you have, with the wheels that are on it. A 1725 rpm grinder and/or cooler-running wheels may help you develop your technique but a few practice sessions with whatever you have will do wonders as well.

The adjustability of the Veritas tool rest allows for versatility in positioning the table. It comes with the sliding blade holder and angle setup guide. The hole in the table accommodates the skew grinding jig, sold separately.

This sturdy plywood tool rest slides back and forth and tilts to present most any angle to the wheel. TOOL REST AND PHOTOS BY PAT ROCK

Please read and follow all safety information that comes with your grinder and its wheels. Read the grinding wheel safety section in Chapter Three on abrasives. Grinders can hurt you and anyone nearby in a variety of awful ways. *Pay attention.*

There are a number of choices in the grinding wheel arena. Some wheels promise to grind cooler than others while some will last longer, etc. This can be said anywhere in this book but it's especially true with bench grinders: nothing makes up for poor technique. While the margin for error may be greater with the most expensive, coolest-running wheel, it can still overheat a tool's edge in a blink. Practice grinding on scrap steel and graduate to your second-string tools before grinding – and risking – your best edges.

Truing and *dressing* the wheel are vital and are routine operations. Truing is the process of making the wheel round after it has worn unevenly. Dressing shapes the face of the wheel and cleans it of embedded metal particles while exposing sharp new grit. Available in three different styles, the same tool is used for both of these operations. Star dressers are a metal holder with a pack of star wheels that look like cowboys' spurs. These spurs are pressed against the grinding wheel while it's running, matching the speed of the wheel while pressed hard enough to crush the surface slightly. This crushing action dresses the face of the wheel.

There are also diamond dressers, either a single diamond mounted on the end of a rod, or a matrix of diamonds on the T-head of a handheld tool. Dressing sticks are made from a very hard material such as silicon carbide or boron nitride in a hard bond. Sometimes a dressing stick is a piece of hard material held in a handle. The diamond or hard bit of the dressing stick is pressed against the wheel while it is running and moved across the face to scrape it to the desired shape. Star dressers have "feet" that can slide along the tool rest to create a flat face on the wheel. Diamond and stick dressers can be advanced by hand or held in a simple holder that slides along the tool rest. Some people recommend dressing a crown in the wheel, claiming that it reduces the problem of burning edges on the corners. However, I believe good technique can be learned to avoid such problems and the crown in the wheel simply reduces the wheel's effective width.

A star-wheel dresser (above) crushes the surface to true and dress the grinding wheel. A diamond (below) scrapes the high spots off to achieve the same result. A close-up (bottom) of both dressing tools. Wear a respirator – both jobs are very gritty.

I never used to like bench grinders much. I used one frequently when I first started out making knives in the 1980s. I found it to be gritty and bouncy – no matter how much I dressed them, the wheels never seemed round. I switched to belt grinders exclusively until quite recently, when I discovered that by simply balancing the wheel, the bouncy problem could be solved. Oneway Manufacturing (www. oneway.ca), the ones who make the wood lathes and the Wolverine grinding jig for turning tools, makes the Wolverine Precision Balancing System. Now my bench grinder runs smoothly for the first time. The system replaces the flanges that hold the wheel to the grinder. The Oneway flanges have a concentric raceway that allows you to move weights around while the wheel is on a bearing stand, not unlike balancing a car's wheel and tire. You slide the weights in the raceway until the wheel stays put at any position and it's balanced. This takes a few minutes of patient fussing but the results are worth it: smoother, quieter grinding and a better surface finish on the tool. Plus, the wheel will last longer because you're not dressing it as often. My grinder still makes a gritty mess but it finally runs smoothly and I'm much more inclined to use it.

This simple system from Oneway Manufactiuring will take the shakes out of your grinder.

BELT SANDERS

Bench-mounted belt sanders (in the metalworking world we call them belt grinders) can perform a number of sharpening chores. They run cooler than bench-grinder wheels (you still must be careful, though,) and can switch among many grits in seconds. Because you need only swap belts when they get dull, there is no wheel truing and dressing as there is with bench grinders, so there's less dust in the shop. Belts are available in a variety of abrasives and grit sizes. We use the basic aluminum oxide metalworking belts. However, I also recommend that you try out some of the newer aluminum-zirconia belts and 3M's Trizac belts that cut quickly and come in very fine grit sizes for real polishing. There seem to be new belt innovations hitting the marketplace all the time, so it might be wise to shop around and try out the latest offerings.

The small, inexpensive, 1" × 30" belt grinder models are very handy and take up little space. The table that comes with them may not adjust enough for the acute angles we so often need, but it's a simple matter to cut a wooden wedge to give the table a more effective angle at the belt.

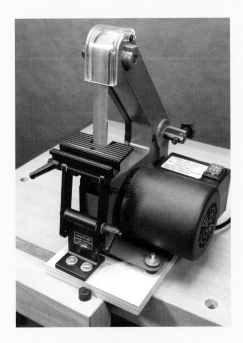

You'll find many uses for a small, affordable, 1" x 30" belt grinder. Mounted to a plywood base, it's easily clamped in a bench vise to a horizontal position. And, it can benefit from an after-market tool rest like the Veritas model shown here.

When using the table that came with it, this table-top belt grinder (sander) needed a little help to set the angle for the plane iron. A simple wooden wedge did the trick.

VERTICAL GRINDERS
Tormek

Tormek leads the pack in the division I'll wordily call "Vertical, Water-Cooled, Low-RPM Grinders." While similar machines are available from Jet and others, Tormek (www.tormek.com) has set the standard by which the others are measured. The Tormek is a well-designed, well-made machine that gives you an amazing amount of control over the creation and accurate re-creation of the cutting edge on just about every tool you own. Over a dozen jigs are available to properly and repeatably hold everything from chisels and scissors to axes and fingernail gouges. The low-speed vertical stone turns in a water trough to keep the stone wet: no burning, no sparks and no dust. The stone can be "graded" by firmly rubbing the included grading stone against it while it turns. This dressing exposes fresh grit for the most aggressive action. The other side of the grading stone does the opposite – it smoothes and refines the wheel so that it performs like a finer-grit stone to put an intermediate edge on the blade. On the other end of the shaft is a wheel with a leather strop "tire" that is charged with a fine abrasive paste for final polishing. Yet another accessory can be attached to the strop end of the shaft that has two shaped strops for polishing the insides of gouges and the like.

I am very impressed with this machine but I feel there is one thing missing: a jig for flattening the backs of chisels and plane irons – a task essential to the whole sharpening process. The official technique is to hold the back of the blade parallel to the side of the stone (unlike high-speed grinders, you can use the side of the stone) and slowly approach the rotating surface until you've made contact. Granted, the stone is moving at only 95rpm but landing askew could dub a corner of a blade and make for more work in flattening. I suggested a fix for this problem to Tormek's U.S. representative – it may already be available as you read this.

You'll want to use these water-cooled grinders in an area that can be allowed to get wet. They can be messy and your recently-flattened bench top may not be the best location for one.

Where a bench grinder is an aggressive tool for rapid stock removal (with all the risks mentioned above) the Tormek-style grinders remove metal much more slowly and with much less risk. They seem calm and almost surgical by comparison.

The Tormek grinder with all the accessories.

The Work Sharp grinder includes an adjustable-angle port that grinds the bevel on the underside of the wheel.

HORIZONTAL GRINDERS
Work Sharp

There are several competitive brands of horizontal, "sandpaper platter" sharpening machines available at this time. They share the advantage of having a wide range of abrasive sizes to choose from, and changing grits is as easy as changing a record on the turntable (er, CD in the DiscMan?) Anyway, the three machines I looked at all share many fundamental similarities, while each enjoys individual features as well.

The Work Sharp WS3000 (www.drilldoctorstore. us) uses glass discs that are over ⅜" (10mm) thick × 6" (150mm) in diameter as the bases for the PSA-backed abrasives that are applied to both sides of the glass. A tool rest spans the top as an aid to free-hand grinding from above, but there is an adjustable "sharpening port" ramp for grinding bevels up to 2" wide from below on the underside of the platter. The port is adjustable for 20°, 25°, 30° and 35° bevel angles and has a skew adjustment to keep things square. The sharpening port ramp has integral fins below to dissipate heat that is generated by grinding though the instructions recommend a "plunge-pull" technique to avoid overheating. The ⅕ hp motor rotates the disc at 580rpm.

An optional wide-blade attachment is available for the Work Sharp that secures to the top of the machine, providing a flat table that can be leveled with the turntable to facilitate flattening backs of chisels and plane irons. This option includes a bevel-

Fitted with the slotted wheel and matching abrasive paper, you can see through the wheel and watch the grinding action while it's happening.

honing guide that rides on the flat table surface to allow sharpening blades that are too wide to fit the sharpening port.

The Work Sharp is a compact, well-made, affordable machine that will speed up many sharpening operations. It comes with a slotted Edge-Vision Wheel that can replace the glass discs. Used with the matching slotted abrasive discs you can actually see through the disc while grinding. The slotted wheel has the abrasive on the bottom, so when you approach from below with, say, a gouge, you can see through the wheel-slots from above while it's spinning and watch your progress with the gouge (good lighting is must). This feature comes in very handy for some freehand sharpening tasks.

LAP-SHARP

In addition to being a top-quality machine, the Lap-Sharp Sharpening System (www.woodartistry.com) incorporates two features that the others here lack: reversibility and a foot switch. Reversing the turntable allows for sharpening a number of edge-shapes that you can't sharpen otherwise. Honing film is tough but you can cut into it when you orient the edge into the direction of rotation. This is especially problematic when sharpening something like a kitchen knife or pocketknife. Being able to reverse the platter allows you to keep the edge trailing away from the abrasive, avoiding the risk of cutting into it.

The Lap-Sharp's foot switch easily solves the back-flattening problems encountered with other machines. Being able to simply position the blade on the stationary surface and hold it in place while you step on the "go" pedal allows flattening of the back of the chisel or plane iron without risk of rounding off a corner when trying to make a landing on a moving deck.

Wood Artistry, maker of the Lap-Sharp, offers a variety of accessories for holding and/or positioning

The Lap-Sharp system, with included foot switch. The honing guide is sold separately.

most any tool you need to sharpen. The 8" (203mm) diameter platter is quickly swapped to change grits and honing film discs are available from 60 grit to 1μ in several abrasive compositions. Their honing guide can be snapped onto a guide rod on the machine or used off it with bench stones or honing film. And, there are jigs and fixtures available for planer and jointer knives as well as carving and turning tools.

The Lap-Sharp's cast, powder-coated aluminum housing is fitted with an integral drain tube for use with a constant flow of water, if so desired. The 170rpm turntable is powered by a ¹⁄₁₅ hp direct-drive gear motor that impressed me with the amount of torque it produces. I could apply substantial pressure on the platter without slowing the motor. This is a well-engineered, well-built machine that will stand up to a lifetime of frequent use.

VERITAS

It seems the engineers at Veritas spend a lot of their time designing excellent sharpening tools, systems and accessories to quickly and easily put fine edges on just about every tool in the shop. Their entry in the sharpening machine category is the Veritas® Mk.II Power Sharpening System (www.leevalley.com), which comes complete with a tool holder for blades up to 2½" (63mm), a tool registration jig, a tool guide rod, a starter-pack of abrasives – everything you need to start sharpening. The tool guide rod assembly fits into a socket on the machine that incorporates a ball plunger that allows the post to "click" into one of seven preset heights that determine the bevel angle. It's as if the machine is a powered honing guide.

The tool registration jig that comes with the Veritas Mk.II Power Sharpening System is a simple extrusion that, when used with the tool holder, sets the edge extension with repeatable accuracy. You vary the bevel angle by raising or lowering the guide rod assembly either to the preset click-stops or somewhere in between.

Two 8" (203mm) platters are included with the system; one 3mm-thick, the other 4mm-thick. You apply the coarse abrasive discs – 80 grit and 100µ – on the 4mm platter and the fine discs – 40µ and 9µ – on the 3mm platter. That way, when you switch from the coarse platter to the thinner, fine-grit one, you will automatically create a 1° microbevel. Very clever.

The Veritas® Mk.II Power Sharpening System is powered by a ¼ horesepower (hp) motor with a belt-driven, ball bearing 650rpm turntable.

The Veritas system includes the honing guide, extension guide and two platters. The thinner platter is for the finer-grits. The change-in-height feature automatically (and cleverly) creates a microbevel.

KOCH

The Koch Sharpening System (www.woodcraft.com) stands apart from the others discussed here in that it was designed by a master woodcarver to sharpen carving tools quickly and easily. It can be used for more than that of course, but it excels at carving tools. The Koch System consists of four wheels on one long shaft that rotates away from the operator so the tools are honed on the top of the wheel using the beefy tool rest as a reference. The 4" (100mm) diameter wheels are a special composite material that acts like a cross between leather and felt. One wheel on each side (red and yellow) is composed of layers that allow it to conform to the convex curves of carving gouges and the like, while the other wheels (blue and green) are for straight-edge tools. Koch supplies two honing compounds – green (fine grinding) and blue (fine honing) – of different grit sizes. The key to the system is to apply compound to the appropriate wheels (green on the left, blue on the right) then press the tool against the wheel until a dark line appears indicating that the compound has melted, which activates the abrasive. Koch claims that the liquefaction of the abrasive sharpens without overheating and leaves no burr on the opposite side of the bevel.

The Koch wheels are available separately for any grinder with a ½" shaft but the Koch machine, ¼ hp, 1725rpm, with the long double-shaft, accommodates all four wheels at the same time, and is heavy enough to handle that long shaft and still run smoothly and quietly. Koch says that you can use their system for any blade but I'd be concerned about maintaining flatness on the backs of "flatness-critical" blades like bevel-edge chisels and plane irons when using any charged wheel. This machine will be a time saver for the carver who demands sharp tools (and is there one who doesn't?)

DREMEL

I find all kinds of uses for a Dremel-style hand grinder including a few specialty sharpening functions. The small sanding drums, mounted stones, diamond burrs, chain saw stones, etc. are perfectly suited for that serrated knife edge, carving gouge, concave or shaped blade. It's a tool of a thousand uses and I keep mine handy for all sorts of small shop chores.

DRILL PRESS

I wouldn't recommend buying a drill press just for sharpening, but if you already have one, you can use it for a variety of sharpening jobs. For instance, you can use it with a sanding drum to grind the bevel on a concave spokeshave blade or mount a felt, cardboard or leather wheel in the chuck for polishing – use your imagination.

Koch Sharpening System.

Dremel.

Basic Kits

To sharpen anything, you need, at the very least, something to abrade the thing you want to sharpen. That may sound simple but things get complicated from there. For chisels and plane irons the abrasive needs to be flat. And, you need more than one grit size. (Already more complicated.) Here are some thoughts about basic sharpening kits.

First, and I've said this more than once elsewhere, technique is more important than tools. If you under-stand the sharpening process – what is required to create a perfect edge – you can use almost any sharpening system with reasonable results. The following applies mostly to chisels and plane irons – flat blades with straight edges – because they seem to need the most attention in a typical furniture shop. More esoteric tools will need specialized gear mentioned in their respective chapters.

To assemble your sharpening kit I recommend an incremental approach, beginning with the least amount of investment. It's not that I don't want you to spend money, but I would hate to have you waste any buying stuff you won't use. Just like anything, there are many ways to sharpen and what works for one woodworker may annoy another. And, different disciplines need different sharpening gear. For instance, if you have no need to sharpen a saw, you'll have little need for a saw set in your sharpening kit.

LEFT Scary Sharp basics.

BELOW Scary Sharp basics with more accessories added.

Basics with stones. A grinder as add-on above, and also a belt grinder.

SCARY SHARP

The simplest sharpening kit (often dubbed the Scary Sharp System) is a piece of ¼"-thick (6mm) plate glass (or some other flat tile) and some abrasive *honing film* (high-grade sandpaper.) I've used the basic silicon carbide wet-or-dry sandpaper from the hardware store with good results, but it wears out very quickly. The honing films currently available are a superior product for sharpening and are available in a large assortment of grit sizes. I tend to go through the coarsest grits most quickly so I buy more sheets of those when I stock up. The glass I use is large enough that I can apply two strips of honing film on each

side: 80µ, 15µ, 5µ and 1µ, but you can use two pieces of glass with abrasive on each side if you prefer (they're a bit easier to store). The self-stick, PSA-backed option is handy but you can use a spray adhesive such as 3M's "Super 77." That's all you really need for basic freehand honing of chisels, plane irons, etc. Some other things that come in handy (a square, a marker and scribe) you already have in your shop.

If you are unsure of your technique, a honing guide can help. Honing guides are often useful and sometimes required for getting a perfect edge on an angle-critical tool like a plane iron. As your experience increases, you'll find yourself gathering some accessories to make things easier and more comfortable. A non-slip mat to keep the glass plate from sliding around, good lighting, a magnifier of some kind (some swing-arm lamps have a large lens in them). Sharpening is messy so I use disposable gloves so I don't have to scrub my fingers.

A sharpening area can help keep the rest of your shop – and your work – clean. It also makes the routine of sharpening simple, so you'll be less inclined to put it off. Also, a clean and ready sharpening area encourages you to put in the time that it takes to become good at sharpening. A dedicated area can be built to the right height for your own ergonomic comfort and efficiency (usually lower than bench height) and can include storage space for all the gizmos and doodads you'll collect as you slide farther down sharpening's slippery slope.

STONES

Many woodworkers use honing film exclusively for sharpening. They swear by it, but if you get tired of buying honing film (the downside of honing film, by the way, is that it gets dull with use and needs to be replaced) you may want to invest in some stones. With stones, you refresh the abrasive surface time and

Perhaps not basics, but basically very useful options to hand sharpening. Tormek, Work Sharp and Veritas.

again by flattening it instead of replacing it. Your experience with honing films should give you an idea of what grit sizes you prefer and you can use that knowledge to shop for stones that approximate those grits.

Stones demand some sort of storage. The type of waterstone that can be soaked full time needs at the very least a food-storage container, or a fancy, dedicated stone pond that will keep your stone(s) handy and your work area as clean as possible. An apron and a roll of paper towels nearby would not be considered luxuries.

From here, you may want to add some electrical power in the form of a bench grinder or one of the dedicated sharpening machines that I've discussed elsewhere. Most resharpening jobs do not need power tools but they do come in handy for all sorts of things, including reshaping the damaged or neglected edge. In and of itself, the addition of a power tool may necessitate a dedicated area in the shop for sharpening – such as that long counter under the window or a cart or bench built just for this purpose.

If the grinder has a permanent home on a bench or counter, a drawer underneath or nearby would be a good place to keep the rest of the sharpening gear so it stays clean and out of harm's way.

With time and dedication you'll no doubt find yourself acquiring and adapting all sorts of special-purpose doodads for those tools that you, and only you, understand how to sharpen. Your collection will depend entirely on the types of woodworking you do and the tools required for it. A woodcarver will have a different sharpening kit than a turner, etc. All the possibilities let you be creative and open to new ideas. It seems that every woodworking magazine has an article on some nuance of sharpening every few editions. Ask friends or fellow students or club members about their sharpening setups and use all available resources to learn more about your own sharpening needs, then respond accordingly. As I've said before, asking others is a great way to get to know another woodworker. Just ask, "How'd you sharpen that?" and you'll likely make a new friend.

Plane Irons

PLANE IRONS AND SPOKESHAVE BLADES SHARE similar requirements when it comes to sharpening. Of all the tools in your shop, they're about the most straightforward to sharpen. Both need their backs flattened and their bevels honed to the proper angle, and that's about it. Of course, it's not really that simple as there are straight, cambered and skewed edges, back bevels and microbevels to be considered, as well as the subtle differences in bevel-down versus bevel-up planes.

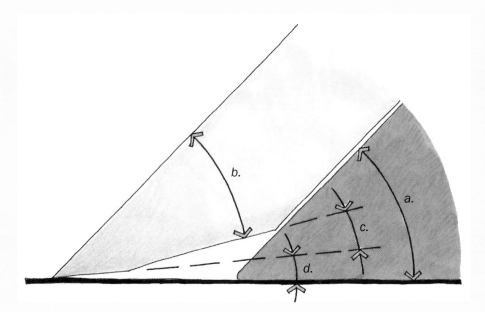

Typical bench plane geometry:
a. Bed (ramp) angle of the plane relative to the sole, most commonly 45°;
b. Primary bevel angle of 25°;
c. Optional microbevel of 5°;
d. Clearance (or relief) angle of 15° (12° minimum).

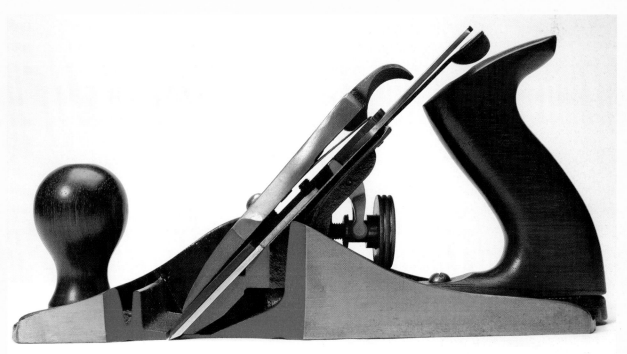

Cut-away bench plane.

It seems there are more words written about sharpening plane blades than any other tool in the shop. (I haven't counted but I'm pretty sure that's true in this book, too.) Part of that is simply because I make plane irons for a living and they're what pulled me into the world of woodworking in the first place, so I have a special place in my heart for them. I also have been considering plane functions for twenty-five years and I know more about them than any other

hand woodworking tool. But if you think about it, few other tools are used for so many operations from rough dimensioning to fussy-fitting to final surfacing. They're remarkably versatile tools and a plane's relationship to its blade is at the heart of all of it. If you are experienced with hand planes you undoubtedly know what I mean. If you're new to them, get to know them. Wonderful tools, planes.

Plane Irons

A plane is just a holder for a blade. Without a blade, a plane is just a … hammer? But a blade without a plane can still do a lot of work.

The standard bench plane uses a blade bevel-down, usually with a cap iron, or chip breaker (also simply breaker). Absent a back bevel (sometimes called a top bevel), the angle of the bed, or ramp, is the angle of attack of the blade into the wood. A clearance – or relief – angle is required and needs to be at least 12°. With a bed angle of 45° (once called common pitch) and a bevel angle of 25°, the clearance angle is 20° – the standard bench plane setup. There are some other bed angles that have been popular in the past for planing more difficult woods: a 50° bed angle is called a York pitch; 55° is called middle pitch, and 60° is called half pitch. Traditionally, the blade will be ground to 25°, which works well, but I recommend a 5° to 10° microbevel to strengthen the edge to help it last longer. Working with a microbevel also speeds up the sharpening process because you only have to work on that narrow strip along the edge.

Over the years I've had a lot of customers inquire about thicker blades for the bench planes, assuming that thicker blades are somehow better. While it may seem true, consider that the cantilevered portion of a bevel-down blade remains the same for thicker blades. It's just moved farther away from the ramp on a larger, thicker cantilever.

In a bevel-down plane, added blade thickness adds to the edge's cantileverage as well. The top illustration is the standard cantileverage with a standard thickness blade. The bottom shows a thicker blade with proportionally larger bevel and cantileverage. The cap iron adds rigidity by preloading the unsupported cutting edge.

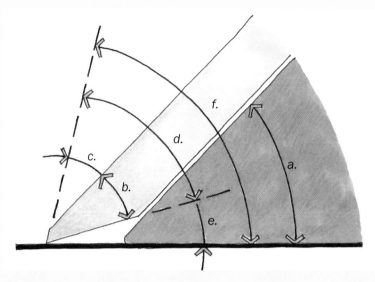

Bench plane geometry with back-bevel added:
a. Bed angle of the plane = 45° (typically); b. Primary bevel = 30° to 33°;
c. Back-bevel = 5° to 20° (or more); d. Included edge angle = 35° to 50°
e. Clearance (or relief) = 12° minimum; f. Angle of attack = e+b+c = 50° to 65° (or more).

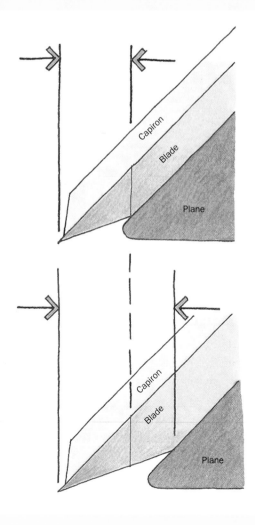

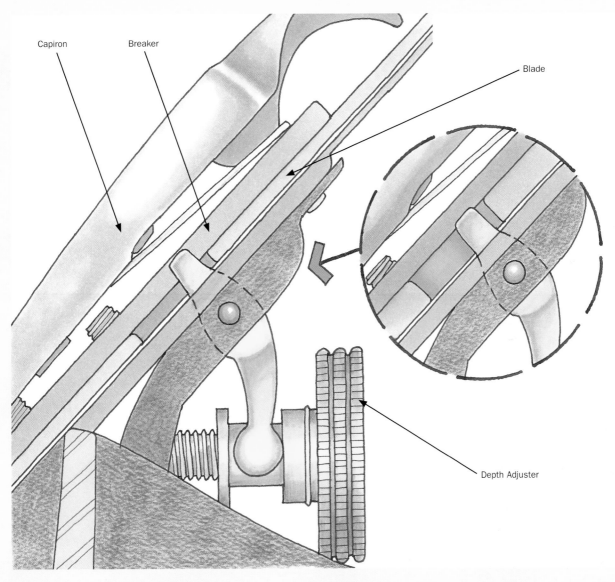

Capiron

Breaker

Blade

Depth Adjuster

Because the depth-adjuster lever reaches through the blade to engage the breaker, a thicker blade may prevent it from reaching and working properly, or at all.

Also, with thicker blades for bench planes, there is a real risk that the depth-adjuster lever, which reaches through the blade to engage the cap iron, may be too short to reach its destination; or, at the very least, not reach through its entire arc. Either way, it won't work properly, if at all.

Thicker blades are easier to handle – their bevel will sit more securely on a stone due to the larger footprint – and can add mass and rigidity to the overall system, but I've found the ubiquitous Bailey pattern bench plane – thin blade and all – to be quite able to perform as well as any plane ever made. All it takes is the fettling described here and if, after that, your plane doesn't function the way you want it to, there is something that still requires cleaning, adjusting, tightening, flattening or sharpening. And, thin blades are faster to sharpen as there is less metal that needs to be honed away.

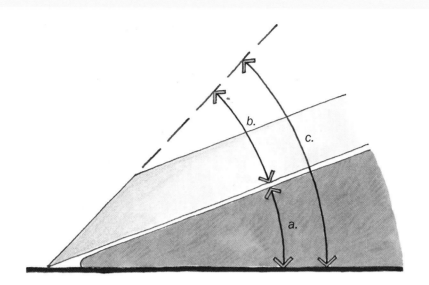

Typical block plane geometry:
a. Bed angle = 20°
b. Bevel angle = 25°
c. Angle of attack = 45°

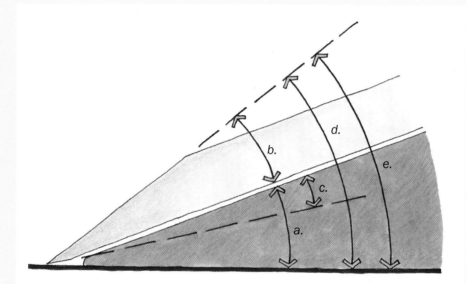

Blockplane geometry with
back bevel added:
a. Bed angle = 20°
b. Primary bevel angle = 17°
c. Back bevel = 8°
d. Included edge angle = 25°
e. Angle of attack = 37°
f. Clearance = 12°

Back bevels are useful to increase the angle of attack and reduce the risk of tear-out in difficult grain. By increasing the plane's angle of attack by adding a back bevel (adding 10° increases a standard pitch plane's angle of attack to 55° – "half pitch") you can more reliably plane grain that frequently changes direction, like quilted maple, with reduced risk of tear-out problems usually encountered. If you choose to use one it needn't be large – just ¹⁄₆₄" (0.4mm) is enough. Brian Burns has self-published *Double Bevel Sharpening*, a book about back-bevels that details the practice and provides suggested angles for bench and block planes in various woods. Back bevels solve tear-out problems by allowing a plane to have an almost

infinitely adjustable angle of attack – suited to any wood and any planing situation simply by altering the small bevel on the back of the blade. The only problems with adding a back bevel are; you increase your sharpening time by adding another bevel, and if you should want to reduce or eliminate the back bevel, you'll have to grind the main bevel until the back bevel is gone, shortening the blade by the length of the back bevel. You can always have an extra blade or two (says the blade-maker) with different back bevels for use in different planing situations. Mark them with their angle specifications to avoid confusion when you need one or the other for a specific job.

Typical block-plane geometry: a. Bed angle = 20°; b. Bevel angle = 25°; c. Angle of attack = 45°.

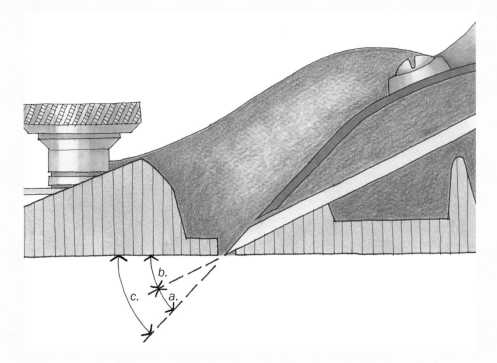

Angle a. is the bevel angle of the blade, angle b. is the bed angle of the plane = 20°, angle c. is the angle of attack, the combination of a + b.

Block plane blades are used bevel-up without a cap iron. Remember that the angle of attack with a block plane is the sum of the bed angle added to the bevel angle. A standard block plane has a bed angle of 20° so if you add that to your bevel angle of 25° you end up cutting at the same angle as a bench plane, 45°. To reduce the angle of attack, perhaps for cutting end grain, a smaller bevel angle, and hence a lower cutting angle, may be desirable. A back bevel here can increase the strength of the edge by increasing the overall bevel angle, but be careful not to add too much back bevel or you can interfere with the clearance angle of the blade. You can reduce the angle of attack to 37° with a bevel angle of 17° and, by adding an 8° back bevel, retain the strength of an included bevel angle of 25°.

Low angle block planes, with a bed angle of 12° should not have any back bevel added to their blades. The 12° bed angle is about the minimum for clearance behind the edge and any back bevel would reduce that, eliminating the necessary relief.

Getting Started

New blades come in all stages of readiness. Some will require grinding on a powered grinder to establish the initial bevel. Others will be much closer to usably sharp and may only need final honing to meet your standards. If you're lucky, some may even come ready to use. Let's imagine a blade that comes to you only rough-ground from the factory or in terrible shape from the flea market.

FLATTEN THE BACK

Using whichever tools, system or machine you prefer, start flattening the back of the blade (the Ruler Trick, at right, is a great, quick way to flatten a blade). Use the finest abrasive grit size that will do the job efficiently but don't be shy about using a coarser grit if your progress seems too slow. If you grind with too coarse an abrasive, you'll remove more metal than necessary and make more work for the finer grits. With too fine an abrasive, you risk merely polishing the high spots instead of grinding them down. Start with a middle-range grit size and if it isn't taking the metal off quickly enough, switch to a coarser grit. Some people prefer to flatten the back all the way to final polish and then do the bevel honing, starting at the coarse grits again. Others do both as they go so they don't have to "back up" to the coarser grits: your choice.

This old blade is not sharp or square. The edge has too much crown and there's a deep, ugly rust spot on the back.

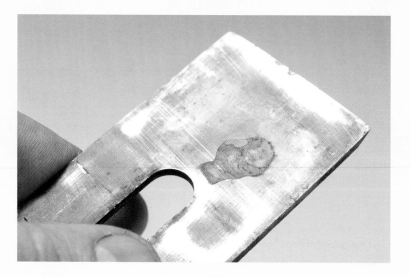

Starting with a grit that's too fine just polishes the high spots – you won't remove them efficiently.

FLATTENING WITH THE RULER TRICK

I need to stress the importance of flattening and polishing the flat back of the blade, the side opposite the bevel. Many beginners worry like crazy about honing the bevel and give short shrift to the back of the blade. Think about this for a moment: the back of the blade *is* the cutting edge. The steel that you see when you look at the back of the blade is made of the molecules that comprise the cutting edge as the bevel is worn and sharpened away. So take care to do a good job on the backs of your blades.

If the back is not flat, the cutting edge can never be straight. Any curvature, undulations or scratches in the back will show as irregularities on the edge. Sharpening a back flat requires a flat abrasive surface. Waterstones are quite soft and wear quickly (exposing fresh, sharp grit – which we like) but need to be flattened periodically or they tend to wear hollow in the center. If you use them like this, the blade you're honing will take on a rounded shape. Natural oilstones, like Arkansas stones, tend to stay flatter but still require occasional maintenance. If you use sandpaper, use it on a surface that is truly flat, like thick glass.

There is a simple trick for expediting the flattening process. The "ruler trick," made popular by David Charlesworth, is as simple as laying a stainless steel rule under the back of the blade.

By lifting the blade that little bit, you're now flattening only the very front portion of the back of the blade. You'll polish a narrow strip – maybe only ⅛" wide (3mm) along the cutting edge – instead of flattening the entire back surface. You'll be surprised how much faster this is. But, you say, aren't you putting a back bevel on the blade? Well, yes, but it's a very small angle – less than a degree – and won't effect the performance of the blade at all. However, do not do this with chisels. They need to be truly flat right to the edge.

Traditionally, flattening the back of a blade meant keeping the back of the blade flat against the stone or abrasive film.

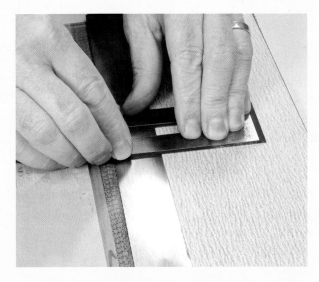

A thin metal ruler (or strip of plastic, or whatever) lifts the rear of the blade to minimize the effort required to flatten the business end.

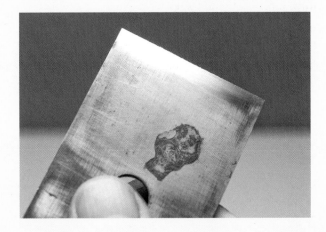

In just a few seconds, I've managed to flatten enough of the back to last for dozens of bevel honings; and, if I'm careful, I won't have to deal with that ugly rust spot for years.

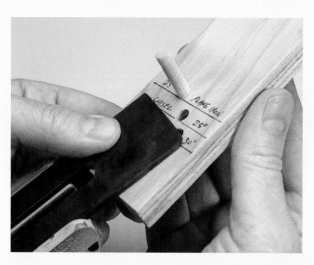

You can measure the extension of the blade from the honing guide each time or make a simple wooden jig with preset stops for various blades at various angles. Or, just put marks on your bench top to align the edge with. And, of course, an adjustable square works, too.

A honing guide with 15µ honing film adhered to a piece of glass. You can see a sheet of 80µ film on the far edge of the glass; 5µ and 1µ sheets are on the other sides. The whole sheet of glass is on a nonslip mat.

You can flatten the back as you go by flipping over both the blade and honing guide.

ESTABLISH THE BEVEL

With flea market blades the bevel is rarely straight and square and handheld truing up is difficult. A jig or honing guide to hold the blade against the grinder or abrasive surface is advised. See Chapter Seven on chisels for more about marking and grinding a cutting edge straight and square and reshaping the bevel on a bench grinder. To reshape the edge on stones or abrasive film, clamp the blade in the honing jig and make sure that it is square and projects the correct amount for the bevel angle you want to create. For repeatability, make a simple jig with stops to indicate the amount of projection from your jig for each bevel

angle you want to use, or make a note of the projection and measure it into place each time. Low-speed grinders, both vertical and horizontal, have guides, fixtures or jigs to help hold the blade against the abrasive while reshaping the edge.

Establish the bevel at the desired angle holding it straight and square while using the finest grit that will get it done in a minute or two. If it's taking longer than that, you may need to switch to a coarser grit.

If you use a honing guide, just flip it and the blade over to hone the back as you go through the succession of finer grit sizes (unless you've already finished with the back-flattening process).

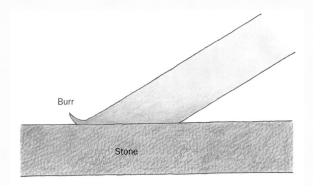

A burr forms when the two planes being honed intersect. When you have a burr, it's time to switch to a finer grit.

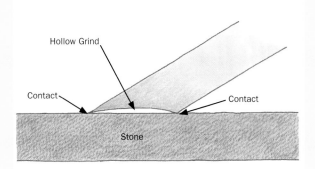

In addition to requiring less metal to be removed during honing, a hollow-ground bevel acts like a honing guide, resting securely on the stone at the proper angle.

THE BURR

When you've raised a burr, change to a finer grit. The burr is a ragged, wiry edge made of small fragments of steel that cling to the edge instead of being scraped off by the grit grains. Remember, that it will only form when the surface you're working on meets the intersecting surface at zero-radius. So, when the burr forms, you've gone as far as you need to on that surface with that abrasive. Don't take the burr off by bending it back and forth; just let the next grit abrade it away. The finer the grit the smaller the burr until, with the polishing stones, you may not be able to see it easily. Use magnification to see it or you can usually feel it with a fingernail.

Refine and polish the bevel on finer grits. Be sure to clean all traces of grit off the blade, your hands and your honing guide's wheel before switching to a finer one. You don't want any stray grains of a coarser grit to scratch up your ever finer surface or you'll have to back up to that coarser grit and start over from there.

HOLLOW GROUND

If the bevel was hollow-ground, you may be able to eliminate the honing guide with some thicker blades. The edge and the heel of the bevel will contact the stone, minimizing the area that you need to abrade away. You can feel it when the edge and heel are both in contact with the stone – it's a tactile honing guide. (See Freehand Honing on page 108.)

Handheld honing is facilitated with a hollow ground bevel. You simply register the edge and the heel of the bevel against the stone and hone two thin stripes.

FREEHAND HONING

Much of honing can be done entirely freehand and it's a skill I encourage you to develop. Use the jigs and guides to teach yourself the basic requirements – try out different grips and stances with the "training wheels" until you begin to habituate them. You'll use the same grips and stance when you go it alone. The only difficult part about honing freehand is maintaining the bevel angle on the stone. If you rock it back and forth while you slide it to and fro, you'll hone a round, convex bevel. You may want this rounded bevel but it shouldn't happen if you don't. I find it easier to slide the bevel at an angle to the axis of the stone, turning the blade almost sideways such that the bevel is going side to side (even though I'm pushing and pulling it to and fro). I also appreciate a hollow-ground bevel when freehand honing. With the edge and the heel of the bevel as reference lines, the bevel almost clicks into the correct position on the stone and does so with very tactile feedback.

It's easier to maintain the angle this way. When I push the blade straight ahead, held as if it was in a honing guide, it's too easy to rock it up and down on its bevel, constantly changing the angle a little bit and rounding the whole bevel. Skewing the blade works better for me. One advantage with freehand honing is that, as you change grits, you can change the angle of the blade on the stone. That way, when all the previous grit's scratches are replaced by the current grit's scratches you can clearly see that it's time to change grits again.

And freehand honing is quicker – you don't have to find and attach the guides, etc. On blades that require a specific angle, by all means, use the guides. For initial edge shaping and other rough work, powered grinders and honing guides can

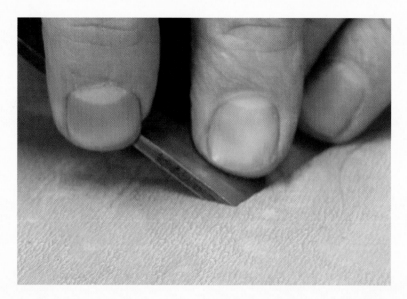

Freehand honing can be fast and easy.

By changing the angle slightly during honing, you can quickly see when one set of scratches is obscured by the next, and it's time to change grits.

save a lot of time. But for a large portion of routine sharpening, freehand is the way to go and you'll find you sharpen more often as your confidence increases. You won't tend to wait so long and risk damaging your work with a dull plane blade if touching it up is as simple as taking it out of the plane, giving it a couple of quick passes on a fine stone and going back to work. Try it. It's a skill worth learning.

CAMBERED IRONS

There are many proponents of cambered (slightly rounded) plane irons for performing any number of planing tasks from rough dimensioning to precision edge jointing. The details of the whys and wherefores are beyond the scope of this book and opinions for and against abound, but here's how to get there.

One simple method is to use a honing guide and, taking advantage of the play between the wheel and axle, just push on one corner during the stroke on the stone. If you're not looking for a lot of curve, a small amount of loading and unloading the two corners during normal honing is enough. Toshio Odate has developed a diamond honing plate that has a 0.0025" (0.06mm) dish in it. You simply use the dished plate for your initial bevel-shaping and the camber is automatic. Or use the Odate convex dressing plate to put the groove in your waterstones.

Some woodworkers use as much as $\frac{1}{16}$" (1.5mm) of crown on a blade used for flattening a rough board. For a lot of camber like that, Veritas makes a camber roller assembly for their honing guide that replaces the cylindrical wheel with one that's slightly barrel-shaped to allow a small amount of rock and roll while you push and pull the blade to and fro. And, Jet makes a camber jig for their slow-speed wet sharpener that also fits the Tormek.

Cambering a plane iron by loading the blade on one side while honing. I'm using the Veritas Honing Guide with the camber roller but most honing guides can be loaded in this same way to camber a blade.

The amount of camber is different for different planes. Use more camber when roughing and dimensioning [as much as $\frac{1}{16}$" (1.5mm)], less for smoothing and finishing [.005" (0.12mm)].

Use gentle pressure when stropping to avoid rounding the edge.

POLISHING AND STROPPING

For most stock-prep woodworking, 2000 to 4000 grit will be plenty of sharpness. But for finish smoothing, creating the perfect surface with the perfect edge, use the finest grits you can find: 6000- and 8000-grit waterstones are available, Shapton offers stones as fine as 15000 and 30000 grit. Beyond that, there are coated abrasives – Mylar sheets with grit size as small as 0.3 micron and chromium oxide powder with half-micron grit size that can be used with a strop. I usually hone a plane iron to 8000 grit.

I like stropping a blade but not everyone does. If you polish with a very fine abrasive, say an 8000-grit stone, you'll have an edge that's hard to improve. But something about a gentle swipe on a green chrome-oxide-charged leather strop makes me feel like I've done all I can. Care must be taken, however, with leather strops. They have some "give" on the surface and if you push too hard you can round the edge. If the flat back gets rounded, it will change its angle of attack for a bevel-down plane, or its clearance angle for a bevel-up one. You can also use boxboard (the inside surface of cracker-box cardboard), hardboard, or a piece of smooth, fine-grained wood as a strop to avoid the "give" of the leather and the risk of rounding the edge.

Your blade should now shave the hair on your arm with little effort. If it won't shave, or fails any of the sharpness tests mentioned in Chapter Five, you may

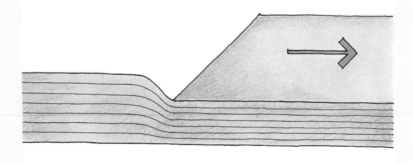

Be careful when using a leather strop that the natural compressibility of the leather doesn't round off the edge.

need to back up a bit and analyze your method. The odds are that you failed to raise a burr at some step, or missed some other vital milestone along the way. Use a magnifier to look closely at the edge and you should be able to see what's wrong. If it passes the sharpness tests, you're ready to go. A coating of oil or wax will help prevent rust.

If this blade is for your block plane, take a look inside the plane where the blade beds and make sure it's clean and rust-free anywhere the blade makes contact. Flatten the sole if necessary (see page 118) and you're done.

Resharpen often as the edge dulls. If you allow the blade to get too dull, it will take a lot more time to resharpen. You'll have to regrind the bevel and follow the subsequent finer grits back to zero-radius. When regrinding an edge that is dull, but still square and undamaged, avoid grinding all the way to the edge. If you can leave a thin strip of the dull edge in front of the new hollow grind, you'll have less work to do on the stones. A dull edge usually needs less work than a freshly ground one does, so stop short and save some time.

If the edge is simply dull but the bevel needs a new hollow, stop just short of the edge when grinding. The dull edge may require less honing than a freshly ground one.

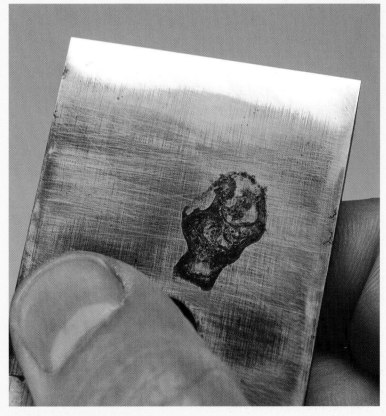

The plane blade, front and back, ready for use.

TAPPING OUT A JAPANESE PLANE IRON

Tapping out is a process of "bumping out" the flat surface along the back of a Japanese plane blade or wider [more than 7/8" (22mm)] chisel. Japanese chisels and plane blades have a hollow ground into their backs. The purpose of this hollow is to make flattening easier. The perimeter of the hollow becomes the flat back of the tool and the scooped out part no longer needs to be removed when flattening. Generally this is a great idea and makes flattening and polishing the back of these tools very quick and efficient. There are, however, some exceptions and considerations.

First the plane; a Japanese-style plane blade has a wedge shape in profile. It drops into a pair of wedge-shaped ways in the wooden body that holds it. Because these blades are individually custom-forged and therefore slightly different, each wooden body is custom-made for each individual blade by a blacksmith and a block (*Dai*) maker. This means that the dimensions of the wedge shape of the blade along the sides are critical. If the blade gets thinner along its sides, it will drop through the wooden body. Flattening the back of the blade on a stone will make the blade thinner. To avoid this we "tap out" the blade.

A Japanese chisel does not need to be fitted into anything like a plane body, so changing its dimensions is not a critical problem. However, Japanese edge tool steel is really hard, about Rc64. Even after hollowing the back it can still take a while to flatten on a stone. This is especially true on big, wide chisel blades. Tapping out is a way to speed the

Chipper Landing

Here is a blade that needs to be tapped out. The chipper landing has become very narrow. This blade has been tapped out and resharpened many, many times. It is more than 1" (25mm) shorter than it started out. The honed stripe behind the edge is the chipper landing (inset) is only 0.04" (1mm) at its narrowest point. I prefer to tap out before the chipper landing completely disappears.

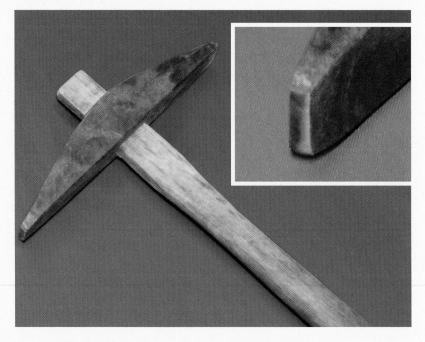

I use a modified saw-tooth setting hammer. The teeth in the original hammer have been filed off and the ends of the hammer have been hardened. Even so, years of use have rounded the sharp corner.

process. Flattening the back on only a stone can also make the pattern of the hollow less elegant. Tapping out can aid in keeping the pattern elegant.

To tap out a blade, I work on a small anvil, as shown at right. I cover the anvil with a piece of lead chimney flashing. (This is a great trick to remember as it will support the blade better by conforming to the shape of the hollow in the "down" side of the blade.) This is really the key point for tapping out. If the blade is not in good contact with the anvil, tapping out could crack the blade – a common fear associated with tapping out. Keeping your elbow close to your body and swinging with lots of little strikes will make the process much more consistent. The idea is to tap right through the blade into the anvil.

– Harrelson Stanley, (GetSharper.com)

I support the blade over an anvil. In this case I'm using a smaller anvil set in the top of my larger one.

The narrowest part of the chipper landing is a little off-center on this blade so I am working a little off-center. Don't worry about the dents in the iron above the hard steel, they will disappear after a couple of resharpenings. Keep your hammering high on the bevel. Do not strike the hardened steel at the edge.

This picture shows the newly bumped-out chipper landing. By honing off the top of this bump, the chipper landing will be widened without changing the thickness of the blade at its edges.

Cap Iron

If this blade is for your bench plane, take some time to work on the plane's *cap iron* (also called a *chip breaker* or *back iron*). It doesn't matter how crusty and rusty it is as long as it meets the back of the blade with no gap at all and that the ramp that deflects the shaving up and out of the plane is clean and smooth. You can use any of the sharpening techniques you like on the cap iron; honing it is similar to honing the blade.

Start by polishing the ramp from the sharp edge of the cap iron to the top of the ramp. If it's rounded, you may need to use a rocking motion while rubbing it on the stone. Now hang the cap iron off the edge of the stone (or whatever you're using) and straighten and polish the underside of the edge. Match the factory angle of the underside surface of the cap iron – don't change it or a gap may open up when the cap iron is tightened against the iron.

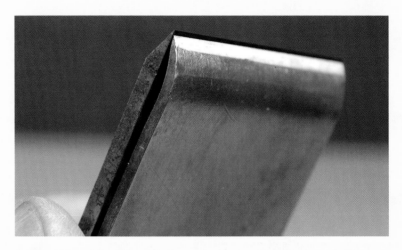

A close-up view of the cap and blade together, as they occur when mounted in the plane body.

This cap iron is corroded and rough and could benefit from a bit of elbow grease.

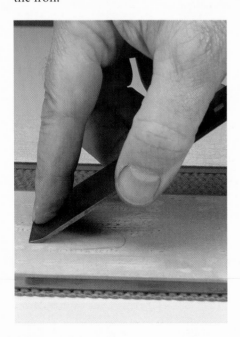

Freehand polishing of the cap iron is usually adequate but you can set it up in a honing guide if it needs to be straightened or squared up.

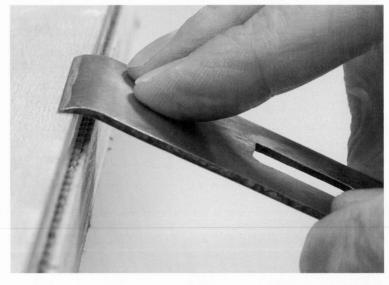

Sometimes the underside of the cap iron edge needs some straightening. Hold it off the edge of the abrasive to hone it at the proper angle.

A gap like this between the blade and cap iron (left) will usually pull closed when the screw is tightened (right).
If not, you need to bend or grind and polish it until it closes with no gap.

Polish a smooth ramp for the shaving to flow over.

Next, while the blade is out of the plane remove the frog and clean the machined areas where the frog and plane make contact. You don't want any rust or crud between them; just good metal-to-metal contact. Flatten the frog mating areas (I can't believe I just wrote that) on a coarse grit stone or paper. Use a file to clean and flatten the upper flats in the plane body. The lower flats are hard to get to so I just use a screwdriver or whatever to scrape off as much of the crud as I can. The Dremel with a small wire wheel brush can be useful here (as well as for cleaning all manner of nooks and crannies in a plane). Also, remove the hold-down screw from the frog and flatten the face of the frog so the blade will bed securely.

Disassemble the plane as needed.

Close-up of the inside of the plane body.

Filing the inside of the plane body flats.

The machined flats that the frog rests on need to be cleaned (quite badly in this case). Scrape or file as necessary to insure good metal-to-metal contact between the frog and the plane body.

Close-up of the underside of the frog.

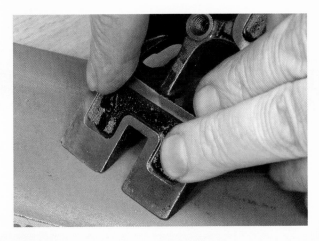

Honing the frog's flats.

Frog flats after honing.

Work around the central adjuster lever (much easier than removing it) to flatten the frog's face. (That sounds terrible, doesn't it?)

The frog flats that rest on the plane body flats need to be just as clean. Hone them flat, along with the face of the frog – the ramp the blade rests on – as needed to ensure a solid connection from the blade to the plane.

Examine the mouth of the plane. To properly hold down the shaving as it is being sheared by the blade, the front edge of the mouth should be straight across, square and sharp. That edge will wear with use, as shavings slide over it, wearing it down, like ancient stone steps. That wear is usually more so at the center, also like the steps, and usually more obvious and problematic with older planes. If it's worn noticeably, scribe a line across and file that edge to true it up.

Replace the frog and just snug in the screws for now. Assemble the blade and cap iron tightly with the cap iron about ¹⁄₃₂" (1mm) back from the cutting edge. Insert the blade assembly into the plane and clamp it to the frog with the lever cap. Adjust the blade as if for a fine cut – just enough to clear the sole. Use the frog adjusting screw to set the mouth opening. It needn't be much wider than the thickness of the shaving you intend to take, but an opening of ¹⁄₁₆" (2mm) or so for now is close enough. Remove the blade and cap iron to tighten the frog screws securely.

Plane soles need to be fairly flat to work properly. What's "fairly flat?" I don't have a specification* but it's easy to make a telltale rubbing by gluing a piece of 220-grit paper to a flat surface. Retract the blade well out of harm's way, but leave it clamped in place just in case it's causing any distortion in the sole when it's under clamping pressure. Rub the plane on the paper lightly and look at the sole. You should see clearly where the sole contacted the paper – the "high spots." If the new, shiny spots are randomly distributed, continue lapping the sole until it is mostly shiny.

Lie-Nielsen's website states that the soles of their bronze planes are lapped to a tolerance of .0015".

How flat is flat enough? How much time do you have? The pits in this neglected plane's sole will take a lot longer to lap out and have little or no effect on the plane's performance. I say, get it "close" and try it out.

It needn't be completely, perfectly flat (whatever that means). If you have large contact indicated at all four corners and in front of the mouth, that's good enough. You don't want a bump behind the mouth. If it's high there the plane will never work well, so continue lapping on the sandpaper until you're sure that bump is gone. If you're fussy, you'll want to rub the plane on the paper until the entire sole is uniformly honed. 220 grit is plenty good enough, too, but I wouldn't stop you from polishing it a bit more. Clean off all the swarf – the mixture of grit and metal that's been removed – and apply a coat of oil or wax to keep all that freshly exposed iron from rusting.

Now get ready to test it out. Use a scrap of wood, secured in a vise or clamped to a bench, to test the plane. Slowly lower the blade a fraction of a turn at a time while making passes over the wood until it just barely starts to cut. Angle the blade to one side or the other with the lateral adjuster lever until it cuts uniformly from side to side.

Ta-da!

Skew & T Blades

Skew blades can be inserted at an angle in some of the available honing guides. The Veritas skew alignment jig (see photo in Chapter Seven: Chisels) works with their honing guide to set skew and bevel angles.

T blades from shoulder planes can be hard to hold but, other than that, they get sharpened the same as any other plane iron. You may need to apply some creativity about how to set the blade squarely in the

honing guide. A short try-square can help, or you can mark the honing guide with "guide lines" to help with accurate alignment. As with full-width irons, pay attention to bevel angles and grit progressions to get the edge you want.

Some rabbet planes incorporate a nicker to shear wood fibers ahead of the cut. These are sharpened by simply honing and polishing the flat side.

Spokeshaves

METAL SPOKESHAVES

Metal spokeshaves are simply short-soled, bevel-down planes without cap irons. So what, you say? Well, in order for a spokeshave to make fine shavings, and hence, fine surfaces, most of the tuning requirements mentioned above for planes apply to your spokeshave.

Take it apart and clean it up as needed. Sharpen the blade – the procedure is the same as it is for plane irons – but before re-installing the blade in the spokeshave, take a look at the ramp where it beds. The average cast-iron spokeshave is a fairly rough affair as it comes from the factory. If the ramp is rough with casting bumps (and they usually are) and covered with a heavy coat of paint (ditto) remove the screw and use a file to dress the ramp reasonably flat and smooth. You want the blade to bear down on the ramp uniformly. Don't go to extremes; reasonably good contact along the mouth opening and a few more contacts distributed evenly around the rest of the ramp should suffice. Polish the lever-cap a bit as its as close to a shaving-diverter that you possess in a spokeshave (no cap iron) and a little attention will help prevent shavings from clogging as they bump into the too-steep, leading edge of the clamp ramp. Flatten and polish the sole, too.

The Stanley #151 spokeshave. This one was left unattended for far too long.

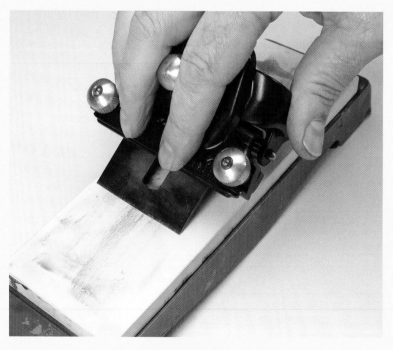

This blade proved barely good enough to bother with (and these blades aren't all that great to begin with, either). There are (ahem) better quality after-market blades available, some of which are a bit thicker, to close the gaping mouth that the factory thought was good enough.

Use a file to clean the ramp. Close is close enough.

The underside of the lever cap needs to be flattened a bit to make good contact with the blade. And the ramp-bevel on top needs to be ground to an edge so shavings will flow over it – not collect under it.

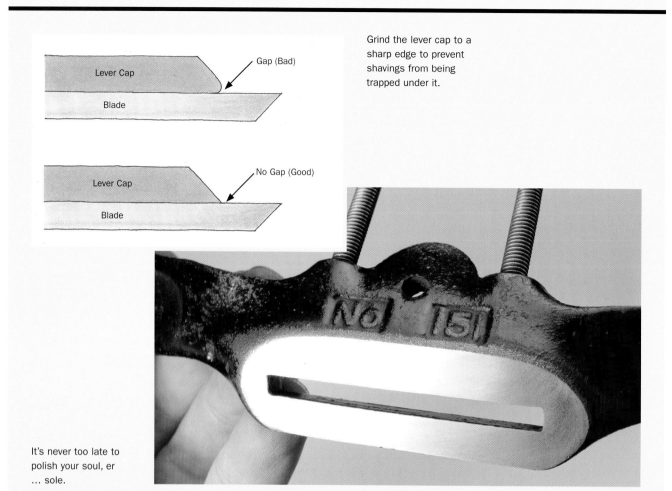

Grind the lever cap to a sharp edge to prevent shavings from being trapped under it.

It's never too late to polish your soul, er … sole.

A handy tool saved from the junk heap – just in the nick of time.

Wooden spokeshaves are very handy tools for jobs that require a short sole and a low-angle cutter. They make a great do-it-yourself tool-making project, too. But the threaded posts can make sharpening difficult. A narrow stone, or a piece of MDF with sandpaper just for this purpose, can make honing easier. Or, you can simply hang the posts over the edge and sharpen side to side. Don't forget to flatten and polish the back.

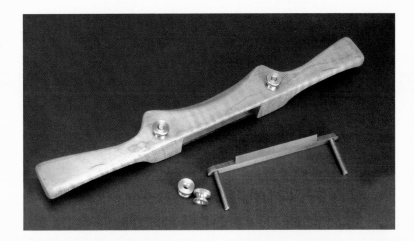

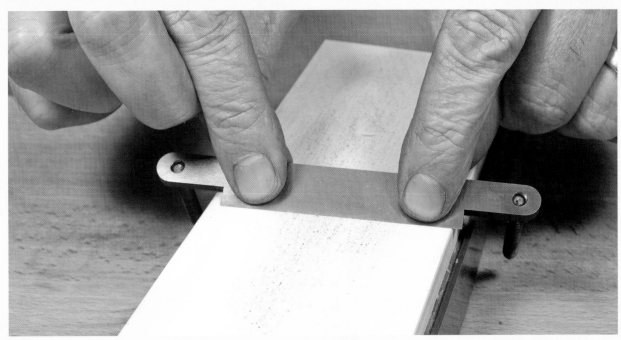

7 Chisels

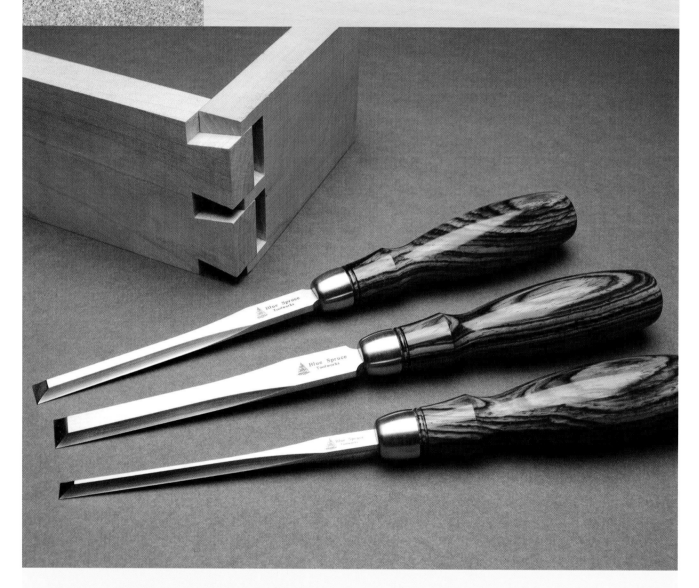

CHISELS MAKE UP A LARGE AND IMPORTANT part of the woodworker's tool kit. The apparent simplicity of a chisel — a blade on a stick — belies the numerous variations on that theme. At the very least, a well-tuned chisel will help you do the work intended with a minimum of effort. And a well-tuned chisel, performing the task for which it was designed, is a truly pleasant and confidence-building experience.

A set of Dovetail Paring chisels from Blue Spruce Toolworks (www.bluesprucetoolworks.com).

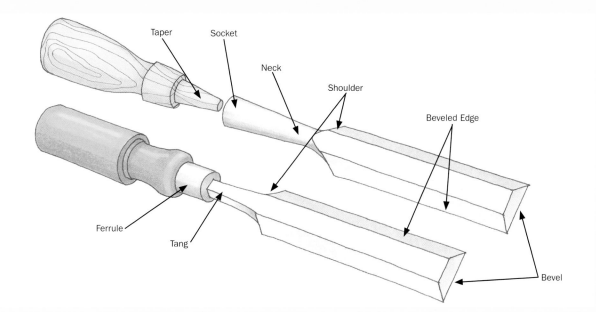

Proper honing of a chisel relies on properly flattening the back. As with plane irons, a flat, polished back is essential to a sharp edge. A chisel is frequently used by sliding it on its flat back so that the edge can clean a chip out of a corner or flatten a surface. If the chisel's back is not flat, the cutting edge will arc up and off the surface, so in order to get to and cut that last bit of chip, you'd have to lift the handle or it will just ride up and over the bumps you're trying to shear off.

A concavity on the back is not as serious a problem as a convexity. In fact, Japanese chisel-makers grind a hollow recess on the backs of their chisels to reduce the effort required to sharpen them. If the Japanese chisel-maker went to all that trouble, the least we can do is to use only hand-honing methods on our Japanese chisels. Powered grinders, certainly the high-speed variety, are too harsh for steel that is often very hard and brittle.

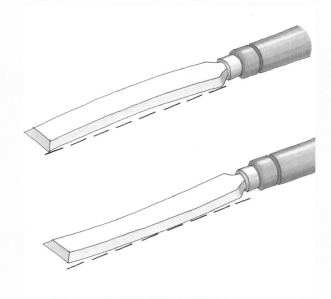

A concave or convex chisel blade are both problems that require attention in order for the chisel to work properly.

Japanese chisels are hollow ground on the back to reduce the amount of steel that needs to be removed during sharpening.

A convex back is much more difficult to remedy than a concave one. There is a tendency to rock the convexity to and fro as you slide across the stone, which means you will either polish it as it is, or actually exacerbate the convexity. You need to hold the chisel steady so that your efforts on the abrasive are consistent — unwaveringly parallel to the stone — no rocking as you work the blade back and forth. This is a good job for power tools. A slow disc grinder like the Lap-Sharp, Veritas or the side of a slow-speed Tormek-style wheel can help by allowing you to concentrate on the high-spot you're trying to grind down. A Dremel-type hand grinder can also be used, allowing you to grind down the convexity and even create a concavity on the back like a Japanese chisel. Use a marker to color the entire back surface so you can readily see what's being ground away. Hold the bump in the blade against the abrasive, grinding it down a little at a time, checking your work often with a straightedge, or by rubbing the chisel's edge on a flat stone. The marks left by the stone will clearly indicate how you're progressing.

Some new blades will come with a protective coating that you will need to remove with acetone or lacquer thinner. After that, a new chisel will normally require removal of the grinding marks left on the back by the factory. Choosing the first, coarsest grit is a matter of judgment as some factory grinding marks are deeper than others and will require more aggressive treatment. You can get a sense for what may be needed by starting with 800 grit or 1000 grit to see how things go. If you're simply polishing the tops of the grinding ridges, you may need to step down to a coarser grit to get the job done in a reasonable amount of time. Removing honing scratches usually takes less time using subsequently finer grits than it does when you do all the initial flattening on a stone that is too fine. The edge on a new

The "before" photo of a chisel in need of restoration.

After a short time on the flat grinder.

chisel will probably be reasonably square but check it anyway and correct it if it is out-of-square while you hone the bevel.

Rescuing an abused chisel requires similar evaluation. Often the backs of used, flea-market chisels were never flattened properly in the first place. You'll need to do the 800 grit test to see how much work you will have to do, then proceed from there to prepare the back. The old chisel's bevel is undoubtedly trashed after opening all those paint cans (or was it scraping gum off the sidewalk?) and may benefit from a proper grinding.

Hold the blade of the chisel flat on the stone allowing the rear part of the blade and handle to hang off the stone's edge.

FLATTEN THE BACK

Start with the finest grit that will get the job done in a reasonable amount of time. Be very careful to keep the blade flat on the abrasive surface at all times. Avoid any rocking motion that would round an edge or corner. Once the chisel is flat end-to-end you can concentrate on the cutting end of the back. Because even a slight back bevel is undesirable in a chisel, don't be tempted to use the plane iron "ruler trick" to save time. Let the rear of the chisel's back ride off the side of the stone while honing it and you'll get the front part polished and properly sharp without having to do the entire back.

Clean the blade and your hands and change the angle of the tool on the stone when you change grits (see page 70). When all the old grit's scratches have been replaced with the new grit's scratches, you're ready for the next, finer grit. Continue with finer grits until the back has the polish you want. Prep-work on

This flattened and polished back shouldn't need honing ever again unless it's damaged or allowed to rust.

the back is, for the most part, a one-time chore, and depending on how much of the back you polish, you won't have to worry about it again for a long time. So proceed through the subsequently finer grits all the way to your finest stone for a mirror-like, polished surface. I don't recommend a strop for chisel backs because they tend to slightly round off the edge.

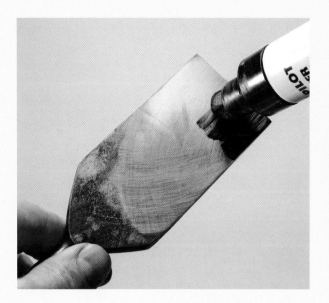

Use a felt-tip marker to color the blade for scribing.

Scribe a guide line square across the blade.

Grind to the line to remove nicks in the edge.

The edge is ground square across, ready for bevel grinding.

HONE THE BEVEL

Now is the time to decide on a bevel angle. For a paring chisel the bevel can be as low as 20° (some woodworkers like the bevel angle even lower, like 15°, but you sacrifice edge strength with a bevel that low). Standard bench and butt chisels are traditionally ground at the factory to 25°, and this is fine for most work, but the edge will last longer if you add a 5° microbevel to make a 30° cutting angle. Some chisels will perform better with a shallow-bevel/microbevel combination, like mortising chisels (more later) but often microbevels are added just to save time. With most powered sharpening systems, adding a microbevel may actually add time to the process. So, unless you believe the tool will indeed work best with a microbevel, just leave it off when using a powered sharpener.

If the edge is in dire need of help – chipped, rusty, out-of-square – the easiest thing to do is to mark a line across the width of the chisel at the extent of the damage, then blunt-grind the edge back to that line and reshape the bevel to your chosen angle.

Establish the bevel angle by setting the blade's

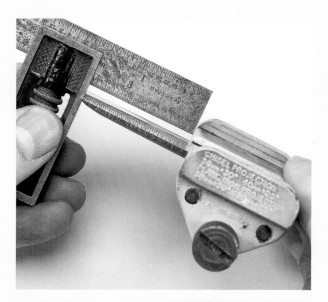

The distance from the guide determines the edge angle. This is a side-clamping, Eclipse-style honing guide.

Establishing the bevel angle on a grinder requires a combination of blade extension and the articulation of the two joints of this Veritas grinder table.

Avoid overheating while grinding the bevel.

Your finished bevel should be even and straight across the blade.

extension from the honing guide, setting the tool rest the correct distance from the grinding wheel, or adjusting the table on the belt grinder.

Low-speed grinders such as Tormek, Veritas, Work Sharp and Lap-Sharp have specific tool holders and angle gauges to help set the bevel angle correctly.

Mortising and firmer chisels take a lot of impact stress as they're chopping and prying – their edges will tend to last longer with a higher bevel angle. Grind a primary bevel of 25° and add a 10° microbevel for strength. If the edge holds up well, you

may be able to reduce the microbevel and improve the cutting action. If the edge doesn't seem to last long, a higher bevel should help. As you strike these chisels, keep in mind that the narrower ones do not need to be hit as hard as the wider ones. The concentration of force discussed in Chapter One is perfectly illustrated here. The same force of impact that you impart to a 2" chisel translates to a force eight times greater when you apply it to a quarter-inch chisel. So adjust your hammer blows accordingly – your chisels will thank you.

ABOVE The chisel on the right has an edge that is half as wide as the other. It only requires half as much force to make the same cut as the one on the left.

LEFT Hold the edge securely against the stone while honing with a guide.

Establishing the bevel is easiest with a powered helper but a simple honing guide will enable you to quickly grind the bevel to the angle you want. Unless you are sharpening a skew chisel, you will probably want to ensure that the edge is square to the sides. While it is not difficult to compensate for an out-of-square edge when using a chisel, most woodworkers prefer that the edge be square. A skew chisel was ground that way for a reason – the edge angle should be maintained. A properly set honing guide can help in either case.

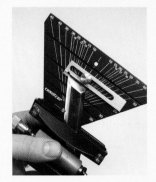

Veritas has a skew alignment jig available for their honing guide that allows you to accurately and repeatably set both skew and bevel angles.

The Sharp Skate serrated clamp pivots to a range of angles for sharpening skew blades.

Rough-out the primary bevel, then add the microbevel angle and proceed through the grits to polish the edge to match the shiny back you worked so hard on.

I've broken the process into two sections (flattening and honing), as if they would be performed separately or sequentially, as is the case when you employ a honing guide. Flatten and polish the back, then set the edge angle in the honing guide and run through all the grits again to prep the bevel. Remove the burr on the back with the finest abrasive only. If you are sharpening by hand, it's more efficient (and reduces the risk of large-grit contamination), to process both bevel and back before changing grits.

Resharpen as needed, starting with the finest grit that will restore the bevel. There's no need to use your coarse-grit stone on a blade that only needs freshening up. The polished back should only be re-polished on the finest abrasive to remove the burr that formed during resharpening of the bevel. The only times the back needs coarser work would be in the event any corrosion or damage needs to be ground away, or when you've resharpened the bevel beyond the polished area of the back.

Do not forget to take rust-prevention measures as soon as you are finished.

Here's the finished chisel, sharpened to 8000 grit.

8 Scrapers

FIRST, A NEWS FLASH: SCRAPERS AREN'T REALLY scrapers. At least, the standard hand scraper (or card scraper) with the burnished hook isn't. The sharp edge created by the hook actually acts like a "micro" plane blade making a shearing cut. The rest of the so-called scraper acts as a radical chip breaker, which is why you get those soft, lacy shavings when using one of these so-called scrapers. The shaving is very thin to start with because the blade is so very short and the shaving immediately bumps up against the forward-leaning wall which shatters the fibers into formless wisps.

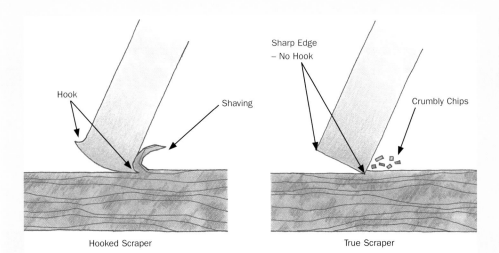

A "hooked" scraper (left) takes a thin, fluffy shaving. A true scraper (right) has no hook and makes fine crumbly chips that are almost like dust.

Veritas™ Variable Burnisher, (far), Hock burnisher rod and Veritas™ Tri-Burnisher, (near).

A true scraper has a negative rake angle to compress fibers and scrape them off the surface of the wood (review Chapter Four). Because of the rebound from the compression of the fibers, true scrapers tend to leave a dull, matte surface and make a formless mass of soft, irregular shavings rather than the satiny surfaces and papery shavings you get with a shearing, plane-type cut. But true scraping can be employed to flatten and smooth almost any surface no matter how difficult or variable the grain. Because the grain direction is unimportant, true scrapers are used for flattening the inlayed patterns in marquetry. "Hooked" scrapers will handle difficult grain due to the very thin shaving they take, the high angle of attack and the severity of the chip-breaking action inherent in their design. Though for some woods, even that small hook may be too aggressive and may cause some tear-out.

For most work, the standard preparation of a scraper goes like this: the edge that will host the cutting edges (the hooks) needs to be *jointed* – filed or stoned square. The flat surfaces on either side of that edge should be dressed flat as well. Then a hooked edge is created with a burnisher – a hardened steel rod (usually round but traditionally burnishers have been oval, triangular with rounded corners, or teardrop shaped. These days, round burnisher rods are the most common.) You can use a number of substitutes, such as automotive valve stems or wrist pins, drill blanks or even a screwdriver shaft, but be sure whatever you use is smooth, polished and harder than the scraper or it may grab and gall the burnisher, damaging both surfaces. If your scraper leaves any mark at all on your burnisher, get a harder burnisher.

Hold the file square against the edge of the scraper. Use your fingers, a block of wood with a slot cut in it or a holder such as the Veritas™ Jointer/Edger.

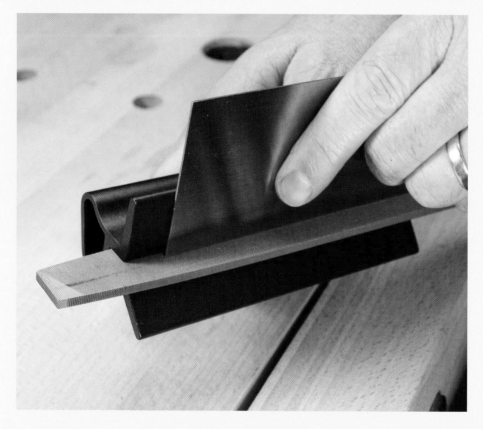

To prepare a scraper with what you already have in your sharpening kit, start with a fine, mill bastard file to joint the edge while holding the scraper in a vise. A smooth, flat, square edge is the goal. The cutting edge is, or will be, formed from the corner that you just created, so the quality of that corner is an issue. For rough surfacing or paint removal, the as-filed edge will suffice, with or even without a hook. For finer surfacing, more honing will allow you to create a sharper cutting edge that will also last longer. A rect-angular hand scraper can be flipped over to prepare the opposite edge, too, giving you four (two-plus-two) cutting edges between sharpenings.

Honing the square edges can be done by simply clamping a 1000-grit stone onto your bench and, using a thin piece of wood to space the blade off the bench surface, sliding the scraper horizontally against the side of the stone. Or, with diamond stones or glass stones with nonabrasive edges, use a block on top of the stone surface to act as a fence and hone

Use a hard stone, like an oil or ceramic stone, or a diamond plate like this one with a square "fence" to polish a scraper edge. If using a soft waterstone, use the edge of the stone to avoid cutting grooves in the surface with the blade on edge.

the scraper in a vertical position along the fence. Finish the edge to 2000 grit or 4000 grit. The cutting quality and longevity of the final edge will be largely determined by the degree of honing and polishing done at this point. Again, for rough work, extra honing may be unnecessary, whereas the finest finishing work will benefit from the extra time spent honing your scraper.

Dress the flats on either side of the edge you just jointed with your 1000- or 1200-grit stone to remove any burrs and to flatten and clean them up as well (use the ruler trick in Chapter Six: Plane Irons to speed up this step). You now have a sharp, honed, square edge on your scraper. When flattening marquetry, for example, this may be all you need. For more aggressive surface finishing, though, you'll want to roll a hook with a burnisher.

The aggressiveness of the scraper's edges can be adjusted by how large and at which angle the hook is. With the blade in a vise, use your burnisher to deform – *roll* – a thin strip of metal off the edge – a hook. (The common terminology is "roll" a "hook" or a "burr" but there is really no rolling going on at all.)

Dressing the flats on either side of the edge removes any burr and ensures a square edge ready for burnishing.

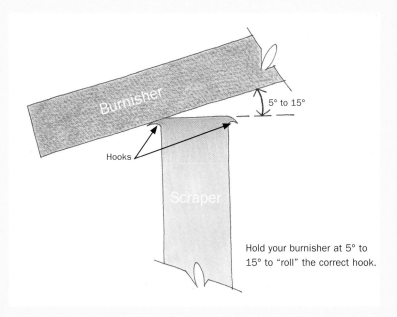

Hold your burnisher at 5° to 15° to "roll" the correct hook.

Apply a stingy amount of oil to the burnisher, hold it at 90°, tilt it slightly, about 5° or so, press down as though you're taking a shaving with a spokeshave – not bearing down hard but applying firm pressure – and slide the burnisher in a uniform pass along the whole edge. Now, tilt a little more – about 10° for now – and take another pass or two or three. You don't need to push hard, start with a light touch; it's easier to take two or three passes than it is to undo a too-big hook. Unfortunately, it's not difficult to make the burr too big. Feel for a burr; maybe even test it on a piece of hardwood to see if it cuts shavings. The angle of the hook is a matter of taste, something between 5° and 15° should work, the larger angle will tend to cut a bit more aggressively and you'll need to hold it with more forward tilt to get the cut started.

Turning a hook with a simple burnishing rod.

If you should form a hook that's too big to be functional, you may be able to correct it. Some vintage burnishers have a sharp point at the end. Gently push the sharp edge under the hook and run it along the length of the scraper. This bends the hook, or burr, up – usually enough to make it usable.

I should mention here that you are creating sharp edges on a piece of steel that's sticking up out of a vise. While it's not the most dangerous operation in the shop, a slip while burnishing, or a just a careless swing of an arm, can cause some part of you to come in contact with a sharp edge. *Be careful.* And don't walk away, leaving the exposed blade in the vise for someone else to bump into.

Protecting your edges keeps them sharp and avoids accidents.

Roll another hook on the other side the same way so you'll have two at the ready. Flip the blade over and form two more hooks on that edge and you'll have four sharp edges ready to use. Be careful when using them, however, as they're sharp and even though they don't project very far, those extra edges can cut your fingers and thumbs while you're using them. A bit of tape can help, either on the edges or on your thumbs.

And there are formal scraper holders available from Veritas and Woodcraft.

Use proper rust-prevention protocol when you're done, and protect edges from the ravages of toolboxes and drawers. The stationery store sells plastic channels for holding pages of a term paper that can be cut to make great edge protectors.

SCRAPER SHARPENING SYSTEMS

Of course, where there is a perceived need, some entrepreneur will invent a gadget:

Woodsmith Cabinet Scraper System

The Woodsmith scraper sharpening system revolves around their extruded aluminum fixture. The fixture has two slots for holding a file at two angles – 90° for hand scrapers and 45° for scraper plane blades – as well as a hole for holding a burnishing rod. For each file position and the rod, the fixture has fins that allow the scraper to encounter the file or rod at the proper angle.

The Woodsmith fixture can be secured to your work surface via the extruded clamping ledge or by screwing it to a piece of 2x4 which can then be clamped in a vise.

Veritas™ Tri-Burnisher, Variable Burnisher (Mk. II) and Jointer/Edger

Veritas also offers help for scraper preparation. Their Triburnisher rod has an egg-shaped cross section designed to replace round, oval and triangular burnishers. It is especially suited to burnish the inside radiuses of curved scrapers. For straight scrapers they offer an extruded aluminum jointer that holds a file and has two fences: 90° for hand scrapers (as well as saw teeth and ski edges) and 45° for scraper-plane blade bevels.

The Veritas Variable Burnisher is a handle with a slot that holds an adjustable-angle carbide rod. You set the desired hook angle with a dial on the side of the device and slide the scraper through the slot to roll the burr to that angle. While hand burnishing is an easy skill to learn, this variable burnisher lets you roll the same hook every time and is a very popular convenience.

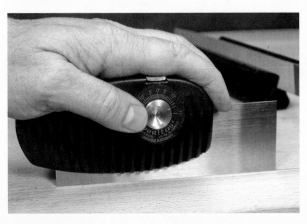

Curved scrapers are prepared the same as straight ones but with the added difficulty of having to work with curves and the need to get creative about filing and honing the concave edges. Use carvers' slipstones, sandpaper on dowels, sanding drums, Dremel, whatever. Just keep the edge square and polished and use the burnisher at the desired angle. You can do it.

You may be able to freshen up a scraper's edge when it starts to dull by simply re-rolling the burr to extend the cutting edge. If the edge wasn't too dull, you may be able to avoid complete resharpening once or twice. Eventually you will need to start over with the file or stones to remove the burr(s), square-up the edges and roll a new, sharp hook(s).

Scraper Planes

Scraper planes are, like all planes, blade-holders. And,
like all planes, they allow the blade to travel with relative independence along the surface contours of the
board. It may be desirable that a hand scraper can
follow surface contours, but if your goal is to flatten
those contours, a scraper blade held in a plane body
will scrape only the high spots to flatten the board.
Scraper plane blades are prepared in essentially the
same way as hand scrapers, but they usually have a
45° bevel ground on them, so you're only dealing with
one cutting edge per blade. You could conceivably
sharpen the other end of the blade but then you'd
have a sharp edge sticking out of the top of your
scraper plane and that, without proper precautions,
would pose a real danger.

Prepare the blade by honing the 45° bevel just as
you would a bench plane blade: flatten and polish the
back, hone the bevel sharp. With the blade in a vise,
burnish the edge at 15° to produce the burr.

Scraper plane blades are usually ground to a 45° bevel and
burnished at about 15°.

9 Handsaws

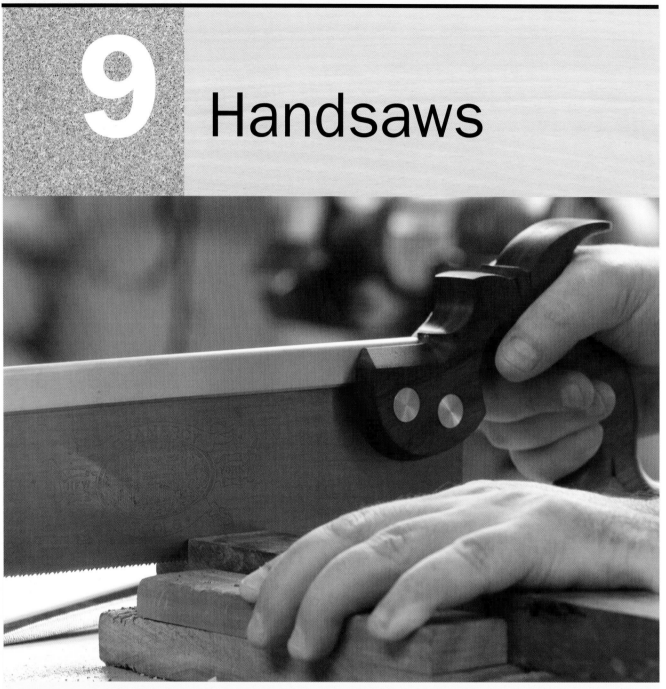

COURTESY WWW.TOOLSFORWORKINGWOOD.COM / GRAMERCY TOOLS.

A SAW IS A LONG ROW OF SMALL CHISELS – sort of. It helps if I keep that image in mind when I think about sharpening one. But the row-of-chisels analogy is only so good; my imagining must also include the *set* of the teeth. As the row of chisels cuts through the wood, the rest of the saw, the flat blade that the teeth are part of, follows along through the cut. The path through the wood, the gap or slit, created by the teeth is the *kerf*, and if the kerf is the same width as the saw blade, the saw will rub, drag and bind during cutting, making the cut difficult if not impossible to finish. To solve this problem, the teeth of a saw are set by bending them slightly outward, one tooth bends one way, the next tooth the other way and so on along the edge of the saw, so that they cut a wider kerf and allow the rest of the blade to travel unimpeded. Bending the teeth is possible because saws are usually hardened to a midrange hardness – hard enough to hold an edge for sawing but still soft enough to set and to sharpen with a file.

Unfortunately, my "row of chisels" image does not take into account the fact that most saw teeth are sharpened to a negative rake angle and actually cut more like scrapers than chisels. My powers to visualize reach only so far.

A saw tooth's singular purpose is to remove wood. While a chisel or a plane iron may be called on to do the same thing, we often demand that they leave behind a fine, smooth surface at the same time. To ensure that fine surface, we hone and polish the edges on plane irons, chisels, carving tools, anything that we use to create a smooth surface. Though all the wood-cutting edge geometry applies, saw teeth are sharpened to achieve a different goal: they must simply remove material efficiently. A smooth, finely honed, polished cutting edge is not called for; therefore, we sharpen saws with a file – an efficient tool to do an efficient job of making an efficient tooth.

Some contemporary saws have induction hardened teeth that can't be sharpened or reset; they're too hard for filing or bending. You can tell induction hardened teeth by the rainbow discoloration at the toothline. These saws will tend to stay sharp for a long time but, when one is finally dull, you will have to replace it. Being able to file a saw yourself isn't only about keeping it sharp. You can also modify the shape of the teeth for different cutting situations. A saw's edge geometry can be adjusted for optimum performance in, say, green softwoods, which require more set – more bend – compared to dry hardwoods.

There are two fundamentally different sawing tasks: *ripping* and *crosscutting*. Ripping is cutting more or less in the same direction as the grain runs in the wood (with-grain) while crosscutting, as the name implies, is cutting across the grain (crossgrain, see Chapter Four: How Wood is Cut). A ripsaw is usually used to narrow a board while a crosscut saw usually shortens one. Each cutting action calls for a different cutting-edge geometry. A crosscut saw is used for almost any angle of crosscutting, whereas ripsawing is most commonly used to cut close to parallel with the grain.

Ripping is done with teeth that resemble square-edged chisels held at a near-vertical scraping angle. Each tooth makes a small, curly shaving much like a small version of the shaving made during with-grain planing. Ripsaw teeth are usually filed with a rake

angle between an aggressive 0° and a more laid-back 15°. The larger rake angle makes it easier to start a cut; the more vertical teeth will cut faster. Pete Taran (www.vintagesaws.com) suggests a 4° rake as a good compromise for ripsaws.

Crosscutting wood fibers requires some special cutting action. The end-grain fibers that line the kerf must be severed then rolled up and out of the path of the blade. So, to facilitate crosscut sawing we add an angle to the tooth of the saw in order for it to achieve the fiber-severing goal, allowing a clean cut that leaves a relatively smooth surface along the sides of the kerf. This angle on crosscut teeth is called *fleam*, which is also the old-fashioned term for the lancet used to open a vein for bloodletting. Fleam is an angle on the face of the tooth (and generally on the back as well) much like a skew-chisel, compared to a rip tooth's similarity to a square-edged chisel. The sharp point of the skew cuts deeper than the rest of the tooth in order to sever the wood fibers along the sides of the cut, while the rest of the tooth cleans out the kerf.

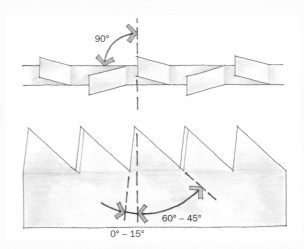

Tooth geometry of a typical ripsaw.

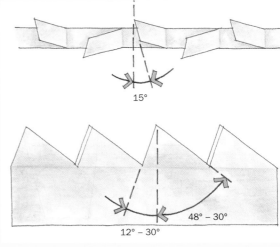

Tooth geometry of a typical crosscut saw.

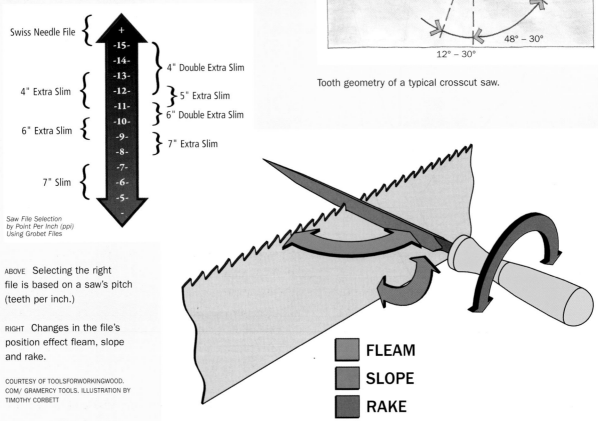

Saw File Selection by Point Per Inch (ppi) Using Grobet Files

ABOVE Selecting the right file is based on a saw's pitch (teeth per inch.)

RIGHT Changes in the file's position effect fleam, slope and rake.

FLEAM
SLOPE
RAKE

★ ELEMENTS OF SAW TOOTH DESIGN ★

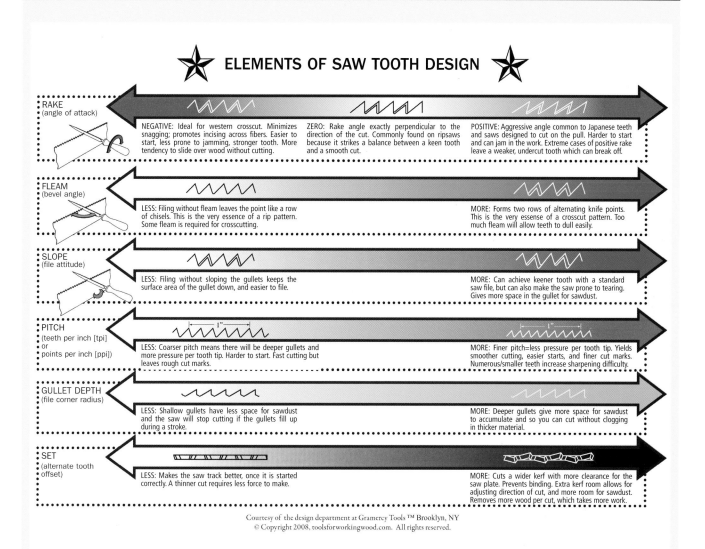

RAKE
(angle of attack)

NEGATIVE: Ideal for western crosscut. Minimizes snagging; promotes incising across fibers. Easier to start, less prone to jamming, stronger tooth. More tendency to slide over wood without cutting.

ZERO: Rake angle exactly perpendicular to the direction of the cut. Commonly found on ripsaws because it strikes a balance between a keen tooth and a smooth cut.

POSITIVE: Aggressive angle common to Japanese teeth and saws designed to cut on the pull. Harder to start and can jam in the work. Extreme cases of positive rake leave a weaker, undercut tooth which can break off.

FLEAM
(bevel angle)

LESS: Filing without fleam leaves the point like a row of chisels. This is the very essence of a rip pattern. Some fleam is required for crosscutting.

MORE: Forms two rows of alternating knife points. This is the very essense of a crosscut pattern. Too much fleam will allow teeth to dull easily.

SLOPE
(file attitude)

LESS: Filing without sloping the gullets keeps the surface area of the gullet down, and easier to file.

MORE: Can achieve keener tooth with a standard saw file, but can also make the saw prone to tearing. Gives more space in the gullet for sawdust.

PITCH
(teeth per inch [tpi]
or
points per inch [ppi])

LESS: Coarser pitch means there will be deeper gullets and more pressure per tooth tip. Harder to start. Fast cutting but leaves rough cut marks.

MORE: Finer pitch=less pressure per tooth tip. Yields smoother cutting, easier starts, and finer cut marks. Numerous/smaller teeth increase sharpening difficulty.

GULLET DEPTH
(file corner radius)

LESS: Shallow gullets have less space for sawdust and the saw will stop cutting if the gullets fill up during a stroke.

MORE: Deeper gullets give more space for sawdust to accumulate and so you can cut without clogging in thicker material.

SET
(alternate tooth
offset)

LESS: Makes the saw track better, once it is started correctly. A thinner cut requires less force to make.

MORE: Cuts a wider kerf with more clearance for the saw plate. Prevents binding. Extra kerf room allows for adjusting direction of cut, and more room for sawdust. Removes more wood per cut, which takes more work.

Courtesy of the design department at Gramercy Tools ™ Brooklyn, NY
© Copyright 2008, toolsforworkingwood.com. All rights reserved.

Ripsaw teeth are filed straight across, the file held at 90° to the saw blade. Crosscut teeth are filed at an angle from 10° to 45° with 15° being popular for a general-purpose crosscut saw. Crosscut teeth have a less aggressive, negative rake angle of 12° for a fast, aggressive cut, to 30°, which is more typical and gives a smoother though slower cut. Another aspect of saw tooth geometry is *slope*, which refers to the angle of the file from horizontal.

Though it may seem a daunting task (all those teeth!) you can sharpen your handsaw yourself. Most power-saw blades are either carbide, which is sent to a specialized shop for sharpening, or disposable and simply replaced with new blades when dull. Keep in mind, though, that a good handsaw is another of the many hand tools that will last for generations if cared for and kept sharp. There's nothing difficult about fil-ing a saw; like everything else it's a skill to learn and, with a small amount of practice, you can make your saw work better than it did new – a finely tuned tool that you'll find myriad uses for.

These days, most of your sawing tasks are likely done with one of the power saws that we all seem to have, but there will always be a place for handsaws and hand sawing in any fine-woodworker's tool kit, and skill set. As your saw sharpening skills improve, you'll find yourself sharpening your saw more often because you are using it more often, and vice versa. A handsaw is frequently your best tool for many sawing tasks. When you keep your handsaw in good fettle, you're likely to find yourself turning your back on the noise, dust and danger of power saws in favor of your uncle's classic, well-tuned Disston (et al), or one of the beautiful new generation of saws being produced today.

ABOVE It only requires a few specialized tools and some practice to sharpen a saw.

LEFT A little solvent or kerosene and 320-grit paper cleaned this old Disston crosscut saw that my uncle Vern gave me.

FLEA-MARKET SAWS

If you find an older saw in good shape at a second-hand store or flea market, consider that it may easily be over 50 years old and still perfectly useable. In fact, the older saws were often made with greater care and the handles were comfortable works of art because they were made when handsaws were woodworkers' primary tools for sawing wood. The blade needn't be shiny or even rust-free to be worthy of consideration. Most surface rust can be cleaned off; discoloration

is typical and no problem. Even a missing tooth or two is not sufficient to disqualify a saw. Dull? Not a big deal because you can joint the teeth to the same height, file them to the same sharp shape, and then set them to cut the desired kerf.

When you get your new/used saw home, remove the handle and clean the saw to remove all surface roughness. The closer to smooth and shiny it is, the better it will slide through the cut when sawing.

Mike Wenzloff files a saw with a "make-do" saw vice. PHOTO BY LOUIS BOIS

TOOLS
SAW VISE

To sharpen a saw, you need a way to hold it securely while you're filing it. "Official" saw vises are available at secondhand sources but it's very easy to make a superior one from a scrap or two of plywood. And, you can make a saw vise that's closer to the length of your saw than commercial ones, which will save you time repositioning the saw as you're working on it. Be sure to have good lighting available. One or two easily adjusted, swing-arm lamps are perfect for the task.

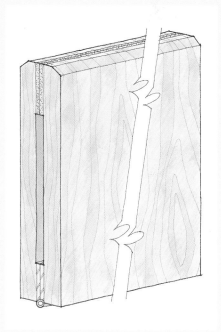

A simple saw vice can be made from a couple of solid, or plywood boards 8" to 10" and up to the length of the saw. Hinges keep it aligned; leather or rubber jaw liners help with "grip" and dampen some of the noise generated by filing.

TAGE FRID ON HAND SAWS

"The first time I sharpen a crosscut saw I change it to a ripsaw by changing the teeth from a point to a chisel edge. This makes ripping faster and easier because there are more teeth per inch than would normally be available on a ripsaw, and I find the saw works better even for crosscutting. I usually demonstrate this to my new students because the difference in cutting speed is dramatic."

— *Tage Frid Teaches Woodworking*, Tage Frid, Taunton Press, 1979.

SAW SET

Saw sets are readily available and affordable, both new and used. The basic "pistol-grip" style works well. As you squeeze the handle, a small steel plunger pushes against an adjustable, beveled anvil. Some saw sets have a rotating disc with a ramp that's beveled such that as you turn the adjuster, a different part of the ramp is presented to act as the anvil, modifying the amount of set that the tool will perform with each squeeze. Others have a sliding beveled anvil that is adjusted up and down to dial in the amount of set. The teeth are set in the same direction that they were set previously. Setting a tooth the wrong way – bending it all the way to the other side – can weaken it or even break it off. Take care to match the set direction. The saw set is positioned over the saw blade, a suitable tooth is located, the handle squeezed and the plunger pushes the tooth against the anvil, bending it the right amount (more later).

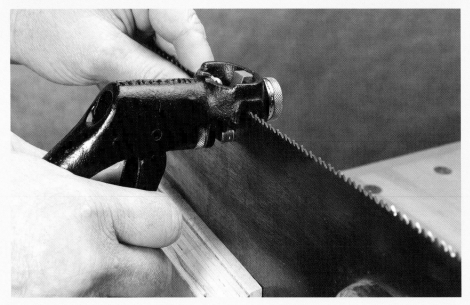

ABOVE A typical saw set. I've colored the plunger red for visibility in this photo.

LEFT It's easy to set teeth too much. The dial on the saw set should be used as a rough guide, so use caution and calipers to check the set.

FILES

You'll need an 8" or 10" smooth-cut flat file for jointing and a small triangular file for tooth shaping and filing. There is plenty of advice available about triangular file sizes, but Mike Wenzloff (www.wenzloffandsons.com) says to use the smallest file that will fully file the back of the next tooth. A smaller file has a sharper corner and will cut the gullet – the concavity between teeth – deeper for better chip clearance. He also tells me that he can sharpen over 20 saws with a file before the file wears out.

Always use a file handle. The control required, and the comfort you deserve, make this mandatory. Also, those small triangular files have tangs that will hurt you if left unhandled. You can make a handle easily enough but they're inexpensive to buy and reusable. Filing is usually a two-handed job so some sort of "handle" on the other end of the file is a good idea.

This outboard handle can be a simple scrap of wood with a hole drilled all the way through to receive the file. The hole should be small enough that the file can be lightly driven in. This additional handle will act as a guide to keep the file rotated so it can file the proper rake angle in the teeth. To make it easier to reuse this rake angle guide, you may want to mark the rake angle on both sides and to identify which side the handle of the saw is on so you can line everything up next time you use it.

Speaking of guides, a fleam or bevel-angle guide is handy for filing crosscut saws. You can lay a bevel gauge set for the correct angle on the bench behind the saw vise or cut a slot in a scrap of wood (both sides) that you slip over the teeth near where you are filing. Either will serve as a visual aid and help keep your file at the proper angle.

The simple guide on the end of the file offers a visual reference to keep the file cutting the proper rake angle on each tooth. The fleam guide, the parallelogram with a slot, pictured here on the bench, gives a similar reference when filing crosscut teeth that need an angled bevel. You simply hold your file parallel to the fleam guide as it sits over the saw blade.

Setting (before jointing)

Setting saw teeth before jointing assures that the tops of the teeth will all cut in the same plane. If you set after filing, your flat-topped, jointed teeth will be bent slightly outwards. And, those flat tops will be bent out of plane with each other. Because professional saw sharpeners debate whether to set before or after sharpening, it seems to me to be a matter of personal preference. As your experience with saw sharpening grows, the difference(s) should become more obvious and you'll probably end up in one camp or the other.

To set the teeth, you can clamp the blade in the saw vise such that the teeth are enough above the jaws to allow comfortable access with the saw set. As sawmaker Kevin Drake says: "I find it more comfortable to just hold the saw in my left hand and set the teeth with my right. My hands sort of wiggle down the

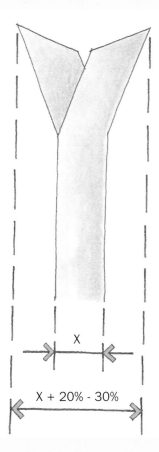

The set (exaggerated here) should increase the overall thickness of the blade by 20% for dry hardwoods to 30% for soft- or green woods.

saw as this happens." Sawmaker Mike Wenzloff adds: "Holding a saw in one's lap works with smaller backsaws. Not so well on 28", 4tpi rips."

Begin setting with the teeth closest to the handle. Because those teeth get far less use you can use them to fine-tune your settings. Adjust your saw set according to the manufacturer's instructions. Often, the anvil adjustment is based on a scale of teeth per inch, but when it comes to any one saw, this may not be accurate. And some saw-set scales are just arbitrary reference numbers. Start with a setting that corresponds to more teeth per inch than your saw actually has. That should make for a smaller amount of set; it's a good place to start as the saw set's settings aren't the code, they're more what you'd call guidelines than actual rules. Select a tooth that's set away from you and position the saw set over it with the plunger pointing at the tip of the tooth. Squeeze the handle to set the tooth. Move the saw set over, skip a tooth, and set the next one that's going away from you. Do a couple more, applying pressure evenly with each tooth, turn the saw around and set the teeth you jumped over in that same section so that you have an inch or so of set teeth. Now measure. Compare the width of the blade stock to the overall width of the teeth you just set. The set of the teeth should increase the thickness of the blade by about 20% for dry hardwoods; up to 30% for soft- and green woods. Saw blade thickness + 20–30 % = the width of the teeth after setting.

Example: A saw blade with a thickness of 0.035" (0.9mm) should be set to a width of 0.042" (1.1mm) for hardwoods and 0.045" (1.2mm) for softwoods. Notice how little set there really is: the total thickness is increased by only 0.007" (0.18mm) to 0.010" (0.25mm) so any one tooth is set just 0.0035" (0.09mm) to 0.005" (0.13mm) – that's only three and a half to five thousandths of an inch. That's not very much, and because it is easier to add more set than it is to remove, use care not to overdo it. After measuring and subtracting, adjust your setting procedure to accommodate the new data and continue to set the saw.

Jointing

Careful sharpening can help avoid the need for jointing the teeth but when the teeth are of an uneven height, the first step in saw sharpening is jointing them even. It is extremely easy to joint the teeth with nothing more than a flat file, but there are scads of saw jointer file holders on the market. Use an 8" or 10" smooth-cut flat file and just run the file lightly along the entire length in one pass.

With your lamp adjusted properly you should be able to see a small, shiny flat on the top of each tooth. Different tooth heights will make different sizes of flats. If there are any teeth without a flat, take another jointing pass. If there are any teeth missing or, much shorter than the others, don't try to joint all the others to match unless there are many missing in a row (in which case you will have to joint all the way down to them and reshape all the teeth to match). Just leave them for now and subsequent sharpenings will eventually catch up to them as the other teeth are jointed and shaped over time.

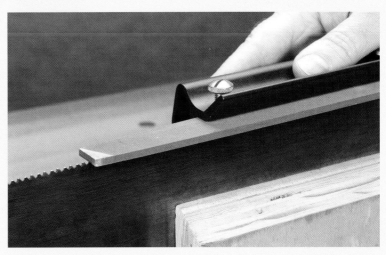

These file holders work well for saws and scrapers. One or two light passes will usually suffice.

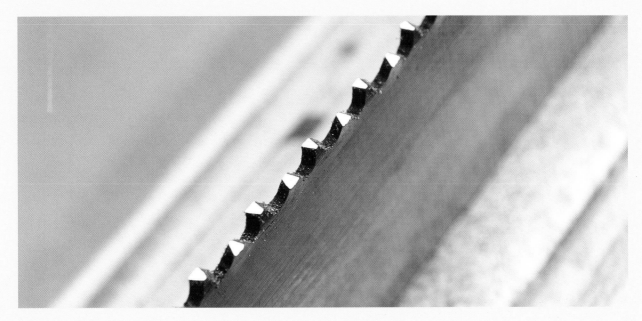

The shiny flats produced by jointing. They're different sizes because the teeth were different heights.

Shaping

Skip this step if the teeth on your saw are uniform, properly shaped already and simply in need of sharpening. However, if the teeth are in need of re-shaping, get the right file, the prepared alignment guide – that scrap of wood with the hole in it – and clamp the saw tightly in the vise, with the teeth just clear of the vise jaws. Start at the handle end and work toward the toe of the blade. Study the flats on the tops of the teeth that were made when you jointed the saw. The goal is to reshape each tooth, with the proper rake angle, such that the flat disappears – but no more than that. Assuming you are working from right to left, at each gullet you are filing the face of the right tooth and the back of the left. You need to reduce the flat on the left tooth by half, and, while doing so you will finish shaping the face of the right tooth (whose flat was already reduced by half during filing in the previous gullet). If one tooth's flat is larger than average, press harder against it when filing – favor it, or crowd it, slightly – so that all the teeth are filed to the same shape. When you finish here, joint lightly to check your work. If the teeth are still not uniform, do the shape-filing again.

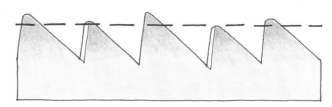

Uneven teeth need to be filed – jointed – to the height of the lowest tooth.

Jointed teeth will have flat tops of varying sizes.

Newly shaped teeth are uniform in height and spacing, ready for filing.

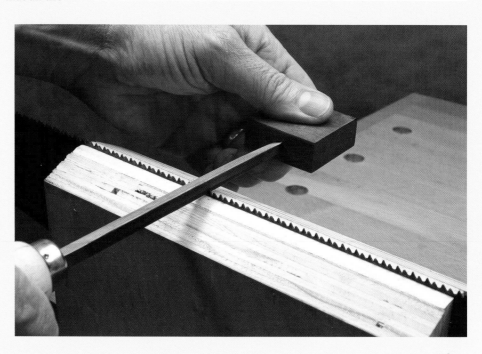

Hold the file so that it is horizontal (0° slope) front to back and the rake angle guide horizontal side to side.

Filing

Check your file to be sure it's still sharp. Filing is the step that actually sharpens each tooth and deserves a sharp file. Assuming the handle of the saw is on the right, and you are working toward the left, find a tooth that is set away from you. Place the file in the gullet to the left of that tooth. You want to file the face of the tooth that's set away from you (you'll be filing the back of the tooth to the left, the one that's facing toward you). It is the faces of the saw teeth that are doing the cutting of the wood. Filing them in the same direction that they are set allows the file to chatter less and do a neater job on this more critical surface. The surface of the back of a tooth isn't as vital to the saw's performance as the surface of the face, so you want the face to receive the best treatment from the file.

Filing requires that you maintain three angles: *rake*, *fleam*, and *slope*. The rake angle guide is the scrap of wood with the file stuck in it. The fleam guide is another scrap with the angle-slot sawed in it that rests over the blade (or an angle guide on the bench behind the vise). With ripsaws, you probably don't need a fleam guide because the fleam is 90° and fairly easy to maintain by dead reckoning. The slope angle is the angle of the file relative to the floor. It hasn't been mentioned yet because it should simply be square to the blade, parallel to the floor. Some saw filers adjust the slope angle in relationship to the fleam angle, but for most common fleam angles it makes little difference in the performance of the saw.

If it seems that all these angles pose something of a juggling act, you're right. But it only takes a few teeth to get into the rhythm and keep all the balls in the air. Check your setup for all the angles and file a tooth. Don't be surprised by the noise it makes; that chattering and screeching comes from the back of the tooth that's set toward you. The closer the teeth are to the vise jaws the quieter it will be – to a point. Ear plugs are a good idea. Filing should only require light file strokes because the shape of each tooth was created during the shaping step. The goal here is to remove whichever flat spot may remain, creating a sharp, zero-radius tooth. Skip a tooth – remember, you're filing every other tooth so that you're filing in the direction of the set – align your file in the gullet, check your coordinates and file another tooth. Slide the fleam guide as needed so that it's a useful reference. Reposition the saw in the vise as needed. When you reach the end of the saw, turn it around and start again from the handle end going left to right, then flip the fleam guide over so it's angled the correct way. Remember too, to reverse the rake guide in order to file the proper angle on the rest of the teeth.

Advance the fleam angle guide as you progress down the blade, filing every other tooth (the ones that are facing away from you). Turn the saw around and repeat for the rest of the teeth.

Setting (after filing)

Some sawyers think it best to set the teeth after all the filing is done. Pete Taran says: *The conventional wisdom is to set a saw's teeth before it is sharpened. I disagree with this approach for several reasons. If a saw is set before it is sharpened, then part of the set is removed when the teeth are filed. It is very difficult to try to figure out how much the set is decreased in filing as it is dependent on many factors, such as how sharp the file is, how hard you bear on the tooth with the file, and how uniform the saw teeth are filed. I prefer to set the saw after it has been sharpened. By setting the saw's teeth after it has been filed, a very uniform set can be achieved, which not only makes the saw cut well, but also makes a very nice finish on the piece being cut. It only takes one or two teeth to be over-set to make the edge of a cut piece of wood ragged and rough.*

Mike Wenzloff disagrees: When being set, *a tooth will rotate outward at the face. For a rip, it presents the face all wrong. For a crosscut, the fleam angle changes at the point of the set upwards to the tip of the tooth. One cannot escape this. While reducing the fleam on a crosscut isn't too big a deal, the rotation is on a rip. Very little set is removed if the setting is done precisely before the final light filing. It is just a couple light swipes per tooth except on the larger rip-profile teeth.*

Quite often, the previous setting from the last sharpening is still within specifications and you don't need to do it again. Because, after shaping and filing, you've removed some of the set, why do it beforehand? Make a test-cut to verify. If the saw cuts well: straight and clean. Ta-da! Go saw something. If it drags or binds: add wax. If it still drags, you need to set the teeth. The set gets a little smaller with each filing but you may be able to file the teeth three or four times before needing to set them again.

If a test-cut wanders off-line, the teeth on the side that the saw is cutting toward are set too much. Use a fine stone on the side with too much set and gently hone those teeth a bit. Lay the saw flat and run the stone flat on the side of the blade to hone down the teeth on that side. Take one or two passes with the stone, test again and repeat if necessary. If the saw cut is difficult to control or wobbles around in the kerf, you may have too much set altogether. Measure it with the above specs in mind and if you find you need to reduce it, try clamping the teeth in a vise with smooth, metal jaws and squeezing them to reduce the set. Squeeze a vise-worth section, advance the blade, squeeze again trying to use the same amount of pressure, advance the blade, etc. Check the cut, hone or reset as needed.

Kevin Drake adds: *I much prefer resetting over honing here, mostly because it has worked for me when honing has just made matters worse. Besides that, the set diminishes with use, so just resetting may make a saw behave as if it has been recently sharpened.*

Be sure to coat those freshly cut teeth with rust-preventative and you're done!

10 Carving Tools

Artist-carver Paul Reiber at work.

I WROTE AT THE BEGINNING THAT "SHARP tools are better tools." Nowhere in woodworking is that more true than carving – and for a number of reasons. A sharp carving tool requires less force to push through the wood and is thus more easily and accurately controlled; cuts through wood fibers at virtually any angle the work demands; leaves a surface that needs no sanding, which is vital for carvings where some surfaces cannot be reached with

sandpaper; and can cut adjacent grooves with crisp definition between them. The precision and control demanded of carving tools coupled with the need for a smooth finished surface are the reasons sharpening is so important to carvers. There's nothing magical or tricky about sharpening carving tools. In fact, though the final edge must be polished and, well, perfect, get-

ting there is quite straightforward – no honing guides or gadgets required – just steel and stone. Sure, there are motor-powered conveniences like the Tormek and Koch machines. The Veritas, Lap-Sharp and Work Sharp can all be pressed into duty to save sharpening time. Though bench grinders can help repair major damage or reshape a tool, they may be too aggressive for fine-carving tools. Because the angle of attack varies with the tilt of your hand and arm, sharpening carving tools by any method involves some intuition. And with carving being primarily a hand-tool activity, many carvers eschew power tools as much as possible and treat sharpening as a meditative activity, similar to the carving itself.

When shopping for carving tools you'll encounter what may appear to be an infinite selection of shapes and sizes, but they're all based on three fundamental shapes: gouge, chisel and V-tool in a progression of widths and curvatures (for the gouges), or depths and angles of "V" (for the V-tools). Although the offerings get quite exotic with bent shafts, curved bowls, etc., the variously populated field of carving tools begins

to make some sense with the understanding that they all start with these three basic shapes.

The straight-edge carving chisel is not sharpened like a bench chisel. It has two bevels that meet at the cutting edge in the approximate center of the blade. This edge is honed to a straight edge, usually square to the tool's axis. Gouges have a curved cutting edge defined by the "sweep", which ranges from #1 to #11. A gouge with a #1 sweep is a straight chisel with a flat

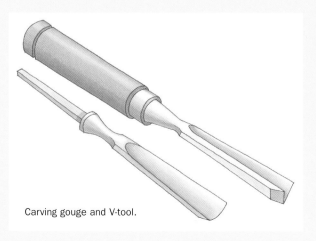

Carving gouge and V-tool.

edge. As the sweep numbers increase the arc increases, like a half cylinder, and are segments of a circle up to a #9 sweep, #10 and #11 are more "U"-shaped. V-tools are … V-shaped, made by two straight edges that meet at a vertex. Other than for the few skewed edge tools, carving tool's cutting edges should be perpendicular to the centerline of the blade.

The basic bevel angle of a carving tool is determined by ergonomics. The angle you seek when sharpening this tool is established by the comfort of the angle when using it. So *you* are the honing "guide". By holding the tool at a comfortable angle on the stones, you will establish a bevel that will cut when lifted a mere degree or two. While this angle may create a too-thin bevel, you can strengthen it by adding an inner bevel.

I'll relay the basics of carving tool sharpening here, but for greater depth I highly recommend Chris Pye's *Woodcarving: Tools, Materials & Equipment Volume I*. The importance of sharpening to the carver is evidenced by the fact that fully half of Mr. Pye's excellent book is devoted to sharpening.

Let's assume your carving tool's bevel requires reshaping with coarse abrasives. This could be the case after many resharpenings where one tends to tilt the edge up higher each time to save effort. Eventually, the bevel at the cutting edge will be too steep and the whole bevel will have to be flattened out and reground to the desired angle. Or, let's say that some damage has occurred to the edge necessitating re-grinding, or even that a new tool was ground to some "theoretical" angle at the factory and it's up to you to make it right for your style of use.

Even though the actual bevel angles will vary according to the wood being carved and the carver's preference, the bevel angles will tend to fall between 20° and 30°. Shallow bevel angles are desired in carving for the most part because the thinner edge will shear wood fibers more easily, allowing you to realize the benefits of greater control and ease of use. Beware, however, that thinner bevels will be weaker and the edge will tend to degrade more quickly. In that case, consider adding an inner bevel of 5° to 10° to strengthen the edge, similar to a back-bevel on a plane blade. This inner bevel provides the ergonomic comfort and control afforded by the low outer bevel angle, and the edge toughening of an inner bevel.

A small sampling of the many things used in hand sharpening carving tools.

THE STARTING POINT

The sharpening process is simple for most carving tools. Hold the tool at the desired cutting angle and rub the bevel along the stone at that angle, holding it steady for straight-edge chisels and each side of V-tools, or rotating it to follow the sweep of a gouge, moving either forward and back or side to side.

Create a reference on the cutting edge by dubbing it off on a fine stone. This will create a thin flat where the edge should be that will reflect light. Creating this light-reflecting flat gives you an opportunity to square up the edge and create fresh, sharp corners. It should show up as an even bright line called a light-line. If it's not even, the bevel thickness is not uniform and

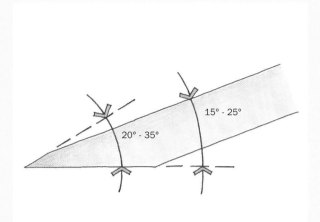

Bevel angles.

Approach the stone as if it were the carving surface. That's about the right angle.

It looks all wrong – lightly grind off the edge flat and square …

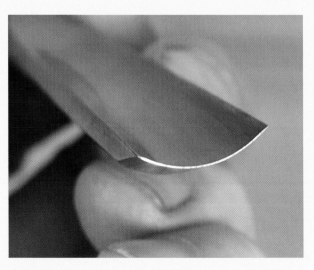

… to create a reflective "light line".

will need to be refined until it is. Once even, start grinding, or reshaping, the bevel. Because of the point-pressure required to grind a curved gouge, for instance, this is an application for harder stones. Oilstones, diamond plates and hard ceramic stones can handle the pressure generated by grinding a small tool, a tool that would, under the same pressure, leave a gouge in a soft waterstone.

Even though they tend to wear a deep hollow quickly, artist-carver Paul Reiber uses coarse, hardware-store carborundum stones for rough shaping. He then uses a translucent white Arkansas stone for fine honing, and tells me how he appreciates the process of "rubbing steel on a rock."

Rubbing steel on a rock. A side to side motion works best for me.

The bevel should be flat – a straight line from heel to edge. If it was rounded to start with (a common problem), you'll see your newly ground flat grow toward the edge as you progress, assuming you are holding the angle steady. When the last of the previous bevel has been ground away, and the flat, dubbed cutting edge has disappeared, move to finer grits, eventually to the strop to polish the edge. Take care to keep the bevel uniform from side to side, which helps maintain the sharp corners.

A small inside bevel will strengthen the edge. Use slipstones or what-have-you for the various shaped tools.

The tool itself can cut a negative shape in a piece of wood, which can be used for honing. Commercial honing compounds, or the fine residue collected from using an 8000-grit waterstone can be applied to the wooden form.

You can use the tool itself to cut its own shape into a fine-grained piece of wood, then charge that groove with abrasive and proceed to hone that particular tool. In many carving cuts the bevel rubs along behind the edge so it is important to polish the bevel, especially at the heel, to leave the smoothest possible surface on the wood.

The inner bevel can be addressed with any number of slipstones or pieces of sandpaper folded or wrapped around a mandrel to fit the inside shape of the tool. A typical carver's sharpening station will have a large variety of shaped stones, custom-shaped wooden scraps for sandpaper, etc. – all evidence of previous efforts to address the insides of the tools. Again, you can use the tool itself to cut a "negative" shape onto a piece of wood. Flex-Cut's honing kit includes a block of wood milled with a variety of shapes like an intricate moulding. It also has two leather pieces glued to it for stropping – one flat, one gently convex – and comes with a stick of their own Flex-Cut Gold stropping compound. Dremel-type hand grinders with rubberized wheels or felt polishing bobs can also be very handy for polishing the inside shapes of some carving tools.

Use a strop for the final polish.

Once the edge is stropped to a mirror finish, test it by cutting across the grain into a piece of wood. It should glide through with little effort and you should hear a satisfying hiss as the new edge cuts cleanly from corner to corner, all along the edge. I recommend that you take time while using the tool to re-strop before it's needed. I know that sounds like a fortune-telling stunt but it is important to touch up your edges often. Whenever you stop work to assess your progress, make it a habit to lightly strop the edge you've been using.

And, while we're discussing work habits, let me recommend that you keep your work area as uncluttered as possible. I don't mean to nag you about cleaning up a busy work surface; it isn't that at all. There are disciplines that result in efficiency. Swapping tools in the heat of creative expression may subject them to abuse because they may bump into each other. Even the smallest nick will leave a track in the cut, so protect your edges while you work and store them safely afterward.

REGRINDING THE BEVEL
As you touch up the edge, again and again, the cutting angle will tend to increase. Eventually, it won't cut properly without lifting the tool too high for comfort or design. You'll have to push harder and your control will diminish. That's when it's time to start over and re-grind the bevel to the right angle, all the way to the cutting edge, re-hone and re-polish.

On the next two pages I've walked (pictorially) through the stages required to re-grind carving tool's edges using a variety of the machines described elsewhere in this book. While all can be used quite well with carving tools, the Koch machine was designed for polishing carving tools and works very well, imparting a high polish on edges. The Tormek has specific jigs for carving tools and a knife-edge leather wheel is available as a strop for the insides of carving tools – very effective as a final polishing step.

Hard felt wheels, flat or shaped, can be mounted on a grinder and charged with fine abrasive compound to polish carving tool edges. The Koch machine's wheels spin opposite to the way a grinder's do. Never let a sharp edge point into the direction of rotation – always trail the edge so it does not get caught by the wheel and thrown into you. It's embar-

A sharp tool should cut across the grain with no tear-out, leaving sharp ridges between grooves.

Here's the Tormek sharpening a V-tool. You sharpen each edge of a V-tool as if it is a separate flat chisel. Unfortunately, that leaves an outside corner that will be too sharp and at the wrong relief angle. So, you have to concentrate on that corner, holding the tool at the desired angle and rounding it over as if it is its own tiny gouge.

rassing to walk into the ER with a gouge handle sticking out of you. And, it's hell on that expensive wheel.

Avoid embarrassment and further expense and, as I've said before: Please Pay Attention!

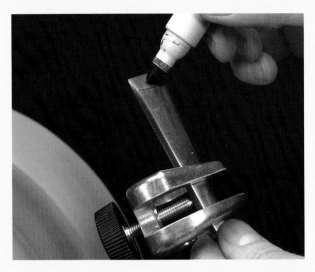

Mark the bevel before you start so you can adjust the bevel angle to see your progress.

Use Tormek's knife-edge strop-wheel accessory to polish the inside of the V-tool ...

... and the standard strop wheel for the outside edges.

Tormek's small tool holder is made for small carving gouges.

Use the round strop-wheel accessory for the inside of gouges.

The outside of the gouge is polished on the standard strop wheel.

The Koch sharpening machine has two wheels of different grits on each side. One is flat for straight-edged tools, the other "gives" for curved edges.

Platter-style grinders like this Veritas, and the Work Sharp and Lap-Sharp, can be used for carving tools. Move the tool around to avoid wearing a circular groove in the abrasive.

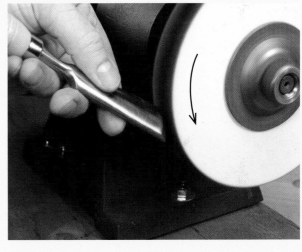

A simple felt wheel on your bench grinder does an amazing job polishing edges. Use it lightly to avoid rounding the bevel. And, always keep the direction of rotation in mind.

The inexpensive and remarkably versatile belt grinder grinding a gouge bevel.

Drawknives

I include drawknives with the carving tools because they're used in a similar freehand manner, though on a larger scale. I could have justified grouping them with chisels for the same reason, or with spokeshaves as they perform a similar duty with a bit more abandon. Because they are used for, and can do so many things, Dan Stalzer calls drawknives "the band saw of hand tools." (I promised to give him credit for that quote.) Dan is a green-wood furniture maker, and instructor, with a collection of old drawknives and a mountain range's worth of shavings made with one of them in his able hands over the years.

He's not a stickler about bevel angles – coming in around 25° – sharpening his drawknives mostly by experience and feel. A very simple modification to his bench grinder made for a useable guide that keeps the handles of the drawknives from hitting the motor: he just flips the tool rest upside down so that it sticks up vertically. Using that vertical piece as a backstop, Dan grinds against the corner of the wheel (you can see

in the photo that the wheel's corner is beveled quite a ways back. He reverses the wheel when the bevel gets too large and starts "beveling" the other corner.) Then it's on to the waterstones for a 1000-grit honing and a 4000-grit final edge. "Plenty sharp enough," he says.

Not all bench-grinders will be able to be modified in this simple way, but a backstop/guide can be added as simply as placing a small C-clamp at the right spot on the tool rest to set the bevel at the correct angle to the wheel. Like it does for so many other tools, the Tormek has a holder that works with drawknives, too.

Drawknives can be sharpened by hand using the same stones and techniques used for your other tools. Sure, they have a very long cutting edge but that's just a matter of scaling up what you already know how to do: hold the bevel against the stone at a consistent angle through the sharpening stroke. Experiment with different abrasive solutions; many drawknife users simply use sandpaper wrapped around a dowel or block that's long enough to keep your hands safe. Drawknives are famous for their bloodlust, so take extra care with that long, sharp edge.

By simply flipping the tool rest over you can use this bench grinder on drawknives. Using the corner of the wheel keeps the handles from hitting the motor. (The rough-looking post in front of the rest is a stalagmite formed from molten steel sparks.)

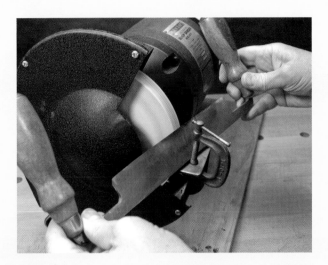

Dan's tool rest flip is simple, but there are other ways to get there. A small C-clamp positioned to set the bevel at the desired angle is simple and effective.

Again, the handles will get in the way with normal stones and methods. Build a stone peninsula that clamps into/onto your bench to access both the drawknife's bevel surfaces. It may not be obvious in the photo, but the stones are not very flat. Dan says, "some hollow in the stone is fine and, in fact, a bit of convexity on the back of the drawknife helps keep it from digging in."

Tormek's knife jig holds drawknives at a consistent angle to the wheel.

11 Turning Tools

Bowl by Kevin Drake.

WOODTURNING SEEMS TO GENERATE MORE innovation in tool development than any other area of woodworking. Planes, chisels and knives have changed very little since their invention, but turning tools are in a constant state of creative engineering. Perhaps this innovative urge is a response to the large number of variables involved in woodturning. Turning tools are handheld which makes for an infinite number of angles of attack, and the wood itself is variable from one spot to the next, with the grain that the edge encounters varying during each revolution. The very shape of the wood is altered as it is worked,

changing the attitude of the tool relative to the surface. The turner constantly adjusts the tool on the fly to accommodate all of these conditions. I've often said that "a plane is just a holder for a blade" and a millenia ago was some clever woodworker's solution to the variables that made it so difficult to surface a board with a handheld blade. With turning, if all we wanted was a cylinder or other repeated shape, we could build a device to eliminate the many variables and crank out cylinders or repetitive geegaws like crazy. (And we do – there are lots of methods and machines for mass-producing turned things in wood or metal, or anything – just look around – that mop handle probably wasn't made by some turner with a handheld spindle gouge.) Turning-tool innovation makes it easier and more reliable to obtain the desired result: the finest surface, hollowest vessel, least fatigue or whatever problem your clever mind perceives and decides to solve by inventing or innovating a new tool for lathe work.

The ongoing innovation in turning tools makes it unlikely that I will address every tool, but I've tried to discuss the basics of the basics. By analyzing the cutting action taking place (Chapter Four: How Wood Is Cut) and adding the constraints of edge geometry (Chapter Five: The Fundamentals) you should be able to sharpen whichever new and improved turning tool finds its way into your kit. And while I'm putting the onus on you to adapt to new tools and their edge requirements, I must add that if you ask 100 turners how they sharpen their tools you will likely get more than 100 answers. This should tell you that there may be more than one way to get there from here. So keep an open mind and experiment with your tools, abrasives and applications to find the path that works for you – for *your* woods on *your* machines with *your* tools in *your* shop.

Woodturning lathe tools are power tools. Sure, they're handheld but the wood is turning under power and the forces at work on their cutting edges demand some different sharpening protocols than those required for true hand tools. A lathe tool is usually expected to cut much more wood between sharpenings than other hand tools. If you have experience turning or have even simply watched a turner at work, you may recall the amount of shavings produced. Comparing that pile of shavings with the one produced while planing for the same amount of time will give you some idea of the stresses at work on your lathe tool edges.

Each of the various turning tools has a specific job to do in a similar way that different planes are preferred for different work. A roughing gouge is used for rough dimensioning of the turning stock similar to the rough dimensioning of a scrub plane. Smooth finish cutting is performed by a skew on the lathe similar to the way a smoothing plane finishes a board.

And like planes, any one lathe tool can be called upon to perform satisfactorily in situations that it may not have been designed for.

Again, as with planes, the need for a finely honed and polished edge is situational. A scrub plane doesn't need a polished edge while a smoother does. Most turners use their tools directly from the grinder with no further honing at all, and there are rarely times when any more edge refinement is called for. Many have the grinder mounted right beside the lathe for quick, convenient touch-ups. The edge from the grinder, while ground to zero-radius, will be quite coarse compared to what is optimal for chisels and plane irons. If you were to use that coarse edge to cut in one spot – hold it at only one circumference of the turning wood – it would undoubtedly leave visible striations on the wood. However, with the wood turning as fast as it is, as you move the tool along the piece, the coarse edge has many chances to level those striations and leave a smooth surface.

Though most contemporary turning tools are made from high-speed steel and can withstand considerable heat without softening, take care to avoid overheating when using powered grinders. Always exercise caution to avoid overheating the steel. Keep the edge moving on the wheel – don't hesitate – and dunk the edge often in water. Don't wipe off the water drops that remain – they're a helpful indicator of overheating; as you continue grinding, when the drops on the edge start to boil, dunk again. Be especially careful with the tool's corners. There is less metal there to sink away the heat and they tend to overheat and display those beautiful/horrible colors in a blink (see Chapter Five: The Fundamentals). Low-speed, water-cooled grinders, like the Tormek, avoid the overheating problem and have jigs for accuracy and repeatability but may be too slow at routine sharpening for turners who have the experience to grind their tools efficiently on a high-speed grinder.

Grinding a uniform edge requires a properly dressed wheel. There are a variety of wheel-dressing products but one of the simplest is a one-point diamond dresser that can be held in an easily made guide that rides the tool rest, or the star-wheel style that crushes the surface of the grindstone as it is pressed against it. (See Chapter Five for more about grinding wheel maintenance.)

Many turners keep the grinder beside the lathe for quick, easy sharpening.

Belt grinders are handy for some of these tools but the flat grind they produce may not be ideal for some "rub-the-bevel" turning operations that would be better performed with a hollow-ground bevel. A flat grind works well inside a bowl or vessel where the concavity of the piece allows the edge to cut while the heel rubs. On the outside however, a hollow grind allows you to register the bevel against the work the same way a hollow grind on a chisel registers the edge on a stone. The heel of the bevel rubs while the edge cuts.

With experience and practice freehand grinding is the fastest way to get back to turning.

Water-cooled grinding avoids the risk of over-heating and the fixturing provides accurate, repeatable angles. But the low-speed wheel takes longer to sharpen the edge.

Gouges

The basic roughing gouge is used to turn rectangular stock round. The edge is straight and square across the front. A large, strong bevel angle is desirable as that edge is being repeatedly pounded by each corner of the stock as it spins. An average bevel angle is 45°, adjusted for softer or harder woods by subtracting or adding as much as 10°, respectively, to reduce the cutting force in softwoods and add strength for hardwoods. Adjust the grinder's tool rest so the bevel encounters the wheel at the desired angle and grind the bevel by rolling it side to side against the wheel.

Socket-style fixtures, like the Wolverine from Oneway, and Tormek's jigs, make grinding a roughing gouge easier by providing a fixed reference angle for the bevel while allowing the rotation necessary for the task. Adjust the Wolverine socket – with the grinder

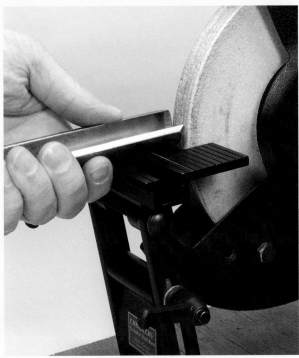

Gouges should be ground square across to start.

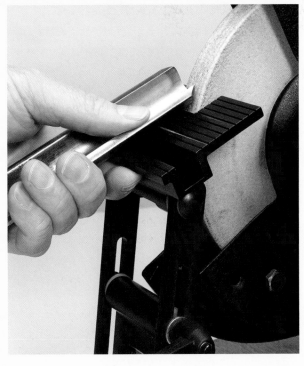

An adjustable tool rest for the grinder makes setting and holding the angle easier.

The Oneway Jig, in use here, allows repeatable grinding of the bevel on tools, including this gouge.
The Wolverine Grinding Jig is the core component of the Oneway Wolverine line of grinding products.

off – so that the bevel is resting on the wheel. Remove the gouge, turn on the grinder and replace the gouge in the socket. Grind the bevel evenly, rotating the tool in complete arcs. Mark your fixture with a scribe or tape so you can re-grind that tool to the same angle with a simple, repeatable setting. Tormek provides an angle setting tool as well as "recipe stickers" for each tool to record the necessary adjustment parameters to make resharpening easier. Their kit even includes a marker for the stickers.

To match the bevel angle for resharpening, color it with a marker then set the angle at the wheel by eye. Rotate the wheel by hand a few inches and examine the stripe that it makes. If the stripe is of uniform width from edge to heel of bevel, the angle is correct. If it tapers, adjust the angle accordingly until the stripe is uniform.

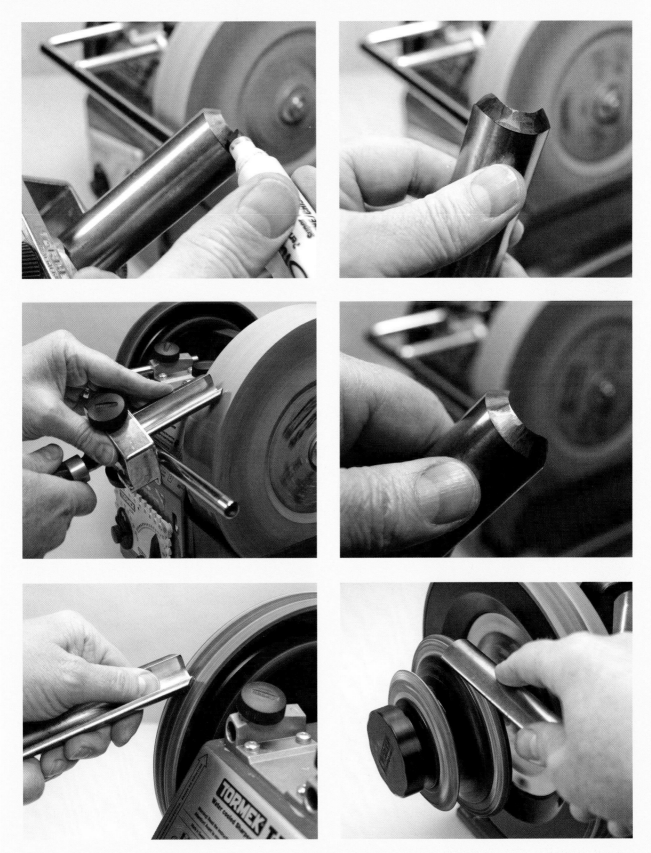

Color the bevel to adjust and verify your angle setup. You want the color removed in a uniform stripe on the bevel from edge to heel. This method is recommended when you're using a bench grinder as well. After grinding, polish the edge inside and out with the leather strop-wheel.

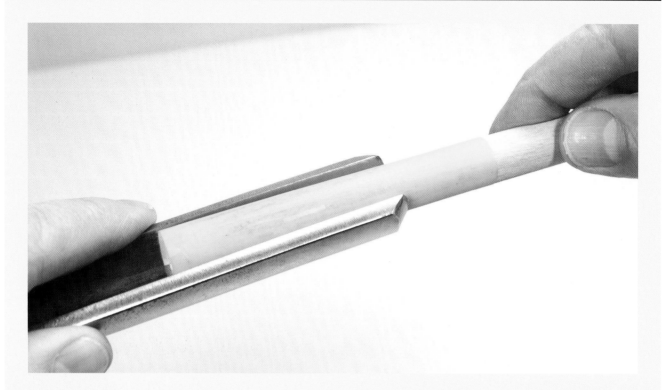

Most turners just use their tools straight from the grinder but it never hurts to polish off the burr and refine the edge a bit more.

Whether or not the inside of the gouge should be polished is a matter of some debate. While unnecessary for rough work, honing the flute will remove the burr left from grinding and a polished surface will reduce friction and heat generated by the fast-moving shavings. Use round, slipstones or abrasive paper wrapped around a dowel of appropriate diameter to deburr from grinding and polish the inside surface.

Spindle gouges employ a fingernail grind at a bevel angle of 25° (again, somewhat higher for hardwoods and lower for softwoods). These can be ground using the same setup you used to grind your roughing gouge. Reduce the grinding angle to 25° and, as we want to radius the edge around the tip, hesitate at the corners to produce the desired fingernail shape while being careful to keep that shape symmetric and avoid overheating.

The exact shape of the bevel on a bowl gouge is a matter of much debate and personal preference. Traditional bowl gouges had square-ground ends with approximately 40° bevels. More recently, side-cutting bowl gouges have become increasingly popular. The shape of the business end of these gouges is sufficiently difficult to produce and reproduce that the use

The Tormek-style machines use a pivoting jig to grind bowl gouges to the proper elliptical shape.

The Wolverine Vari-Grind accessory will properly shape and maintain the edge on standard bowl gouges, the modern side grind (also known as the Ellsworth grind, Liam O'Neil, or Irish grind), and the traditional fingernail shape for spindle-work detailing.

of a jig and fixture is highly recommended. Fixtures, such as the Wolverine system, that work with your bench grinder are available. Designs for shop-made fixtures that use a similar sliding socket backstop can be found online and Tormek offers jigs with their machine for grinding all the popular turning tool edge geometries. All of these systems use fixtures that attach to the machine and work with a jig that attaches to the tool. The jig can be adjusted for blade extension and bevel angle. Combined with the adjustment of the fixture's distance from the wheel, you can dial in all the adjustments to grind the perfect confluence of bevel angle and ellipticality for the perfect cutting edge.

Even with jigs and fixtures, there is some art to grinding the side-cutting bowl gouge. The gouge must be symmetrical with the side-cutting edges straight or slightly convex. If you'll be using a skew or scraper for the final surface you can use the gouge as-ground. If you will be using this gouge for finish work, the inside of the gouge should be polished as with the roughing and spindle gouges. Refinement of the cutting edge with finer grits may be desirable in some applications. Polish the edge on Tormek's leather honing wheel or use stones for a finer finish than that left by the grinder.

To be able to reproduce these complex edges in the future, take measurements and notes or use scraps of wood as spacers to reset the jig and fixture to the same place relative to the grinding wheel each time. Tormek provides stickers, as I mentioned before. Use them. For the socket-style fixture, scraps of wood can serve to gauge the distance from socket to wheel, marked with the information about which chisel it is used with as well as the setting for the pivot and the blade extension dimension.

Skews

Skew chisels can be used right from the grinder. A skew angle of 70° to 80° is common but the exact angle is a matter of preference and experience. Try an included cutting angle for the bevels of 25° for softwoods. That can be increased up to 40° to improve cutting performance and edge life when turning harder woods. Straight skews can be ground using the grinder table set to the correct bevel angle and sliding the chisel across the grindstone at the correct skew angle. Mark both left and right skew angles on the table as a reference so you can match both sides and be careful to maintain symmetry – keep the bevels the same length and the edge centered. The Veritas adjustable grinder tool rest can be used with the chisel clamped in their grinding jig at the proper skew angle. A bevel gauge can be handy to help set both sides of the blade to the same skew angle. Mark a line on the skew chisel to use as a reference when you flip it over to grind the other bevel.

Many turners prefer to use radiused skew chisels as they tend to avoid catches better than straight-edge skews and allow more flexibility while cutting. Some grind their radiused skews freehand, using the grinder's table as if it

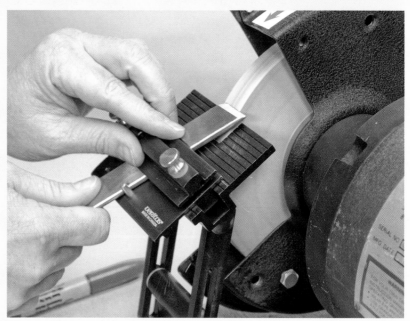

Marking the skew angle (above) and straight skew grinding with the Veritas grinder table and jig (below).

were the lathe's tool rest. This takes a bit of practice and you can learn the required moves by setting your grinder table to the bevel angle to give you an accurate bevel as you move the blade past the wheel by hand. The Veritas skew grinding jig works with their variable grinder tool rest or you can drill a hole in your grinder's tool rest to accommodate it. Set the blade extension to obtain the desired bevel angle and arc, then swing the tool on the pivot pin to grind the

bevel. Reposition the skew on the other side of the jig and repeat, being careful to maintain symmetry so the tool will cut the same when you change directions or turn the tool over.

The Tormek-style systems include jigs for grinding straight or radiused skews. They remove metal more slowly than a dry bench grinder for shaping an edge but can resharpen one quickly without the risk of overheating.

Practicing freehand grinding will save time in the long run.

The Veritas skew grinding jig pivots on a pin in a hole in the grinder table.

Polishing the edge may not be necessary for turning tools but it can't hurt as long as you avoid any microbevel that could interfere with the "bevel rubbing" employed by turners.

When you're finished sharpening, the skew makes quick work of material removal.

Scrapers

While a turning scraper may not look like the card scraper that you use to surface flat stock, the cutting action is essentially the same. The edge encounters the wood at a high scraping angle and the burr, if any, acts as a short shearing blade with a radical chip breaker (the face of the blade breaks the shaving's fibers before they can lever up and tear out). Lathe scrapers are usually round-nosed tools but the shape is easy to modify for a specific purpose.

Grinding a turning scraper is simply a matter of adjusting the grinder table to the proper angle – 70° to 80° is standard – and grinding the scraper to the desired shape and zero-radius at the edge. The burr that is left by the grinder is not the best for cutting and I recommend that you hone that off with a fine stone, polishing the face of the tool. Then use a burnisher to form a stronger and sharper burr. A handheld burnisher will do, but can be awkward to use on such a small target. The Veritas Scraper Burnisher is a small table with two hardened pins, one of which is tapered 5°, the other 10°. The scraper is pivoted against one pin while rolling a hook against the other. The use of one pin or the other depends on the bevel angle, allowing a 5° adjustment of the burr angle.

PHOTO COURTESY OF LEE VALLEY TOOLS.

Parting Tools

The diamond-shaped parting tool needs to be ground symmetrically so that both edges meet at the widest point in the center at an angle of about 30° to 50°. The angle is not critical and you can hand hold the tool at the grinder or use a Tormek-style jig or a pocket-style fixture to keep it steady. The straight-from-the-grinder edge will suffice for most parting jobs.

12 Axes and Adzes

OF ALL THE AXES, HATCHETS AND adzes developed and used throughout the ages, few are still in use today by woodworkers. I use an ax when I have to limb a fallen tree – I prefer it to a chainsaw for small work like that. The broadax (also broadaxe and broad axe) and adze are still used by hand-tool purists and timber-frame traditionalists but I know of few woodworkers whose work has at any point been touched by an axe or adze.

ESF's Woodsmen's Team Takes Top Honors at Competition SYRACUSE – The crisp spring air in Syracuse crackled with the sound of wood splitting and the smell of sawdust as the State University of New York's College of Environmental Science and Forestry Woodsmen's Team took top honors at the 2007 East Coast Lumberjack Roundup.

Still, that does not mean they aren't the right tools for certain woodcutting jobs; and so long as that is the case, axes and adzes should be properly sharp. These tools are straightforward to sharpen with either a grinder or file. If using a bench grinder, all the appropriate cautions apply: protect yourself and others from flying sparks, grit and potential wheel fragments, and keep the tool cool. A general-purpose axe or hatchet should be ground to about a 25° included bevel angle. If it is to be cutting softwoods, 20° serves to help it cut more aggressively, but for hardwoods try 30° for edge durability. This assumes you will be cutting the wood rather than splitting it. If splitting with the grain is the goal, a steeper bevel will encourage the wood to split, whereas an axe or hatchet with a too-shallow bevel may become embedded in the grain and be difficult to remove.

An *adze* is an axe with the cutting edge turned sideways and is used for surfacing and dimensioning rough timber into lumber. A carvers' adze is smaller, its curved blade used for hollowing. Lipped adzes are used to cut cross-grain. The same bevel angles apply but, as an adze is often used to create a flat surface, a shallower angle and a sharper edge will help with that finer work, leaving a smoother surface. Adzes should be beveled on the inside of the blade with the back left unbeveled. Both surfaces should be honed smooth for best performance.

A *broad axe* is a wide, single-bevel tool that is also used for turning timber into useable lumber. Keep the flat side flat by honing on stones or sandpaper. File or grind only the beveled side and again, as with the adze, a shallower bevel will make fine work a little easier and smoother.

The maul, left, has a large bevel to split wood for firewood. The axe, on the right, has a much smaller bevel angle to chop perpendicularly through wood fibers.

Underhand Chop' 2007.
COURTESY RAE ALLEN

All the grinder precautions regarding safety and heat apply to axes, too.

I find it easier to use the belt grinder for this operation when it's mounted horizontally. I just bolted it to a piece of plywood that I can clamp to the bench.

Axes, et al, are often used right from the grinder – little honing or polishing is required for rough timberwork – but it never hurts to continue the sharpening with finer grits. I doubt any job would require an edge finer than 1000-grit but I suspect that competitive woodchoppers would find even that too coarse.

Axes can be sharpened with grinders (low- or high-speed, wet or dry, horizontal or vertical), files, stones, belt grinder, what-have-you. If you use a high-speed grinder, take the usual care to keep from overheating the edge. With that large chunk of steel in hand, it's easy to overestimate the blade's resistance to overheating at the thin edge. Unless you have a specific need for a specific angle, freehand approximation of the bevel angle will usually suffice. Belt grinders tend to run cooler but still require vigilance to prevent overheating. Water-cooled Tormek-style grinders offer an attachment just for holding axe heads but require patience as they remove metal much more slowly than a high-speed grinder.

Low-speed, water-cooled grinders eliminate the risk of overheating and, with the right attachment, make axe sharpening easy by holding the edge at a consistent angle against the wheel.

Axes are usually softer than plane irons, knives or chisels to resist impact damage, and can be sharpened with a file. A broadax should be beveled on one side only. Flatten the back with no bevel.

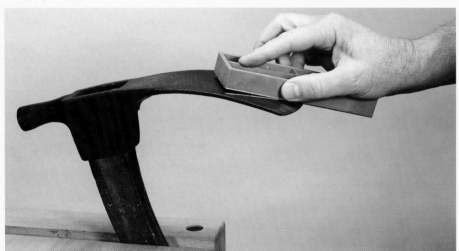

An adze, like a broadax, is only beveled on one side. Here, I'm using a diamond "stone" to hone the flat side.

The inside curves of the lipped adze's edge can be sharpened with a small sanding drum or cylindrical stone in a drill motor. Or, you can wrap sandpaper around a piece of pipe or dowel to hone those inside radii. Don't bevel the outside at all. Just hone it flat.

13 Knives

A BOOK ABOUT SHARPENING WOULDN'T BE complete without a section about knives. After clubs, knives are mankind's most basic tools. Knives come in all shapes and sizes, in all kinds of steels. Like all edged tools, how you sharpen any one of them depends on its intended use: whether in the kitchen, where it may be used to chop through bones or slice through raw

tuna, or in your shop, or on your boat, or out in the backyard doing, well, who knows what? A working knife may be called upon to perform any number of tasks, including the one it was designed for.

Most Western knives have a long, primary bevel and employ a small secondary bevel that is the actual cutting edge. The secondary bevel will have a larger included angle – the angle at which two bevels meet to form the cutting edge – than the primary bevel. Many Japanese knives, on the other hand, have a single long bevel all the way to the edge with no secondary bevel at all.

For tough chopping work, the kind you'd use a cleaver to perform, an included edge angle as large as 50° or 60° may be needed, while the slicing of fish or vegetables may call for an edge angle as small as 10°. This is why most kitchens have more than one knife. You can get by with just one, and it will work for most jobs, but like the old Honda "Street Scrambler" motorcycle I had when I was a teenager, it was never a great street bike and it didn't "scramble" very well either. So, the "no free lunch" rule applies here as well: specific tasks are easier with the right blade.

That fussy cook's array of kitchen knives serves a purpose by making available knives specifically designed for certain cutting tasks. Most of these knives should have an edge angle of between 15° and 30°. Some of the edges will be honed and polished, but for most kitchen prep work, some "tooth" left on the edge will improve performance by giving the edge a bit of grip. I'm not talking about a dull edge. An edge with a bit of tooth will cut like crazy through paper or tomato skins. If you've ever mashed a ripe tomato while slicing it with a polished edge, you know what I'm talking about – an edge with a 1000-grit finish will bite in and cut through the skin. This is how TV hucksters do so well cutting all sorts of difficult things in the infomercials. Their knives have serrations that aggressively dig in and cut aggressively. (… but "never need sharpening?" No way! Don't buy it – or them. Again, there is no free lunch – sorry, you cannot have eternal sharpness.)

Bread knives are usually serrated – they are actually bread saws. Most woodworking blades – chisels and plane irons – cut while being pushed straight through the wood, so a finely honed and polished edge performs best. While some kitchen cutting is done by simply pushing the blade directly through the carrot or whatever, much of the paring done in the kitchen uses a sawing action. If you tried to cut French bread the way you chop a carrot you'd mash it flat. So we not only have different edge geometry for different tasks, we also have different abrasive requirements.

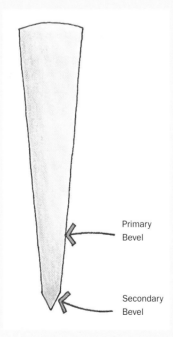

Primary Bevel

Secondary Bevel

A typical Western-style chef's knife blade has a large, symmetric, double-primary bevel with smaller secondary bevels that meet to form the cutting edge.

Top: The flat side of the chef's knife is the primary bevel. The secondary bevel is the bright strip at the cutting edge. Bottom: The bevel on this sashimi knife is the large (mostly) bright surface that's over half the width of the blade. There is no secondary bevel.

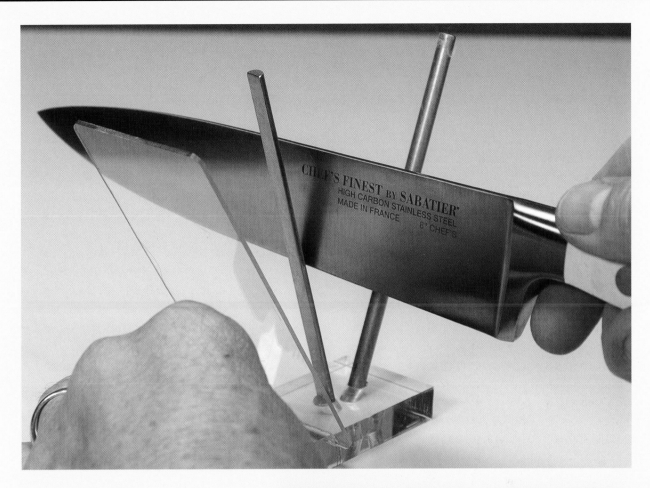

Devices

Double-beveled Western-style knives are fairly easy to sharpen. The angles are rarely critical and there are only a few tricks to learn, with many devices available to help. There are crock-stick-, or V-stick-style devices, slot-style devices and rod-guided devices. Follow the manufacturer's instructions for best results but do not forget about the basic needs of bevel angles and intended use.

CROCK & V STICK SHARPENERS

The V stick sharpener employs two abrasive sticks set at the correct angle like a "V" sticking out of a base of wood or plastic. The sticks are ceramic rods or diamond-coated metal rods.

The knife is held vertically and passed up and down along the sticks to hone the edge. As long as you hold the knife more or less vertically, you can't

Sharpening stick systems by Spyderco (left) and DMT. With these systems, the knife is held vertically and passed up and down along the abrasive sticks to hone the edge at the angles established by the sticks.

help but hone the edge at the correct angle. Different sticks are available with different grits to help you get the tooth or polish that you want on the edge.

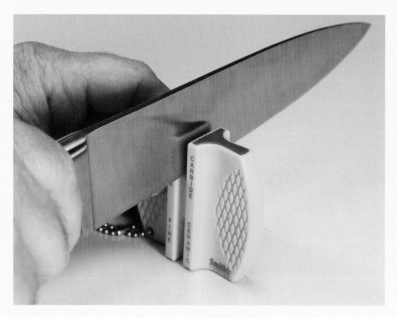

This slot-style sharpener has crossed carbide bits on one side to aggressively shape an edge and ceramic rods on the other for finer honing.

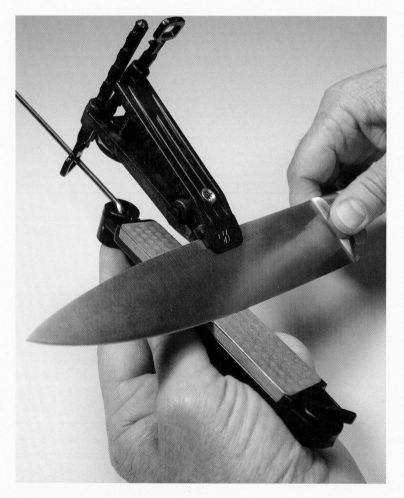

Rod-guided devices use a stone attached to a rod that slides through an aperture that maintains the desired bevel angle. DMT's Aligner ™, shown here, comes with three easily changed diamond hones.

SLOT-STYLE

Slot-style devices have ceramic rods or carbide inserts set at a fixed angle. The knife is drawn through the slot to scrape off or abrade some metal at the correct angle.

These work fairly well; however, the carbide inserts can scrape off an excessive amount of metal and should be used sparingly. The ceramic rods are less aggressive, but the contact area on each rod is small, which tends to increase honing time. Another drawback to slot-style sharpeners is that they do not allow for any adjustment to the bevel angle, which limits the number of tasks you might need the blade to perform.

ROD-GUIDED

Rod-guided devices clamp the blade to a fixture with a hole or slot for a guide rod to pass through. The guide rod extends from the abrasive stone and, while the rod is in the slot, the stone is held at the proper angle relative to the blade, which is adjustable by raising or lowering the fixture relative to the knife.

Some systems clamp a jig to the blade to hold it at the correct angle while honing. With others, the jig rides on the stone and lifts the edge up the correct amount, whereas still other systems have the jig ride directly on the table surface. These are all fundamentally the same as rod-guided systems in that the blade is held in such a way that the abrasive must act on the blade at a prescribed angle.

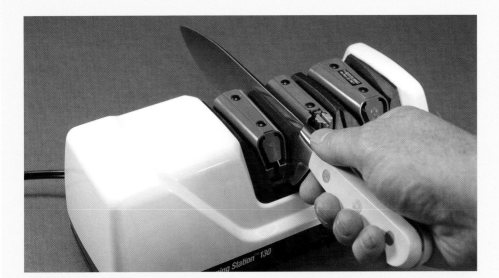

Sharpening machines like this Chef's Choice model come in handy if you have a lot of sharpening to do. And they work a lot better than the edge-mangler on the back side of the electric can opener.

The Tormek's jigs hold the bevel angle throughout the grinding process.

ELECTRIC-POWERED

There are so-called knife sharpeners piggy-backed onto electric can openers. Please don't use these on anything you care about. The grinding wheels employed in most electric-powered knife sharpeners are much too coarse, much too aggressive, and may do more damage than good. That said, the concept of the powered knife sharpener has seen improvement in recent years. I tested the Chef's Choice knife sharpener and found it to do a capable job of sharpening. It has three slots: one with a coarse diamond grinding disc, the next one has a short, non-powered "steel" for refining the burr left from coarse grinding, or you can skip the steel and finish the edge on a fine diamond disc in the third and last slot. The slots are set at a fixed angle and the whole process is relatively foolproof and easy to learn. There are also competitive brands of electric-powered sharpeners. I've given only the Chef's Choice brand a test, but was impressed by its performance and ease of use.

The Tormek-style sharpening machines have jigs for holding knives at a consistent angle while sharpening them on the vertical water-cooled wheel. Once the bevel angles are established and zero-radius has been achieved (burr!), a pass or two on the leather stropping wheel will refine the edge to "ripe-tomato-slicing" sharp.

BELT GRINDER

Although we use 2" × 72" belt grinders in the Hock Shop for all of our grinding needs, a grinder that size may prove unnecessary for the average woodshop. So, for this book, I bought one of the inexpensive, 1" × 30" belt grinders at a local hardware store. I mounted it onto a piece of plywood so the Veritas grinding fixture can be used with it; I can also clamp the edge of the plywood base in a vise to use the belt horizontally. With numerous grits available, the 1" × 30" belts prove handy for all kinds of rapid edge shaping, as well as honing and polishing. Plus, for knives, you can use the slack section of the unsupported belt to add a small amount of concavity to a blade.

When I need to sharpen a knife I head for the belt grinder in the shop. I first analyze the edge to determine how much work is needed. For most sharpening, I use a slightly worn 320-grit belt. If the edge needs reshaping, I start with a 220-grit belt. The belt grinder can remove a lot of metal in a short time so anything coarser is usually too aggressive for knife edges. I estimate the bevel angle, hold it freehand and sweep the blade over the slack portion of the belt. I flip the blade to do the same on the other side and continue

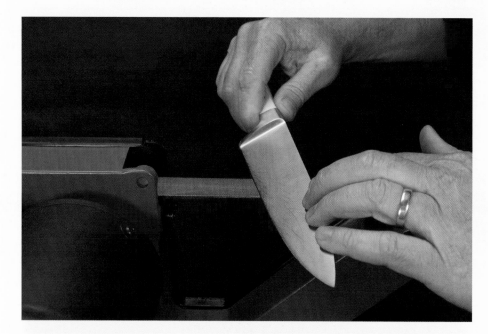

Hold the bevel angle as you pass the blade along the belt. I find this easier to do with the belt grinder clamped in a horizontal position. I use a 320-grit belt for most sharpening jobs.

The white line at the cutting edge is the burr. If you angle your lamp just right, you can watch it form as you move the edge along the belt.

Buff off the burr with light pressure at a steep angle against the buffing wheel.

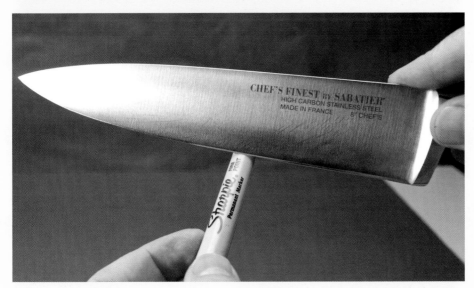

The "fingernail test" for sharpness in Chapter Five: The Fundamentals can also be performed with a plastic pen barrel.

to flip, grinding each side until a burr forms. With a swing-arm lamp adjusted properly, the burr will appear as a thin bright line along the edge. If I started with 220 grit, I now switch to 320 or 400 grit and make one or two more passes. The burr will still show but the bright line will be smaller with a finer abrasive.

I prefer not to use a stitched muslin buff for sharpening chisels or plane irons due to its tendency to round edges, but I do use one charged with chromium oxide compound (that's the green-crayon buffing compound) to buff the burr off knife edges. I press the edge into the buff at a fairly steep angle and sweep it across the face of the buff once or twice on

each side to remove the burr. A quick fingernail test tells me that the burr has been removed and that the edge is sharp.

Be careful when using the buffer with a sharp blade. If you move across the buffing wheel too quickly, you are apt to slide the tip of the knife off the face of the wheel where it can be caught and thrown viciously by the side of the spinning buff. This is not a place to be in a hurry. For me, it all happened so fast that it wasn't until I got home from the emergency room and studied the cut in the wheel that I understood what I had done to end up with that knife stuck in my leg.

STEELS

Sharpening steels – real steels, not just abrasive rods that are shaped like a sharpening steel – come in a variety of styles. Some are simple rod-shaped files with longitudinal teeth that cut knife edges very aggressively. They are often magnetized to catch the filings that would otherwise fall onto the Thanksgiving turkey. I don't recommend these and choose not to use them on any of my own knives. They are too aggressive and will file a blade away much too quickly. Plus, they leave a too-rough edge. I prefer frequent use of a smooth steel on my knives, which haven't actually been sharpened in years. Honest. (At least until I tested the Chef's Choice powered sharpener. I had to test something and, well, having been a knifemaker I have many knives available to me. As much as I appreciate the Chef's Choice, I continue to choose my steel to keep my kitchen knives sharp.)

There are also a variety of "steel-like" abrasive rods made from either ceramic or diamond-coated steel. These are simply sharpening stones shaped into something familiar to steel users. They work well when used properly (see photo) but a real steel does the job a little differently.

A smooth steel will reshape the edge by "flowing" a small amount of metal into alignment, like turning a hook on a scraper blade with a burnisher. In fact, though it may be a bit short, your burnisher will work well as a knife steel. First, in order for a steel to work at all, the knife's edge should not be too dull, nicked or otherwise abused. It should only need a bit of "freshening up." To get a feel for the angles, hold the steel vertically against a solid surface. It's easier to see the required angle this way. Tilt the knife away from the steel at the desired angle and stroke down along the steel pulling the blade along the edge at the same time. It's not that different from the honing stroke on a stone. You're moving a bit of metal, don't forget, so some pressure is required. Switch to the other side of the steel with the other side of the bevel and repeat. Switch sides, back and forth a few times. Reduce pressure with the final strokes and check for sharpness. I find that I can resurrect a fairly dull edge by simply bearing harder against the steel, thus upsetting more metal and working up a new edge.

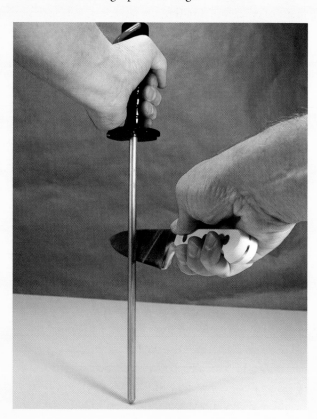

This steel is all too typical and much too aggressive for any of my knives ...

... it scrapes off enough steel that the manufacturer magnetizes it to collect the filings.

Holding the steel vertically makes it a bit easier to see the angle of the bevel. Hold the angle the same on both sides.

Folding the corner of a piece of paper in half (45°), then in half again (22½°) and in half once more (11¼°) will give you an approximate guide to the bevel angle.

How To

You can use your woodshop sharpening kit for your knives with little or no trouble. As you can see from the inventive energy invested in the systems described above, the only difficult part is holding the edge at the correct angle while you rub it on the stone. As I mentioned before, holding the angle can be tricky but it's not often critical. For the most part, close is close enough. A simple paper angle-guide can be made by folding a sheet of paper in half at a corner. You now have a 45° angle gauge. If you fold it again, you'll have a 22½° angle gauge. Fold it one more time for an 11¼° angle gauge. This is about right as a starting point for each side of the average kitchen knife (both edges at 11¼° add up to an included cutting angle of 22½°, which is a good bevel angle for most kitchen knives). Lay the blade flat on the stone, lift the back to match the angle of the paper wedge and, here's the tricky part, hold that angle throughout the stroke along the stone. A little practice and you'll be good to go. You don't have to do the whole edge at a stroke, a section at a time works just fine as long as you maintain the desired angle.

There is one other aspect to consider if you are using your waterstones to sharpen knives. Waterstones are soft and if you are pushing the edge along the stone you can easily dig a knife edge into them. The resulting gouge in the stone's surface will have to be removed before using it for a chisel or plane iron, so it is recommended that you only *pull* the knife

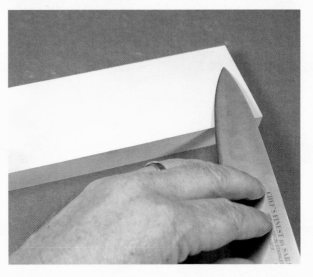

The softness of waterstones demands that the edge be pulled along. If pushed, you risk cutting into the stone.

This edge has been carelessly honed to a concave shape that will no longer cut all the way to the cutting board surface.

edge along the stone to avoid damage to the stone. A similar problem crops up when using sandpaper to sharpen knives. When pushed into the sandpaper, the knife's edge can catch and slice the paper. Yes, it's just a piece of sandpaper and it will probably still work for most other sharpening needs. But a sliced piece of sandpaper is an annoyance that will make further knife-sharpening in the same manner impossible, so it's best to pull the edge along the abrasive.

I've seen a number of classic chef's knives – good ones with forged blades and integral bolsters (that thick finger-guard at the rear of the blade) – where routine sharpening created a concavity along the edge.

Any amount of concavity is too much, as you'll notice the knife leaving behind uncut green onion fibers on the cutting board. You may be tempted to blame the cutting board (and if *it's* not flat it would do the same thing) but often the problem is with the knife. The integral bolster prevents you from sharpening right up to it. So, after some number of sharpenings, you'll have worn away the part of the blade in front of the bolster that is supposed to be flat or convex. It's time to fix it.

When the green onion scenario proves to be a problem with the knife, the forged bolster needs to be ground down and reshaped. I start by grinding the whole edge to the shape I want, bolster and all. I like my chef's knife to have a straight section at the rear of the blade. This way I can rock it back and meet the cutting board with a couple of inches of flat, solid contact.

Now the bolster has a flat on its bottom and needs to be ground round and faired into shape. I use a belt grinder to make short work of this, but any abrasive will do the job. Angle the blade away from the grinder so you're only working the bolster. Roll the bolster to round it off and taper it back away from the edge a bit. Take your time, study your progress closely and often.

Adjust the belt sander platen so the belt doesn't sag when correcting the edge. I removed the plastic grit guard to accommodate the whole edge for this operation and have set up the grinder in a horizontal position. I use a 180- or 220-grit belt for this step.

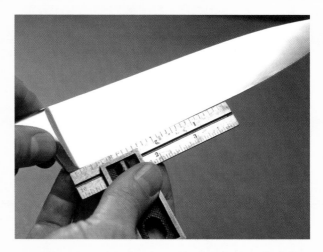

I like a straight section at the rear of the blade of a chef's knife.

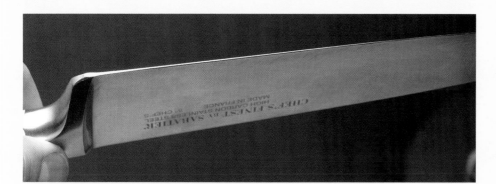

After correcting the shape, the edge and bolster will be flat on the bottom.

Reshape the bolster being careful not to grind the cutting edge. Use 220 or 320 grit.

The bolster is now rounded to shape.

Regrind the edge to the proper angle using about 320 grit.

Once you've shaped the bolster, renew the cutting edge with the belt grinder as described above (320 grit and buff the burr) or with stones to the desired grit. As mentioned above, the intended use determines how fine the grit will be that will ultimately deter-mine the cutting edge. For most kitchen uses 1000 grit or 1200 grit will be plenty sharp and cut satisfy-ingly. However, I like my pocketknife to be as sharp as it can be, so I usually use 1200 grit or finer and then give it a couple of strokes on a strop.

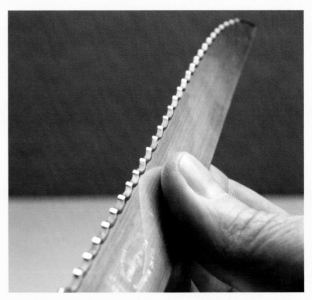

Honing a serrated knife as if it were not, is fast and works quite well. It essentially turns all the serration points into short, sharp chisels.

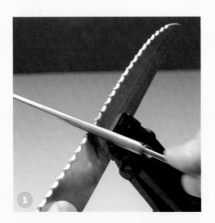

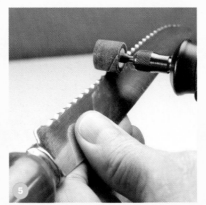

Or you can get into each serrated valley with:
1. DMT's tapered diamond rod used with their slot-style holder
2. & 3. Spyderco's round or teardrop ceramic rods
4. a dowel with PSA-backed honing film wrapped around it
5. Dremel hand grinder with fine drum sander

SERRATED KNIVES

Most serrated knives can be sharpened either by treating them like a regular knife and "flat-topping" the serrations or by using an appropriately sized abrasive rod, diamond or ceramic, and honing each scallop along the blade at the proper angle. Some of the crock-stick-type sharpeners will allow you to sharpen serrations by sliding each serration up and down the sticks, which are held at the proper angle. A hand grinder can be used, but be careful that you do not generate too much heat in that thin scalloped edge.

JAPANESE KNIVES

Sharpen a single-bevel Japanese knife by laying the back flat against a fine stone and work until you raise a burr on the bevel side. Flip the blade, lay the bevel flat against the stone and uniformly hone the entire bevel until it meets the back. Do not use sharpening steels, sticks or rods on your Japanese knife. The edge may be too hard to handle the stress applied to any one point when these tools are used.

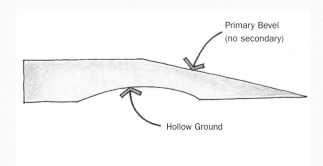

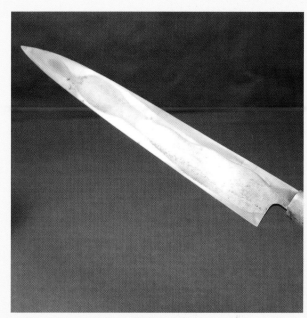

The back of single-bevel Japanese knives have a slight hollow ground into them by the maker to reduce the effort when honing flat against the stone.

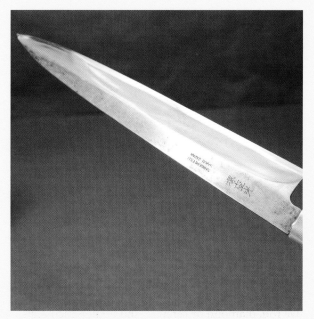

The bevel of my "willow-leaf" (or Yanagi) sashimi knife is flat-honed all the way to the edge.

Carving knife assortment.

CARVING KNIVES

Okay, back to woodworking. All the above information about sharpening knives applies to shop knives as well and every shop has several general purpose knives around for, well, general purposes: carving away that little nubbin left by the table saw blade or opening the box that UPS just dropped off. Consider their intended use and shape and hone the edge accordingly.

Carving knives (woodcarving, not the turkey kind) come in a large variety of shapes and sizes and are all used extremely sharp – usually off the strop. In fact, many carvers use only the strop to keep their knives sharp unless an edge gets damaged in some way and needs to be re-ground. Even that regrinding rarely requires anything coarser than 1000 grit.

A paddle of wood with a piece of 1000-grit paper glued to one side and a strop (made from a piece of leather or boxboard that has been charged with green chromium oxide compound) glued to the other side makes a handy hone for carving knives. Use the strop often and the sandpaper only when needed to keep these knives performing at their best.

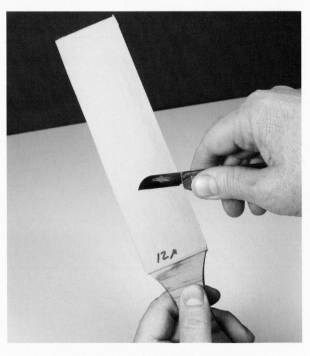

This easily-made honing paddle has a piece of 12-micron film on one side and 5-micron film on the other.

MARKING KNIVES

Marking knives are usually one-sided; so flatten and polish the back, then work on the bevel(s). The tip (skew) angle is often quite acute and won't work well in a honing guide, which means freehand is the way to go. The cutting angle is not critical and the only part that really has to be sharp is the ⅛" (3mm) or so at the tip. In fact, the rest of the edge, back from that ⅛" (3mm) sharp part, can be dulled deliberately to protect your fingers should they slop over the edge of the straightedge. It's embarrassing to slice off the tips of your thumb and forefinger as you concentrate on scribing a line. Messy, too.

Polish the back of your marking knife as you would a chisel.

Hold the bevel angle against the stone by hand.

I stopped at 1200 grit. Good enough.

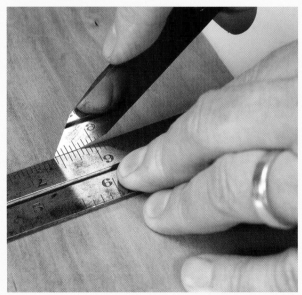

Neglecting your fingers while concentrating on the line being marked may lead to blood loss. DAMHIKT.*
*Don't Ask Me How I Know This

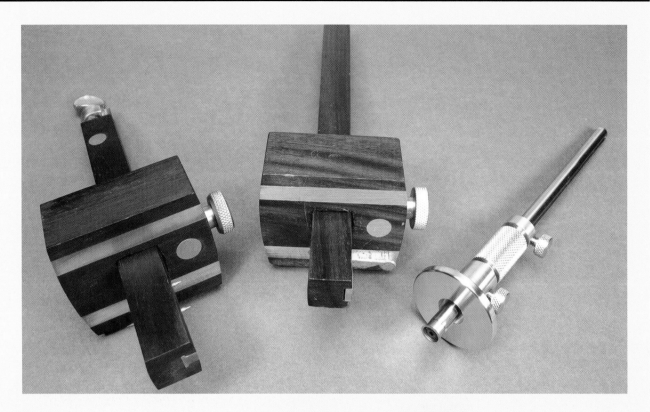

MARKING GAUGES

Marking gauges may use a pin, a wheel or a small knife to incise lines in wood. Even if it seems too small to hold, the small knife needs to be sharpened in the same manner as any other knife blade. To incise the finest possible line across wood fibers, hone and polish the blade to 8000 grit.

ABOVE Marking gauges left-to-right: Garret-Wade's pin-type mortising gauge, Crown Tool's knife-type marking/cutting gauge, Glen-Drake's Tite-Mark™ wheel-type marking/cutting gauge.

LEFT Sharpening knife-type marking cutter.

BELOW Knife-type marking cutter in pieces.

Knife-type marking gauge.

The wheel-type marking gauge can be honed and polished by simply sliding the flat surface across the stones. Unless the wheel, (the term "wheel" is misleading, in that the circular blade doesn't turn but is fixed to the slotted rod) is damaged, rather than simply dull, use your 8000-grit stone for best performance. If it is damaged, you may need to start with a coarser stone before polishing with 8000 grit.

The pins in the pin-type gauges can be difficult or impossible to remove. If they need sharpening, they usually receive a "re-pointing" by removing metal from each side; this may flatten the sides; but, most important, the business end will be usably sharp. Use a small file or stone – either a safe file, such as an auger file, or tape one side to avoid filing the wood – to flatten the pin on the side that faces the stock you want to keep – the bevel should face the waste. You can also make a small hone by gluing a thin strip of honing film to one side of a piece of wood.

Wheel-type marking gauge.

Wheel-type marking cutter on stone.

Pin-type marking gauge with blue-taped ceramic rod.

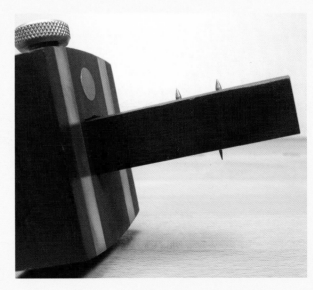

Pin-type marking gauge to show pins.

Scissors

Scissors are simple to sharpen but, as a system, they're a bit more complicated than they appear. Scissors are not really made from two knife blades, at least knives as we've already discussed. As knives (each is called a scissor, which is also a verb) the two pivoting blades possess large-angle single bevels with flat or slightly hollow backs. Usually, one of the blades is straight, the other slightly bent along its length. This generates more pressure between the two as, approaching the tips, they close together. Without the bend in the scissor, the fabric or paper being cut would tend to spring the two shearing blades apart; enough so to fold the fabric between the blades instead cutting it.

Scissors can be ruined by wear and scratches that extend down the flat, inside surfaces of the blades. Scissors that are simply dull will show wear at the meeting, shearing edges, which will be rounded like any other dull edge. Sharpening is a matter of honing the bevels at the proper angle to remove worn edges. Open or disassemble the blades, and grind a new bevel using the old angle as a reference. If you can't tell the angle, try an included angle of 60° to 75°. As with kitchen knives and soft tomatoes, polished edges don't necessarily work better in scissors because the material being cut may just slide along the edges as it is being squeezed between them. Some haircutting scissors have serrations on the bottom edge to hold the hair as it is being cut, so as long as your angles are correct, you needn't hone scissors to a fine polish.

Tormek has a scissor holder that can be easily set to the proper angle. Or you can use your belt sander table set at the proper angle with a medium belt. In addition, you can sharpen scissors by hand. Using a template to set the angle, simply take the blades to the stones and sharpen away. Do not sharpen the inside, facing surfaces at all. If those flats (some with hollows) are badly worn or deeply scratched, that pair of scissors may be relegated to cutting insulation, roofing felt, or discarded altogether.

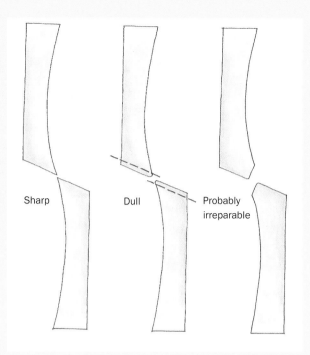

Sharp   Dull   Probably irreparable

Scissors must meet at a point along their edges. When dull, they tend to pull the material being cut in between them.

Tormek's scissor guide in use.

After sharpening the bevel, gently de-burr the edge from the back with a fine hone. Be careful not to add any back bevel at all, just remove the burr. Jeff Farris, the Tormek USA sales manager showed me a trick: to de-burr scissors, spring the blades apart so that they don't touch while you close them. Then just open them up. The burr on each blade rubs the other up and out of the way. If you wanted to, at this point you could hone the burr off the bevel with a fine abrasive.

Stones with scissors.

HANDY TRICK

Sharpen your scissors in three seconds with your burnisher! That's right, unless they've been abused and are very dull, scissors can be restored by simply burnishing them. Couldn't be simpler and almost sounds like one of those free-lunch ads for self-sharpening knives: just work your burnisher between the blades of the scissors as if you were trying to cut the burnisher in half. For me, this was one of those little awakenings. When I was a kid my mother told me that her mother would sharpen scissors by "cutting" the neck of a milk bottle with them. That tidbit of old-country family lore rattled around in my head until I'd been making blades – and burnishers – for many years. I don't know what made the lights of memory and recognition go on after some forty years but I tried a burnisher on a pair of scissors and have since made a number of people happy with this tip.

Looks awful, doesn't it? But your burnisher can freshen up a pair of dull scissors in seconds.

14 Drill Bits

DRILLING A ROUND HOLE IN WOOD IS MORE
complicated than it seems, especially when it's so
easy for us to do – we just pick up the drill (or bit
and brace or hole saw) and drill a hole. But consider
the actions that the cutting edges of the drill are
being asked to perform. The same drill bit or auger,
with no modifications to its edges, cuts with-grain,
cross-grain and end-grain, during the same cut,
alternating between two of those cutting actions
within each revolution.

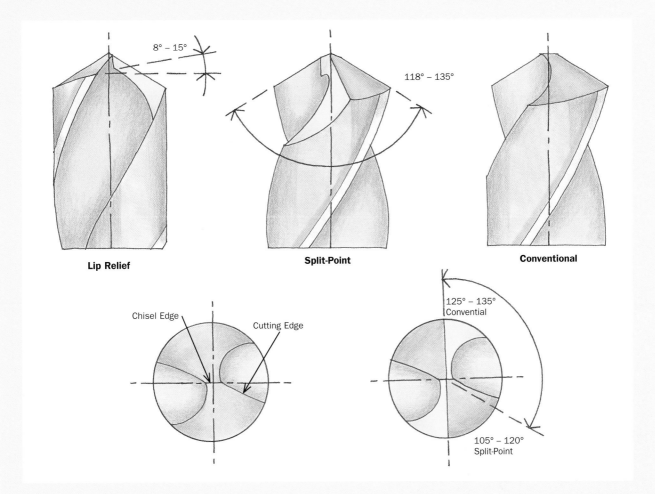

The ever-present twist drill is best suited for drilling metals where grain orientation is not an issue. But woodshops everywhere wouldn't be complete without twist drills that get used for all sorts of chores. Hole saws, spade, Forstner and auger bits are more specialized but most woodshops have an assortment of those, too.

You can sharpen all of the above with some creative application of the sharpening tools you already have. A hand grinder with an assortment of small wheels and bits can make some of these jobs easier. A bit's edge geometry is established at the factory and, as such, is hard to improve upon. So, before getting too deep here, let's consider the economics of sharpening a bit.

I abhor our "throw-away" economy where so many things we use everyday are intended to be used once and tossed. But it comes down to simple economics and the price of labor. Simple tools like bits are made by automated machinery at a very low cost. This translates to a price at retail (where we buy it), of less than five dollars for a basic quarter-inch HSS twist bit. For the sake of easy math, let's say a wood-shop charges its customers at a rate of $60 per hour – a dollar a minute. If it takes you, or your employee, more than five minutes to resharpen that bit, it's not worth doing. It makes good business sense to throw it away and buy another. This won't hold true with all bits, of course. A 3" Forstner bit may run over $30, so if you can sharpen it in less than a half-hour, you are an asset to your business.

Okay, maybe you're not in business, or have never had to weigh the benefits of buying bits by the dozen. No problem. Sharpen away. But, just because your woodworking habit doesn't put food on the table, you needn't devalue what your time is worth. Before you spend a lot of valuable time learning to sharpen a bit, I recommend you do the math.

Now that all that's been said, it's never a bad idea to know how to do something – just in case you really need to someday – like when it's after hours and you're on your last sharp drill bit, or you're at another location and didn't bring the drill bin.

Drill bits cut with two edges at the same time, at the exact same time. It is this fact that makes sharpening bits so difficult, though not impossible. It is possible to sharpen one well enough, even if the bit may not cut perfectly or evenly with both edges. The first bit I ever attempted to sharpen (notice the use of the word "attempted") I ground down to nothing and, in disgust, finally threw away its flute-less, quarter-inch shank. Grind, test … nope. Grind, test … nope. Then I took a good look at a new larger bit, so it was easier for me to see the edge geometry. I studied the factory grind. Then, working much more carefully, I was eventually successful, and today I usually am able to sharpen a bit on the first try. I figure that that first successfully resharpened drill bit cost me about a hundred bucks.

Like every other woodcutting edge, a drill bit needs an angle of attack – in this case the angle of attack is established by the flute-twist – and sufficient clearance behind the cutting edge to keep the edge in the cut – the clearance angle must not allow the metal behind the edge to drag on the wood or it won't cut at all. It will just get hot while it spins on the wood. It's the clearance angle that you regrind to resharpen a bit; doing so establishes a new cutting edge. Another nicety added to some twist drills is a *split point*. If you examine a normal, non-split point, the cutting edges do not meet in the center. When drilling, the space between the edges is not being cut efficiently, which makes the drill difficult to start (it "drunkenly" wanders around instead of getting to work.) Splitting the point extends the cutting edges all the way to meet in the center, so the bit has what it needs to start more easily and drill more efficiently (cutters – drills and end-mills – that cut to the center are what the metalworking world calls *center cutting*).

The freehand procedure goes like this: align one cutting edge horizontally (parallel to the grinder's axle) with the bit angled at 59° to the grinding wheel (half the tip angle of 118°) while holding the shank at a slight down-angle from the wheel. Now, lift the tip against the wheel while pushing the bit slightly forward at the same time. This action should grind a new cutting edge and create the rearward relief behind it. Rotate to the other cutting edge and repeat. By looking straight-on at the tip you can see if you've kept the two edges the same length. Adjust as needed, then test to see if the drill cuts.

Hold the cutting edge horizontally while you lift the tip and advance it against the wheel.

Drill extension and orientation are set and the chuck tightened.

Drill and chuck are inserted into the grinding port and rocked up and down while rotating left and right.

The side port is for splitting the point.

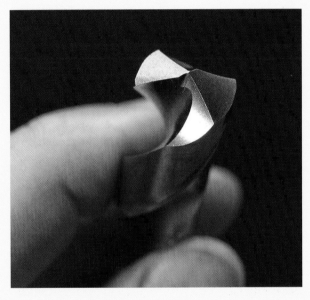

A sharp and split drill point.

DRILL DOCTOR

The same company that manufactures the Work Sharp sharpening system brings us the Drill Doctor (www.drilldoctor.com), a compact and surprisingly effective drill bit sharpening machine. The Drill Doctor uses three stages to re-point a bit. The first step is to clamp the bit into the chuck at the correct extension and angle. Then the chuck-with-bit is inserted into a pivoting socket where it engages the rotating diamond stone. Rock and twist the same number of times for each half of the bit tip and the primary sharpening is done. The bit can be used now, or inserted into the side port to split the point.

GENERIC DRILL JIG

This is a common bit sharpener that is sold under a variety of brand names. It uses the side of the grinding wheel, which, as stated before, is extremely dangerous. Although I am not certain and have only suspicions, it may be that because the bit is applied to the wheel with a relatively light pressure, the manufacturer minimizes what I consider an industrial safety hazard. (This is probably why I deserve my wife's nickname for me, Mr. Safety.) At any rate, the "generic jig" works, albeit with loud safety precautions and red flag warnings from me. That said, it does a good job of sharpening both edges identically.

This jig allows you to sharpen both edges equally.

E-Z SHARP

Here's a simple invention that lends a hand to the woodworker who needs to sharpen a bit only on occasion, not often enough to get good at freehand sharpening and has no real need to buy a dedicated sharpening machine. The E-Z Sharp jig (www.sharpdrillbits.com), an injection-molded metal guide, clamps to your grinder's tool rest. It simulates the by-hand method described above by holding the alignment of the drill bit at the proper angle. It requires a bit of practice but it only takes a couple of tries to get it right.

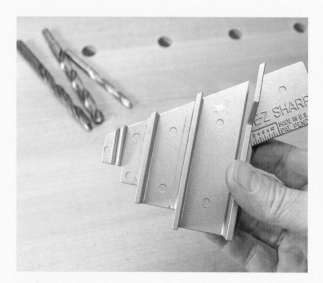

The E-Z Sharp drill sharpening jig helps align the bit with the grinding wheel. You then simply pivot the bit up and slide it forward to sharpen one edge. Flip it over and repeat. There is a cast-in scale to help you keep both edges the same length.

SPADE BITS

Some spade bits have spurs at the corners and some don't. The ones that don't are easier to sharpen – you just use your stones to lightly hone the cutting edges, making an effort to keep them the same length so they'll cut on the same plane and at the same time. The spurred spade bits require a little more finesse, as you must get into the flat cutting edge with a small file (like an auger file) or a slipstone. Same for the spurs themselves, just hone them on the inside edge only – don't work the outside or the bit will bind in the hole. The center spike on either style can probably use a little touch up at the same time. Respect the manufacturer's angles and use them as a guide. Remember, too, before attempting to resurrect a trashed spade bit, that these are inexpensive tools and your time is worth something.

AUGERS

When sharpening an auger bit, try to remove metal from only the flute-side of the cutting edge. This differs from the way twist drills are sharpened. Use a file (an official auger file is a good investment) or a stone, taking care to maintain the original bevel angle. Try to take the same amount off of each edge. The cutting spurs should be filed or honed only on their inside edges. If they are honed on the outside they will bind in the hole. If you use a file, use one with a "safe edge" – an edge that has had the teeth ground off (auger files are made this way) – so that you don't file an adjacent surface that should remain intact. If using a stone, tape one edge to the same effect.

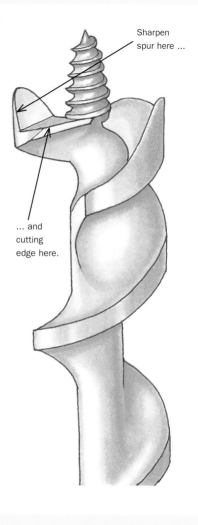

Sharpen spur here ...

... and cutting edge here.

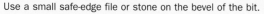

Use a small safe-edge file or stone on the bevel of the bit.

The same safe-edge file or stone is used to sharpen the inside front and top edge of the spurs.

Dress only the inside of the circumferential edges. If a burr is left on the outside, hone it off very carefully with a fine abrasive. Be careful not to reduce the diameter at the cutting edge or the edges will cut a hole smaller than the body of the bit.

A thin, flat stone, or in this case, a cutoff wheel, can be used for the straight edges. Work most aggressively on the face of the bevel, saving the bottoms of the edges for fine adjustment as needed.

The cutting edges should be a few thousandths of an inch recessed from the circumferential edges so the circumferential edges can cut a clean hole ahead of the straight edges and guide the bit in the cut.

FORSTNER BITS

Forstner bits cut clean, flat-bottomed holes of a precise diameter. They are commonly used for drilling large holes, which means the sharp circumferential edges are running at higher speeds than smaller drill bits at the same rpm. That extra cutting speed tends to heat up the circumference. Be careful – they are eager to cut, so it's easy to run them at excessive speed and to over feed them, generating too much heat and ruining the bit. When dull, you can resharpen them. I like the Dremel-style hand grinder for this, with a cylindrical stone for the circumferential edges and a thin cutting disc for the straight edges. Hand-powered tools can do the job, too. For hand tools, think auger file, slipstones, sandpaper on a dowel or some other creative application from your abrasives arsenal.

Toothed Forstner bits add minor complexity to the sharpening task. Again, remove metal only from the insides of the teeth so as not to change the outside diameter. The faces of the teeth can be touched up to restore a sharp tooth point.

BRAD-POINT BITS

Some brad-point drill bits can be resharpened, such as the one shown here where the spurs are formed by simply grinding the edges at an upward angle. Use a hand grinder to re-create the factory grind, making sure the spur tips are sharp points when done and that there is sufficient clearance angle back from the cutting edge. The spur points cut the outside of the hole first, minimizing tear-out at the periphery when starting the hole and when breaking through. This geometry can easily be applied to any drill to turn a metalcutting twist drill into a wood drill.

Follow the factory grind to sharpen brad-point bits.

15 Power Tools

Timberrrrr! COPYRIGHT LARRY GERBRANDT, USED BY PERMISSION.

HAND WOODWORKING TOOLS WERE ALWAYS the intended scope of this book. Power tools rotate their cutting edges through the wood at such high rates of speed that small variations in shape and balance of those cutting edges can create a real danger, well beyond the obvious risk of all that sharp metal whirling at a zillion feet (0.33 zillion meters) per second. That said, there are a few sharpening tasks that you can perform to keep some of your power tools performing at their best.

ROUTER AND SHAPER CUTTERS

Router and shaper cutters are, for the most part, made of carbide these days and should be sent out for proper sharpening. But between professional sharpenings you can freshen up the edge with a flat diamond plate hone; a thin diamond "file" works best for some bits that have too little clearance for a thicker hone. If there is one, you will need to remove the pilot bearing so you can reach the entire carbide blade. Do not remove any metal from the periphery of the cutter; all sharpening must be done on the flat face only, not the shaped outside edge. Try to remove the same amount from each blade and work with moderate pressure against your diamond hones. Progress to finer grits – 1200 grit is probably as fine as you need.

PLANER & JOINTER KNIVES

The new helical, indexed cutterhead inserts for planers and jointers eliminate the need for sharpening. When the square carbide inserts get dull you just rotate each of them to a new edge and get back to work. After four turns, you swap them out for new. The metalworking industry has been using indexed carbide tooling for decades and it looks like the woodworking world is now finding ways to adapt this technology to woodworking machinery.

After removing the pilot bearing and cleaning the resin-gunk off the bit, hone the faces of the carbide blades with a thin diamond hone.

Helical, indexed carbide cutterhead inserts enjoy a number of advantages over traditional cutterheads: long edge-life, quieter operation, no sharpening or adjusting needed – just rotate or replace the carbide inserts for fresh edges.
PHOTO COURTESY SUNHILL MACHINERY (WWW.SUNHILLMACHINERY.COM)

CIRCULAR SAW BLADES

The ubiquity of carbide-tipped circular saw blades combined with the machinery and expertise required to sharpen them puts them outside the scope of this book. Carbide saw-tips can be hand-honed with diamond tools but power saw blades demand a level of precision, uniformity and balance that can be jeopardized by even the slightest bit of improper honing. Therefore, I do not recommend attempting to sharpen your own circular saw blades.

ABOVE LEFT AND RIGHT This inexpensive device can freshen the blades in the jointer (or planer if you can reach the blades). Try to give each blade the same amount of attention. (Unplug the machine first!)

Tormek offers a jig for planer and jointer knives as well. Longer blades are simply repositioned in the jig. It works well but keep a towel handy – this operation is messy. The water runs along the blade and dribbles all over the machine and the bench.

Meanwhile, most of us have jointer and planer blades that are made from high-speed steel that, except for their length, get the same basic treatment as a chisel or plane iron. There are some clever devices and methods for touch-up honing *in situ*, and you can always take them out of the machine and use your stones to sharpen them. If you need to sharpen your jointer and planer knives often, Tormek and Lap-Sharp offer an optional accessory fixture just for long blades, and Veritas has a Jointer Blade Sharpening Jig that holds the blade in a wide honing guide that is used in conjunction with a piece of sandpaper on glass.

Before you spend your money on a special-purpose sharpener or system for your planer and jointer knives, consider how much new blades cost, and how many you can buy for that amount of money. Power tool blades cut wood with significantly more push-force than hand tools and even normal operation tends to make them surprisingly dull. Yes, they are high-speed steel and hold up remarkably well under this punishing task. But think about the volume of shavings they produce between sharpenings and compare that to what you produce with your hand plane between sharpenings. When using a hand plane, chisel or drawknife you know early on that the blade is due for sharpening. With an electron-powered machine, that moment is usually when a blade begins to perform poorly. The deterioration of cutting performance is slow and gradual – barely noticeable until the blades are quite dull. By that time the blades will

need a considerable amount of grinding to restore their edges, and the time required needs to be factored into your cost analysis.

I recently sent out a set of planer knives for professional sharpening and it wasn't until I had them back in the machine that I did some shopping and found that I could have bought new ones for less money than the sharpening had cost me (doh!)

Can you do a better job than the pros? Probably – you'll most certainly hone a finer, more polished edge. However, it wouldn't be a bad idea to start with new or professionally ground edges and hone them to a finer degree using your arsenal of abrasives. A minute or two on your 1000-grit stone will refine the rough-ground edge and you can add a small back-bevel to help cut difficult wood (and strengthen the edge to last a bit longer as well).

I've heard of some who sharpen by holding a stone on the outfeed table while the machine is running. Aside from not adding any relief to the cutting edge, this is insanely dangerous. Never sharpen knives while the machine is running (or even plugged in).

If, while using your jointer or planer, you notice a raised line being left behind, you've nicked the cutters somehow and that nick is showing as a ridge on the wood. The simplest solution is to shift one cutter a fraction of an inch so the un-nicked part of that blade cleans up after the others.

CHAIN SAW

Chain saws are mostly used for timber harvesting and firewood production. Most lumber for woodworking hasn't been touched by a chain saw for quite a while and has been through a lot of processing since. While they don't contribute much to the typical woodworker's woodworking, most of the woodworkers I know own one.

Specific saws and chains will have specific instructions for sharpening relative to angles and limits, and such. Some chains incorporate anti-kickback features that, for safety reasons, must not be modified. Read and follow all instructions that came with your saw and your chain. No matter what you read here, those instructions take precedent. (I'll put on my "Mr. Safety" hat for a moment to remind you that chain saws are aggressively dangerous, able to do grievous

harm to you or those around you in a split second of inattentiveness or inexperience, or even lousy luck – the kind of harm that requires a messy trip to the ER and months of facial reconstructive surgeries).

You'll need a round chainsaw file of the correct diameter for your chain as well as a flat, mill bastard file for adjusting the depthgauges. Instead of a round file there are round chain saw stones available for your hand grinder (Dremel) that work quickly and well. The teeth get filed or ground to new sharp edges and the depth gauges are filed so each tooth will bite to the correct depth in the wood. Your local hardware store will have a variety of file guides to make this job easier but you can do it with just the files and a store-bought depth-gauge tool. There is a service mark on the top of each tooth that indicates the proper angle of the top cutting edge and marks the limit for the size of the tooth: i.e. when you've filed a tooth to that line, it's time for a new chain. The file or stone is held horizontally, at the angle indicated by the service mark on the tooth, with about 20% of the file or stone above the top of the tooth to grind the bevel angle properly.

Unless it's just an on-site touch-up, I remove the bar and chain and clean everything as best I can before I sharpen. The bar needs to be trued-up if the chain has turned a burr on the corner edges. Be careful of those edges – they're just like a scraper's burr and can cut you. Flat-file the burr off the sides and, while

The teeth on the end of this depth-gauge guide are used to clean the crud from the chain groove.

The service mark on each tooth indicates its minimum length and serves as a guide for filing to the correct angle.

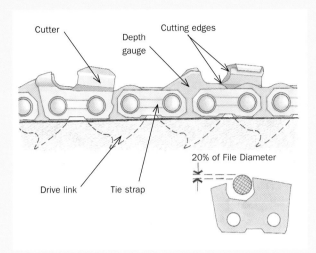

Tooth with parts I.D.'d and file diameter relative to tooth.

Flat-file the bar to keep the chain tracking properly. And file the sides of the corners to remove the burr. This saw-jointing file holder works well but you can file by hand, too. I've protected the bench and vise from grime with a sheet of newsprint. And I should probably be wearing gloves.

the bar is in a vise, even-up the rails with a file. A file holder like the one used for saw jointing is ideal. The chain groove in the bar gets full of gunk and needs to be cleaned out with something thin. My depth-gauge guide has teeth on one end for groove-cleaning but you can use any thin thing such as a utility knife blade. If your bar is symmetrical, flip it over with each sharpening to wear both sides evenly. With everything cleaned up, reassemble the chain onto the bar, and the bar onto the saw. Tighten the chain so that it will still move smoothly by hand. (Gloves are recommended. The only time I've ever hurt myself with my chain saw was when I slipped while advancing the chain during sharpening and sliced into my thumb.)

You can hold the bar in a vise but I usually just set the saw on the bench. Mark a tooth with a felt-tip pen as your starting point. Start with the right-hand teeth (or left, it doesn't matter but it's easier if you do all of one first), trying to remove an equal amount of metal from each tooth. While trying to make each tooth-top the same length (more or less), file or grind each

tooth at the proper angle until the edge and corner are restored to sharp. Unless the chain has been damaged or neglected it should only take two or three strokes with the file, or a second or two of grinding, to sharpen each tooth. When the right (or left) teeth are done, turn the saw around and sharpen the others.

CHAIN SAW SAFETY

"A chain saw is the most dangerous hand tool that can be purchased on the open market. It requires no license and no training to own or operate. Approximately 40,000 injuries and deaths were reported last year in the United States ... and most could have been prevented." – *Carl Smith, Saw Expert*

Align the file with the service mark and ...

Now, file the depth gauges. When you file the teeth, you shorten the length of the tooth-top and also lower the top of the tooth relative to the depth-gauge. To keep the tooth cutting properly, the depth gauges have to be lowered to match. Your depth gauge guide straddles each depth gauge while resting on the tops of two teeth. It lets the tooth's depth gauge protrude through a slot, allowing you to file it flush with the guide. This sets the depth of cut according to the specifications on your depth-gauge guide – 0.025 to 0.030" (0.6 to 0.8mm), or so. The larger the difference between the top of the tooth and the depth-gauge, the more aggressively your saw will cut. Using a depth-gauge guide that shortens the depth-gauges more than is recommended may cause your saw to try to bite too deep, causing it to stall in the cut. Some instructions say to shape the depth-gauge by rounding it off toward the front of the tooth, but I've never bothered and the pros don't either when they sharpen. I've also found that keeping the teeth as close to each other in size as you can is a good idea, it doesn't affect the saw's performance nearly as much as does the correct depth-gauge setting.

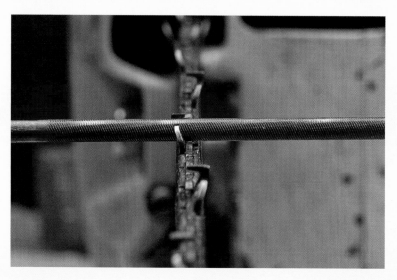

... hold the file (or the grind stone) horizontally. I'm wearing gloves here, mainly so that I can advance the chain by grabbing a tooth without cutting myself.

The same angles, etc. apply if you're using a hand grinder.

The depth gauge guide sits atop adjacent teeth with the depth gauge poking up through the slot. File the depth gauge flush with the guide.

(MICROSCOPIC PHOTOS)

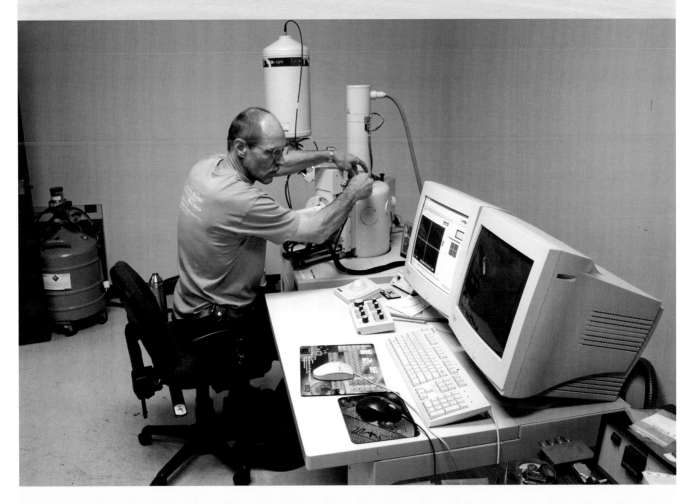

Steve Anderson makes an adjustment to the Hitachi S-3000 scanning electron microscope at Sonoma State University.

I RECENTLY MENTIONED TO CHRIS SCHWARZ, editor of *Popular Woodworking* magazine, something about using a simple USB toy microscope to look at edges before and after sharpening. His reply was, "I got to play with one of those gizmos and it was very ... humbling." I know what he means. Magnifying a sharpened edge can spotlight a dismaying array of results. Even an edge that you are certain is as sharp as any living being could make it, one that passes all the sharpness tests and performs beautifully, will show scratches, nicks and abject irregularities that you'd swear couldn't possibly be there. It's not for the

insecure, but magnifying that edge may show you something that will improve your sharpening technique. Taking that to the extreme, I took some carefully prepared sample edges to the scanning electron microscope (SEM) at Sonoma State University, a beautiful campus north of San Francisco in Cotati, California.

Optical microscopes use light to function – either transmitted through a specimen or reflected off of it.

When most people think of "microscope," the ubiquitous, high-school-biology-lab microscope provides the iconic image. Resolution in microscopy-speak is the smallest distance between two things where you can identify them as two different things. An optical microscope's resolution is limited by the physics of the light waves it depends on. No object smaller than the wavelengths of visible light will be visible as a discrete object in an optical microscope. High-quality optical microscopes have an at-best magnification limit of about 1500x to 2000x. That's where the SEM comes in. An electron beam has a much smaller width (wavelength) than visible light and there are no lenses or even air in the SEM's vacuum chamber to distort the "light" of the electron beam. With that narrow electron beam as a "light" source, Sonoma State's Hitachi S-3000 can resolve objects as small as three nanometers.*

The goal of my foray into the world of electron microscopy was to illustrate the effects of different abrasives and different grit sizes on tool steel edges. If Chris' experience with the toy microscope was humbling, mine with the SEM was, undoubtedly, more so. I had no opportunity to re-do any sharpening during my time with the SEM so what you see here are the images of the honed edges that I brought to Sonoma State that day. The flaws in my sharpening technique are obvious (to me anyway) and … humbling. You'll notice residual burrs and stray scratches on some of the samples and yet, this is how edges look, even after careful honing. Edges that look raggedy at 2000x magnification can

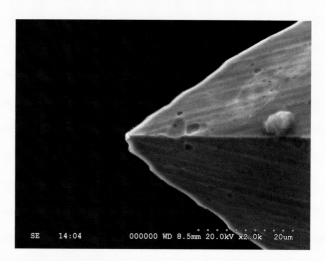

Insulin syringe needle.

perform flawlessly. Take a look at the photo of the BIC razor (yes, that's a burr running along the factory-honed edge). If you saw that image before buying it you wouldn't buy it – and you certainly wouldn't use it. But, burr and all, it performs as intended, and so will your chisel, even if the edge doesn't look perfect when magnified two-thousand times.

Improved sharpening of ever-smaller needles has helped injections become less and less painful over

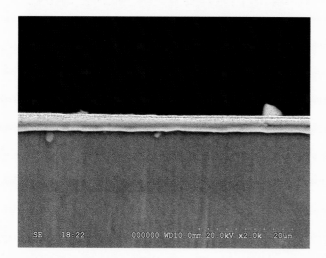

New BIC razor blade. What looks like a wave cresting is a burr left by the honing process.

*A nanometer (nm) is one billionth of a meter. The DNA helix has a diameter of about 3 nanometers and a bacterium can be as large as 10,000 nanometers or 10 micrometers, also called microns (μm or sometimes just μ, the Greek letter mu). Visible light wavelengths range from 400nm (purple) to 700nm (red), so even the best light microscope is limited to "seeing" things not much smaller than a half micron (0.5 μm) when using flawless lenses and blue light for illumination of the specimen. The next order-of-magnitude smaller size designation is the picometer (pm) which is one thousandth of a nanometer or a trillionth of a meter. A hydrogen atom has a diameter of about 50pm. The width of the electron beam used by a SEM is about 300pm, which is why we use it to see such small stuff.

The angstrom (Å) is no longer supported as a unit of measure in the International System of Units (SI) but I mention it because it was the unit for measuring light waves and such when I was young(er). An angstrom was, and still is, one ten-billionth of a meter (10^{-10} or 0.0000000001m), 0.1nm, 100pm, etc.

That scaly diagonal thing is a hair from my head that measures 44.3μ. It is resting against a BIC disposable razor blade. 500x magnification.

the years. So I included a new insulin syringe to show what something that sharp looks like along with a shot of the BIC blade with the obligatory hair (generous of me to part with one) at 500x just to give you a sense of scale.

All but two of these images were shot at 2000x magnification (except the hair that was shot at 500x and the 3-micron diamond paste edge with the deep scratch from a stray grain which is at 400x) but the

actual magnification you see is determined by the size of the image as reproduced here. The info recorded along the bottom of each photo describes the working parameters of the SEM at the time the photo was shot. At the far right on all of the 2000x photos is "20um" below a row of dots. That row of dots is 20-microns long. To the left of that it says "x2.0k" which means the object on the screen of the SEM monitor is magnified by 2000 (2.0k) times (x). If you measure the row of dots and do the math correctly you can calculate the actual magnifications represented in these images. Many of the photos show a lot of debris on the surface of the samples, which is dust that accumulated while we were preparing them for placement in the SEM (nothing like high magnification to bring out every flaw).

These images were never intended as a contest between stone brands; only as a comparison of how they perform. Differences between stone brands of the same grit size should only illustrate that, while there are differences between manufacturer's grit-size specifications, the differences are not material. The

MICROSCOPY

Microscopy has become more accessible recently with the introduction of computer-connected digital microscopes. Several of these are marketed as toys but can come in quite handy for observing things other than pond water or butterfly wings. I use my plastic Digital Blue QX5 all the time for studying edges or finding a sliver in my finger. It is essentially a digital camera with a built-in 10x/60x/200x lens turret that connects to my computer through a USB port. There are several other brands of these computer-connected microscopes available inexpensively and they're fun, durable (toys, after all) and quite useful. The imaging software that comes with the QX5 is designed for kids and drove me nuts with its garish graphical interface and loud bleeps and bloops as feedback for every mouse click. While you can turn off the noise there are much better software interfaces available such as ProScope HR that comes with a micro-

scope of the same name. The bundled software is also available independently as a free download and works well with the QX5, offering image manipulation options unavailable with the toy software. Also, it treats you as though you were an adult.

These microscopes come with a small light for reflective illumination but you'll get much better images with the addition of a much brighter light. A desk lamp can be directed onto your specimen and the angle adjusted to give the best contrast and reveal surface relief.

It's easy to scoff at a bright blue plastic microscope that's being marketed to kids. But a friend of mine resharpens diamond surgical instruments for a living and uses his Intel QX3 to record before-and-after pictures of every knife that is sent to him for honing. And Brent Beach (www3.telus.net/brentbeach/sharpen/index.html) has done remarkable work illustrating the intricacies of sharpening with virtuosic mastery of his QX3.

bonded and coated abrasive products – stones, plates, films – all leave relatively consistent scratches that indicate a high degree of grit size uniformity. The pastes and compounds all show signs of stray larger grains in the mixtures. The 400x image of 3μ diamond paste, for example, clearly shows a deep scratch at the same angle as the others. I assume this was caused by a stray particle of larger grit. How it got there could easily have been my fault – I could have carried the boulder that caused that scratch under a fingernail or whatever – even though I always take measures to avoid grit contamination at every step of my sharpening routine. These deeper scratches are glaring at this extreme magnification, but I doubt they would ever be noticed in the performance of the edge.

These photos may beg more questions than they answer but I think they're interesting to study. You can easily see that my sharpening techniques were not perfect. Many of the edges show scratches that should have been honed out before changing to a finer grit. If I learned anything from these photos it's to take a bit more time with critical honing jobs; don't be so impatient to start the next grit. And, I learned that if, after sharpening, something doesn't seem right, try again. It's easy to leave a raggedy edge or a burr even with careful technique.

These images are all of hardened AISI O1 edges at 2000x magnification except where noted. They are identified by the abrasive used last.

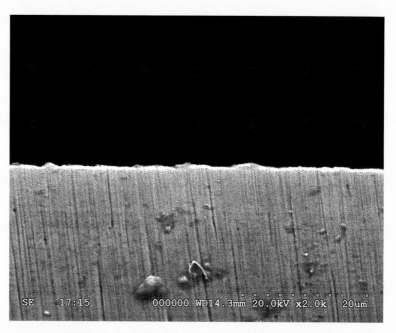

Hard Arkansas oilstone.

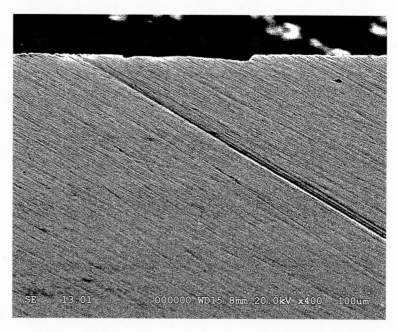

400x magnification of the edge honed with 3μ diamond paste showing a scratch made by a larger particle.

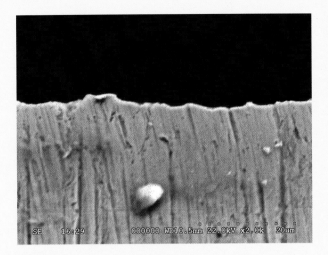

Spiderco Ultra Fine ceramic stone.

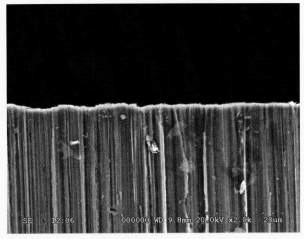

DMT Dia-Sharp 8000-grit diamond plate.

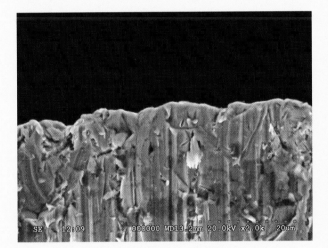

Norton 1000-grit waterstone.

Norton 8000-grit waterstone. It would appear that I left a burr on this edge. Probably when I flipped the blade to polish the back and failed to chase the burr off of the bevel side.

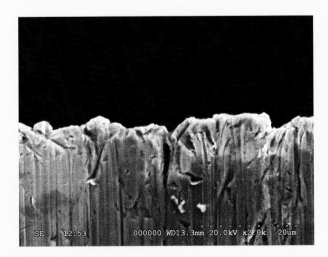

Shapton 1000-grit waterstone.

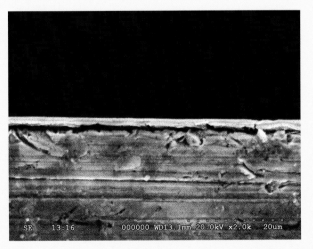

Shapton 1000-grit waterstone using side-to-side sharpening.

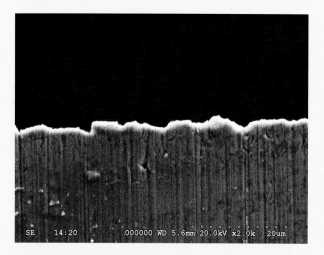

Shapton 8000-grit waterstone.

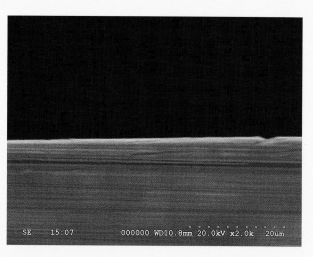

Shapton 16000-grit waterstone using side-to-side sharpening.

Shapton 16000-grit waterstone. I followed Harrelson Stanley's recommendation and lightly "jointed" the edge just before the last passes on the stone.

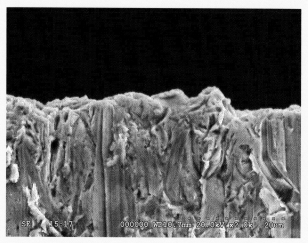

King 800-grit waterstone.

Norton 3μ diamond paste. The vertical scratches are remnants of a previous grit.

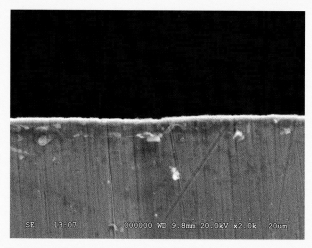

Tormek stropping wheel and compound. The deeper scratches are from larger particles on the wheel.

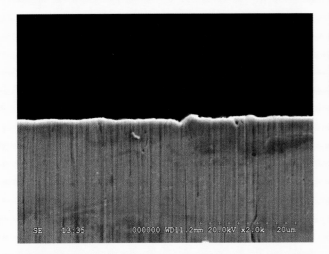

1.0μ honing film.

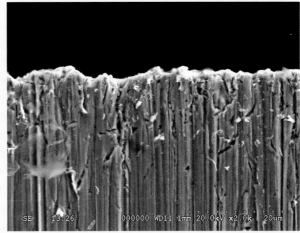

5μ honing film.

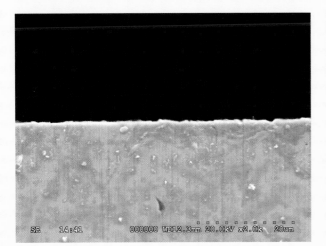

.03μ honing film. Lots of dust on this sample.

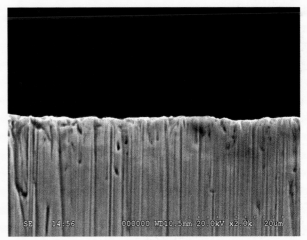

Leather strop with green chromium oxide compound.

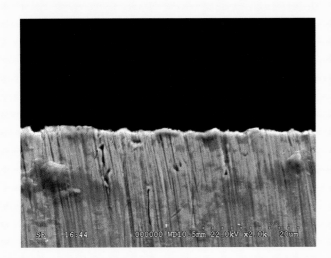

Leather strop with FlexCut Gold compound.

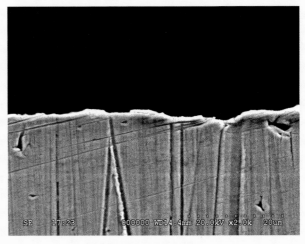

Leather strop with Yellowstone compound.

(RESOURCES)

I don't know everything there is to know about sharpening, and I certainly have not been able to cover all aspects of sharpening every tool. If the instructions you were looking for aren't in this book, I apologize. For you, I've included the following list of resources in the hope that if I didn't take care of your need, the least I can do is point you in the right direction and wish you good luck.

Some of the resources I used doing research for this book include, but are certainly not limited to, the following. And, I've thrown in a few good links, just because I think they're valuable for a greater understanding of the worlds of steel and sharpening and woodworking. As website addresses can be rather impermanent, I've included this list, and will keep it as up-to-date as possible at www.theperfectedgebook.com. Check in often for news about resources and innovations in sharpening as they become available.

Bruce Hoadley's *Understanding Wood*, Taunton Press

Leonard Lee's *The Complete Guide to Sharpening*, Taunton Press

Thomas Lie-Nielsen's *Sharpening*, Taunton Press

Chris Pye's *Woodcarving: Tools, Materials & Equipment Volume I*, Guild of Master Craftsman

Popular Woodworking's blog frequently addresses sharpening issues: blogs.popularwoodworking.com/editorsblog/default.aspx

As does *Woodworking Magazine*'s blog: blog.woodworking-magazine.com/blog/

Joel Moskowitz's sharpening notes at AntiqueTools.com: www.antiquetools.com/sharp/ (his blog is always interesting, too.)

Pete Taran's saw sharpening instructions at VintageSaws.com: www.vintagesaws.com/library/primer/sharp.html

More on sharpening handsaws: www.norsewoodsmith.com/node/87

Chad Ward's Knife Sharpening instructions: forums.egullet.org/index.php?showtopic=26036

In-depth steel information at The Sousa Corporation's technical library:
www.sousacorp.com/tecnical.htm

Lyn J. Mangiameli's High Angle Smoothing Plane Comparison:
www.woodcentral.com/bparticles/haspc.shtml

Molecular Expressions™ Optical Microscope Primer:
www.microscopy.fsu.edu/primer/index.html

Ancient Metallurgy, A Beginner's Guide:
weber.ucsd.edu/~dkjordan/arch/metallurgy.html

Corrosion Doctors (way more about rust than you probably want to know
– downright frightening): www.corrosion-doctors.org/index.htm

Brent Beach's excellent blade sharpening and testing treatise:
www3.telus.net/BrentBeach/Sharpen/index.html

Steve Elliot's also excellent research into sharpening, planing and edge retention:
bladetest.infillplane.com/

More on Tool Steel metallurgy from the University of Cambridge:
www.msm.cam.ac.uk/phase-trans/2002/martensite.html

Classification of Carbon and Low-Alloy Steels from Key to Steel:
steel.keytometals.com/Default.htm

Woodcentral's "Articles of Interest" on hand tools:
www.woodcentral.com/cgi-bin/articles.pl#handtools

More on Material Hardness testing and specs:
www.calce.umd.edu/general/Facilities/Hardness_ad_.htm

Hardness vs. Wear by Robert F. Miller: http:
www.cladtechnologies.com/Articles/Hardness%20vs.%20Wear/hardness.htm

Chainsaw sharpening from Oregon: www.oregonchain.com/faq.htm#sharpening

The Internet has made some research point-and-click easy and I highly recommend using it to expand on whatever in this book you may have found interesting but limited in scope. There are informative commercial sites – sellers of sharpening products, steel suppliers, heat-treat and cryogenic service providers, abrasives, etc. – as well as a plethora of forums and blogs with no shortage of opinions, experiences and contributions from all corners about every aspect of woodworking, tools, sharpening, you name it. Sharpening is a subject that keeps unfolding with more and more information the longer you look. Pursuit of the perfect edge can be a weekend hobby or a lifelong quest – the more you learn, the more there is to learn.

(SUPPLIERS)

BEST THINGS (THE)
299 Herndon Parkway, #210
Herndon, VA 20170
800-884-1373
www.thebestthings.com

CLASSIC HAND TOOLS
Hill Farm Business Park
Witnesham, Ipswich
Suffolk, UK IP6 9EW
+44 (0)1473 784 983
www.classichandtools.com

CRAFTSMAN STUDIO
4848 Ronson Ct - Suite L
San Diego, CA 92111
888-500-9093
www.craftsmanstudio.com

DIETER SCHMID - FINE TOOLS
Georg-Wilhelm Str., 7A
Berlin, Germany 10711
+49 30 342 1757
www.fine-tools.com

DMT
85 Hayes Memorial Drive
Marlborough, MA 01752
800.666.4DMT
www.dmtsharp.com

GLEN-DRAKE TOOLWORKS
P.O. Box 2747
Fort Bragg, CA 95437
800-961-1569
www.glen-drake.com

JAPAN WOODWORKER (THE)
P1731 Clement Ave.
Alameda, CA 94501
800-537-7820
www.japanwoodworker.com

KLINGSPOR ABRASIVES INC.
2555 Tate Blvd. SE
Hickory, N.C. 28602
800-645-5555
www.klingspor.com

LEE VALLEY TOOLS LTD.
P.O. Box 1780
Ogdensburg, NY 13669-6780
800-871-8158 (U.S.)
800-267-8767 (Canada)
www.leevalley.com

HIGHLAND HARDWARE
1045 N. Highland Ave. NE
Atlanta, GA 30306
888-500-4466
www.highlandwoodworking.com

NORTON
Saint-Gobain Abrasives, Inc.
1 New Bond Street
Worcester, MA 01606
800-446-1119
www.nortonabrasives.com

PROFESSIONAL WOODWORKER'S SUPPLY
P.O. Box 10
Patterson Lakes
Victoria, Australia 3197
+03 9776 1521
www.woodworkingsupllies.com.au

**ROCKLER WOODWORKING
AND HARDWARE**
4365 Willow Dr.
Medina, MN 55340
800-279-4441
www.rockler.com

ROSE MILL CO. (HEAT TREATING)
100 Brook Street
West hartford, CT 06110
860-232-9990
www.rosemill.com

SPYDERCO
820 Spyderco Way
Golden, CO 80403-8053
800-525-7770
www.spyderco.com

SHAPTON STONES
HMS Enterprises
51 Shattuck St.
Pepperell, MA 01463
877-692-3624
www.shaptonstones.com
www.getsharper.com

TOOLS FOR WORKING WOOD
32 33rd Street 5th Floor
Brooklyn, NY 11232
800-426-4613
www.toolsforworkingwood.com

WENZLOFF & SONS.
1154 N. Fremont Lane
Cornelius, Oregon 97113
503-359-5255
www.wenzloffandsons.com

WOOD ARTISTRY (LAP SHARP)
408 Moore Lane
Healdsburg, CA 95448
707-473-0593
www.woodartistry.com

WOODCRAFT SUPPLY LLC
1177 Rosemar Rd.
P.O. Box 1686
Parkersburg, WV 26102
800-535-4482
www.woodcraft.com

(INDEX)

 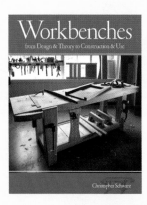 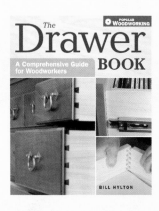